Sex, Salvage and Secrets

(Must Be Present to Win)

The New Atlantian Library

Habent Sua Fata Libelli

The New Atlantian Library

Manhanset House
Shelter Island Hts., New York 11965-0342

bricktower@aol.com • tech@absolutelyamazingebooks.com
• absolutelyamazingebooks.com

The New Atlantian Library is an imprint of Absolutely Amazing ebooks

All rights reserved under the International and Pan-American Copyright Conventions. No part of this publication may be reproduced, stored in a retrieval system, or transmitted in any form or by any means, electronic, or otherwise, without the prior written permission of the copyright holder. The Absolutely Amazing eBooks colophon is a trademark of
J. T. Colby & Company, Inc.

Library of Congress Cataloging-in-Publication Data
Perkins, Reef
Sex, salvage and secrets
p. cm.

1. Biography & Autobiography / Adventurers & Explorers. 2. Biography & Autobiography / Military. 3. Biography & Autobiography / Personal Memoirs I. Title.
ISBN: 978-1-955036-16-0, Trade Paper

Copyright © 2013 by Reef Perkins
Electronic compilation/ paperback edition
copyright © 2022 by Absolutely Amazing eBooks

July 2022

Sex, Salvage and Secrets

(Must Be Present to Win)

Reef Perkins
Born-1946 Published-2012

Contains 100% recyclable thoughts

The New Atlantian Library

Dedicated to my son, Quincy

Dedicated to my wife Glenys

Table of Contents

Foreword

PROLOGUE — 3

Chapter 1, The Early Daze 1950 to 1966 — 5

Chapter 2, European Daze — 9

Chapter 3, Family Daze — 15

Chapter 4, The Loaner — 25

Chapter 5, Leaving Milford — 33

Chapter 6, California or Bust — 39

Chapter 7, Un Frijole Malo — 47

Chapter 8, The Dude Ranch — 53

Chapter 9, Gullible's Travels — 59

Chapter 10, Deep Sea Diving for Fun and Profit — 71

Chapter 11, Return to the Army — 83

Chapter 12. In Country — 89

Chapter 13, Bugs and Bullets — 109

Chapter 14, Almost Normal — 135

Table of Contents (Continued)

Chapter 15, Civilian Daze — 139

Chapter 16, Key West Daze — 153

Chapter 17, Business in the Isthmus — 169

Chapter 18, Plenty Blue, Plenty Green — 181

Chapter 19, California Here I Come — 193

Chapter 20, The Last Run — 199

Chapter 21, A Perp's Life or Once is Enough — 213

Chapter 22, Tropical Rehab — 221

Chapter 23, Friend or Faux — 225

Chapter 24, Salvage Daze — 233

Chapter 25, A Cast of Characters — 251

Chapter 26, Winding Down — 269

About The Author — 275

Foreword

This volume was originally intended to be a one-copy book of vague reminiscences for my son. I got into it. My story jumps around; one thought triggers another; different colors applied at different times on the same, rapidly wrinkling canvas. It is an admittedly vague and dazed recollection, a mixed media of memories. Told through a worn kaleidoscope, time is the mirror and broken glass the memories. Some things are true, some are almost true, and some things are not quite but they are all sincere. It's just a book. Everyone likes his own version of the truth.

Those in search of intellectual stimulation will find they are drawing from a shallow well, diving into an empty pool.

This book began late one night, four years ago in my Key West backyard.

During a conversation with Curtis Gillespie, a well-known Canadian writer imported duty free from the provinces, I began by simply asking, "How do I write a memoir?"

"You must regress. You must go back to find the beginning. It might not be easy," a small cumulus nimbus lingered nearby, "for you ... ah," Curtis looked around "... ah ... where's the wine?"

It wasn't easy.

The sky was so dark I could see my thoughts. Remembering was harder than I remembered. Like a Chinese finger trap, the harder I pulled the tighter it got. I pondered...

To get stoned
Or not to get stoned ... What was the question?

I would like to thank my wife, Roberta, for graciously enduring this endeavor and giving me some of my best unwritten memories; my son Quincy for keeping me almost broke so, as he put it with the voice of a saint, "You can suffer more fully Dad and therefore be inspired to even greater undertakings..." (I knew I should not have sent him to prep school) or something like that; Curtis Gillespie who bravely traveled from the vast lands of the north, insisting on a full TSA pat-down both ways, to listen patiently for days and nights to my ramblings. He added some semblance of dignity to my pleadings. Mrs. Nancy Butler-Ross a writer herself, who encouraged me even when she knew better and patiently undertook to teach me, among other valuable concepts, the rudimentary elements of diction, punctuation and the value of literary sanitation. Ms. Diane Savicky, who boldly undertook the first reading and is still convalescing. The ladies from my writers group, Robin Robinson (leader of the pack), Nina Nolan, Joan Langley and Leah Benner for their generous criticism served with great food. Young Michael Haskins for his quirky insights. Also in the parade of luminaries is Brewster Chamberlin a generous man and wise counsel, Carl Peachey, a writer himself, who after reading a few pages of my early work suggested I seek counseling. Jane Newhagen and Mark Howell for creative insights and Miss Kathy Russ who, on silver steed, along with her faithful Indian companion Steve, rode to my rescue and guided me out of a self-imposed ambush. Ms. Russ is the only person I could find in the Key West literary world who knew how to spell "dingelberry" correctly. My agent, Joyce Holland who advised me to "Stay in the game and don't whine." And the effervescent Ms. Carol Tedesco for undertaking the final edit.

For Mr. Shirrel Rhoades who showed me the crack in the cosmic egg … and finally to Milford High School that gave me my diploma which I have heartily abused.

This book was also made possible in part by a grant from the Anne McKee Artist's Fund of the Florida Keys, Inc.

Then there's White, and for all the words I know I can't find the right ones.

Thank you all for sticking with me. Any tendencies or habits of an excessive nature presented in this story have, of course, been since corrected.

I would like to thank everyone and everything I have come in contact with on this planet, especially myself who has allowed, if not encouraged, me to experience many things and finally to The Great Spirit, Hona Gona, who kept me around so I could be Present to Win. You have made me what I am today. Better luck next time.

—Reef Perkins, 2013

"If I tell you something is a lie, you'll know I'm telling the truth."
—George Burns

Prologue

I lay awake listening to a pair of Bufo toads making more Bufo toads in the swamp I'd built outside our bedroom window. It was not a pleasant sound. Six hours of grainy grunts and bellows took their toll. I flipped. I snapped. I was back in-country. I wanted a beer.

I grabbed my BB gun, put on a black Navy Divers T-shirt, which took longer than it should because I instinctively grabbed the gun first. I donned a black watch cap and with a black heart went out the back door, camouflaging my face with soot from the BBQ grill. I smelled chicken fat as I jacked a BB into the chamber. Locked and loaded. The old ways returned.

Creeping stealthily around the rear of the house toward the pond and avoiding toad detection, I slipped silently into chilly water. I squatted semi-naked in the puckering darkness. There was no time for full battle gear and now my stimulus package was floating free, causing a dangerous tilting moment as I duck-walked across the unforgiving algae. I stifled an Ooo-Rah! as my equipment settled slowly below the surface. My onboard periscope rapidly changed dimension and headed for warmer climes. Without the benefit of camouflage my pod was magnified by the water and looked too much like an albino Bufo on a bad hair day for my comfort. I hoped it would not appear to be a decoy, a toad of interest or a blond to the other Alpha toads. It was a chance I had to take.

Hunkered low behind a slimy pond plant I waited and tracked the Bufo's down for the kill. I had to be in the pond because, as I learned from an earlier mission, if I shot a Bufo from above and missed, the rubber piercing BB blew a hole in my pond liner.

I had to be one with the Bufo. It was them or me, a showdown at the OD corral. Mostly by sound, it was hard to miss, I located the mating crooners. Struggling against aggressive tadpoles gumming my submerged objects, I targeted the amphibious humpers with my tactical night spotting device (TNSD), a flashlight duct-taped to the barrel of my BB gun. The flashlight was heavy and slipped to the side of the barrel. When I moved the gun to sight on the Bufos they went out of the light. I worked hard; I tried to think what they were thinking, got a cold-water faux-boner, a feat in itself, and eventually delivered a single round that nailed both, at once, in the middle of their noisy love fest. It was good way to go. Old skills die hard. So do old toads.

Suddenly, a light came on. My lovely wife Roberta was standing on the porch with a puzzled look on her face. "Your teeth look whiter with the camouflage," she said gently. She always sees the positive side of things. I started to explain, but as I emerged from the pond she shook her head slowly, "I'm worried about you Perkins," she said, pivoted, and went back to bed.

I climbed out of the pond and caught my reflection in the glass panels on the front door. I hadn't been sleep walking and had never been formally diagnosed with schizophrenia, although I had lived in Key West for forty-one years. But now my pot belly, skinny legs and an almost invisible component combined with a rusty BB gun and burnt chicken fat on my face led me to conclude that this was not part of the normal aging process and, for the first time, I was worried about me too.

(Note: The toads described herein are fictional toads. No real toads were harmed.)

Chapter 1

The Early Daze 1950 to 1966

The first thing I remember about living is almost dying. I was four years old.

My senses were in overdrive, bumping into each other trying to explain reality. I chased my shadow across the back yard; I couldn't catch it, but I never felt alone. 1950, summer in Michigan,

I was playing in the shallow pool my dad made with leftover concrete from the house he'd built on Hilltop Drive near Milford. The pool wasn't deep, but the sides were curved and covered in algae, I kept sliding back in. Hundreds of hungry tadpoles surrounded me and tried to eat the tiny hairs off my body. I wasn't supposed to be in the pool alone.

I must have slipped. Suddenly, I was on my back looking up at a blue sky through greenish water It was peaceful but it got darker and I couldn't breathe. Our dog, a St. Bernard named Earl, had been sitting near me, drooling, but now Earl flipped me over and pulled me out of the pool by the back of my neck. My knees scraped on the concrete. It hurt. My face was in the lawn. The grass came toward me at eye level, pieces of it poking up my nose. A yellow flower whizzed by. The grass wasn't moving, I was. I felt a wet, stinky, hot breath on my neck. Earl lifted my head. I could see our black and white TV between the dog's legs as he backed toward the pool house. Earl's nut sack swung like a pendulum, back and forth with each pulling step, contributing to the effort. I didn't know what was happening. Not much has changed.

There was a picture of Earl and me with bandaged knees, in the family album. We were standing by the pool.

Sometimes I wonder if that memory is true. It is true, but... is it accurate? Back that far, sometimes, the truth is lost. Memory is no proof of reality. My memories, like hail stones, hit hard and melt away leaving an undefined welt. I remember my bandaged knees, that much is certain, and I remember my first emotions were pain and wonderment. It was exciting, my first taste of adrenalin. I was dragged face first through the grass and into a new reality, my first world.

I was born Mark T. Perkins. I was born with a sense of urgency.

Michigan was a fine place to grow up. We lived on a hill overlooking Oxbow Lake. We had horses, goats, ducks, raccoons, hornets, beetles, birds, love bugs, ticks, fleas, horse manure, dirt, minks, skunks and a mule. Oxbow Lake was clear and deep. I made my first dives with a Mike Nelson, double tube snorkel mask. The full-face mask had two snorkels and a cage with a ping-pong ball over the end of each tube to keep me from breathing in water. With a sharpened stick, I wordlessly hunted for perch, blue gills and frogs. The silent, weightless escape from reality was exciting. It was an escape from rural life and a different world. That made two.

I kept looking for more worlds and dug a cave over the hill behind our house. I stayed underground for hours smelling the inside of the earth; the deeper I dug the heavier I felt. It was another mystery and more silence. World number three! I was on a roll.

At age six I went to kindergarten where everyone napped on rugs, ate Graham Crackers, drank milk, teased the girls, farted and slept. Could this be number four?

When the Mood Strikes

My dad didn't like being called Dad so, at his request, we called him Bob. He was a civil engineer in the construction business.

We had a big house, four acres of lawn and six horses out in the middle of nowhere, 50 miles west of Detroit, MoTown, the Motor City. Using rabbit ears and tin foil we watched three channels on a black and white TV and sat under a blanket draped over it in order to see during the day. I loved to watch The Lone Ranger, Tarzan of the Jungle and the Adventures of Captain Don Winslow of the Royal Canadian Navy. Bob asked me why all I watched was adventure shows.

"I don't know I just like them better than anything else. I could do that, too! "

"Go for it, Kid," Bob said.

It was a peaceful time. I watched the world expand.

Sex, Salvage & Secrets

Bob liked exotic people and always managed to run across a few when the traveling circuses, carnivals and rodeos came through our country town. When the mood struck Bob, we'd drive to the local rodeo and, after the ambulances left, he'd light up a Pall Mall and nod to those cowboys still able to walk, "You boys want a drink?"

"Why sure pardnr', mighty obliged... don't mind if'n I do," they croaked. The old cowboys got up groaning, holding their backs and headed for their trucks, smacking toothless gums behind leather lips. Bob led them to our house. Our horses snorted, they could smell the wildness of the rodeo. Bob liked the losers, especially the old Brahma Bull riders. If you're still riding Brahma Bulls when you're fifty-years old you probably are a loser, I thought.

Bob explained to his audience that it was the losers who had the best stories. "The winners, what are they going to say? Shucks, it's great to win. Pffffffttt! No Shit! But losers have imagination. It's the losers who tell the real tales, right Boys?" The losers nodded and clicked their beer bottles. They laughed like cowboys at that one. Then Bob looked at me, "Son, all you got to do is figure out, one, if the stories are true and, two, if it makes any difference."

"Huh."

"That old man of yours is crazy as a bucktooth mule, son," an old bull rider cracked.

Bob liked to hang out with "the edge people," people who he said, lived down a side road of life. He particularly liked gypsies for their music and passion, plus the fact they always provided at least one good-looking woman in the clan to dance with him. He let them park their trucks and wagons on the lawn as they went through southern Michigan for harvest. The wagons smelled like every part of life. Smoky, dim, drunken parties with fires, dancing women and exotic instruments and smells created a sense of wildness, but no trouble. The Gypsies never took anything from us that we needed or noticed.

In the 50's folks were hard liquor drinkers. With a cigarette in one hand and a "high ball" in the other, they enjoyed the era of Sinatra and the Big Bands. Nobody drank wine; it was whiskey, scotch and vodka for the men and exotic drinks, the Golden Cadillac, Rusty Nail, Singapore Sling and the elegant Manhattan for the ladies.

We had a big tile bathroom where Bob put ice in the sink and liquor in the medicine cabinet for the parties. Bob made the guys, and sometimes me, go into the bathroom and encouraged us to sing. The room's acoustics were good, everybody sounded great and started loosening up (this was the part Bob loved), thinking, "Hum...Hey...that doesn't sound too bad." Hoo Boy! Off to the living room they'd go, singing and drinking...soon to return to the bathroom to re-fill their glasses and "practice" again, their drunken, but sincere, voices echoed off the cool tile walls. I envied their casual camaraderie.

Milford was comfortably rural and culturally dryer than a popcorn fart, unless you count the Udder Contest at the 4-H show. Our house was the last stop on the school bus route. If I missed the last bus I had to find my own way home. That was the deal, as Bob put it. Because I couldn't find a friend or a parent willing to drive me home I never played team sports and had more animal friends than human. The kids who lived in town did everything. They got to be the president of the class, play baseball, football, make out and drink root beer at the A&W drive-in, everything. Me? I hung with the cows. Since there was no one to talk to I listened to the trees get excited when wind came. A world without words was easy to understand. I liked being alone and vowed I would never be part of the herd, even though I was standing in one.

Everything seemed to go pretty smoothly, a typical American family trying to get by. My mother, Penny, came to this country where she met my dad in 1944. She was from Scotland and twenty-four years old when she left Scotland with her father. My mother's side of the family were full-blown, kilted Scots, right out of the coal mines and moors near Dunfermline, north of Edinburgh. They traveled by train to London and sailed in 3rd class steerage aboard the SS Athenia, a steam ship outbound for Quebec.

My grandfather's name was Thomas Penman but we called him "Dai," Scottish for dad. He looked like Jimmy Durante and was old and tired after a lifetime in the coalmines and factories, but he was gentle and never asked for anything. "Mind ye lad," he always smiled, "coal minin's a job where yee don't want to wear a kilt!" He lived with us for the last few years of his being. Then Dai died and Bob got a job in Europe.

Chapter 2

European Daze

I was seven-years old when the Perkins family of five (Bob, my mother Penny, me, Brother Greg and sister Tammis) moved to Salzburg, Austria. For a year we lived in a chalet on a manicured hillside farm with a gardener, a little creek and a slow turning paddle wheel that reached for silver fish in the stream. I still remember the forever smell of icy mountain water rushing by. Then on to Erlangen, Germany, near Nuremberg, where we lived in a five-floor mansion built into the side of a hill. The street ran behind our house and past our second story windows.

House in Germany

The house in Erlangen was a dream, with servants, a large sunken garden, a music room, a fishpond, a fountain room, a dozen bedrooms and a gymnasium on the top floor. Enter and see high ceilings, chandeliers and a foyer with two curved staircases up to the balcony where Bob, on occasion, dressed up like Sherlock Holmes and played his gypsy violin, bouncing high notes off the marble walls. I often thought about jumping from the inside balcony onto the chandelier twenty feet above the main foyer. It was exciting to think about, but I didn't.

Bob was a civil engineer and although he said he helped with some "projects," the house and staff seemed quite generous for a civil engineer. I thought he was a spy; I was prone to such fantasies.

Bob was convinced that there was nothing manufactured that he couldn't make himself. He made a riding lawnmower, his own ski tow and a machine designed to project our home movies onto the clouds. In Germany, Bob made a trampoline out of cut up inner tubes and, in a moment of sublime inspiration, made a marvellous cotton candy machine. Apparently, cotton candy machines were scarce in Germany in 1954. With our maid Frau Wilde, my accordion teacher Professor Stubble and Bob's friend, the mysterious Herr Bahl gathered in the kitchen, the trial run was undertaken.

The frantically spinning machine, constructed from an Erector set motor, a deformed funnel, a wash tub and a blow torch, made for a wild night with molten sugar and pink dye spewing all over the floor and cabinets. While everyone was running for cover, Bob took a screen door off its hinges and stood behind it so he could "tend the fire." My little brother, Bro, was screaming and careening around the kitchen with a blob of molten sugar on his ear from the "cotton cannon" as my mother later called it. Bro hit the icebox and went out cold. Bob looked out from behind the sugar-spattered screen with a Pall Mall clamped between his yellowed teeth and said, "That's tough." Bob liked to have fun.

My mother, Penny, watched serenely from the doorway. Bro didn't remember what happened. For many years we laughed together when Bob retold the story.

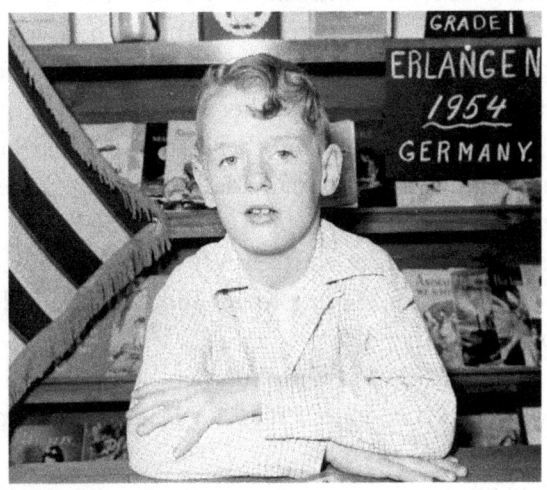

Student Perkins

In those days if a couple boys had a disagreement at the American School in Erlangen, and all first grade boys have disagreements, the teacher stopped the class and said, "OK, fine," and out to the school yard we would go. Once outside the teacher put a pair of six-pound boxing gloves on our tiny hands. "All Right!" she said with some delight, "Form a circle kids, let's watch these two fools beat the snot out of each other."

Everybody laughed at the word "snot." You can't hurt anybody very badly when you're three feet tall with two pillows on your hands. You can hardly see each other. The teachers let the first graders poke at each other until they got tired, or started kicking because they couldn't hold the gloves up any longer. She made us wait until everyone, including the warriors, sat down in the dirt. As soon as everyone sat down, "OK, kids, back to class!" We got up and kicked dust back to the classroom, some still repeating "snot" over and over and laughing like idiots. The opponents had their battle to talk about. Nobody got hurt and, because nobody could lose, each guy felt like a winner. I wish I could have stayed in first grade.

In 1956, we returned to our home in Michigan. After Europe, three kids, and twelve years of American rural life, the stress became too much for my mother's refined temperament. She had been educated in Edinburgh and was artistic in nature and talent. Things didn't work out; my mother wasn't up to raising three kids and said so. Unfortunately, when she made her unhappiness known, my paternal grandmother, who we called "Grandmo," took it upon herself to have my mother psychoanalyzed, a vague and dreary art at best. My mother was declared unstable by the "best doctors," and to "help" my mother, Grandmo had her put in an institution where she wasted too many days of her life undergoing who knows what. It changed her. Compounding the problem, my grandfather, Oakley, liked my mother. That in itself was enough to upset Grandmo. My parents got divorced in the late fifties and we three kids went with Bob. I was about ten years old.

I was 14 the last time I saw my mother. She looked light and dry like a husk once the seed is gone. I told her I didn't want to visit again because I didn't know her anymore.

"That's okay my darling," she said, "I don't know myself anymore." She used my own words to free me and sent me on my way without a hook in my heart. Thanks.

Bob's mother, "Grandmo" was tighter than a horse's asshole in fly season, a woman who lived by H.L. Mencken's definition of Puritanism: "The haunting fear that someone, somewhere, may be happy." She ruled with an iron girdle. Grandmo lived to be 93 on a diet of misery, ghosts and dill pickles. Still, she did spend time with me.

When Grandmo and Oakley came to visit the family for our traditional summer picnic, she and I went outside and sat in her Oldsmobile. I pretended to drive, encountering all types of dangers like alligators and space men from which I always, somehow, managed to save her with my heroic actions. "Oh, for lands sake, Mark, you're always trying to be a hero." She smiled. I tried.

Later, when the dangers were real, I remembered Grandmo and how it felt to be called a hero and how easy it had been to be one, back then.

After the divorce in 1958 Bob remarried. We eventually had five kids in our family. I was the oldest; I was The King. I was in charge, a habit that continued for many years. The original Perkins family had grown and changed. My brother Greg, sister Tammis and myself were joined by Carl and Heidi.

My school was in the Huron Valley School District, near Milford, but we called it Urine Valley, because everybody peed outside during recess. The playground was so big you might not make it to the restroom anyway, so why chance it? We'd go into the bushes, unzip and try to nail an ant or a beetle if we could. I speak only for the guys.

In 1957 the main elementary school was two miles down a tree-lined dirt road from the one room schoolhouse I attended during fourth grade. In that classroom there was an interesting implement, a globe. I spun the ball so fast it became one color. I was the most powerful kid in the universe, spinning the world; my imagination went along for the ride. I was soon asked not to do that.

The schoolroom was on the bottom floor of a farmhouse converted to incarcerate the fourth graders. When the weather was good the windows were open and the classroom smelled of hay, cow dung and clean country air. There were lots of flies and we smeared them on each other's desks with shots from long rubber bands. One day during recess, Carter Hicks and I got to playing war, our camouflage made of mud and weeds. It seemed like a good idea. We must have gotten a bit preoccupied because when we finally returned, late for class, we were reprimanded. Carter apologized, he always was smart, but I must have said something that was unpalatable to the teacher, Mrs. Gillow, who put one of the "big girls" in charge and unceremoniously frog marched me out to her car.

Mrs. Gillow had a Lincoln Continental with power windows that she demonstrated as I was driven to the main school to face my fate. When we pulled up to the principal's office, I began feeling a little edgy and was thinking about escape. My butt was already clenched in anticipation. Mrs. Gillow didn't really want to take me, but she couldn't risk the chance of an uprising in a one-room schoolhouse. These were farmers' kids and they were tough. The door handle on her side of the car didn't work, so when we arrived she leaned out the window to open the door. For reasons I can explain, but won't, I hit "UP" on the power window button and trapped Mrs. Gillow in the door, just below her tits. She was quiet for awhile, almost serene, but then she started to yell. I jumped out my window and started to run, right into the janitor who, while holding me by the scruff of my neck, freed the wailing Mrs. Gillow. Inside we went.

"I'm worried about you, young Perkins," she said as she adjusted her bra and quickly departed the principal's office, not wanting to see what would come next. I proceeded to get my butt whacked by the janitor and the principal. They say there are certain whistling sounds only a dog can hear. The dogs barked that day. My life of authority avoidance took root.

Further on in grade school, it wasn't getting paddled, but writing on the black board that I feared. Writing on the board was real slow. It had to be legible or you'd do it again. "I will not disrupt Mrs. Hornwrath's class," two hundred times. If you weren't tall enough you might run out of room at the bottom of the blackboard and have to stand on a desk to finish at the top. But the worst punishment was not the writing but staying after school. That meant your parents had to come and get you. Mine didn't. That was the punishment. That was the deal. I usually ended up walking home, sometimes missing dinner. I tried hitchhiking but part of the distance was a dirt road where a car only came along every national holiday or so. Hitchhiking was an adventure, but the walk home was a drag especially when combined with the looks from Bob.

High school was more fun. We grew up slowly in the 1960s. Only a few girls had tits at that time in history, so boys could concentrate on other things. In the ninth grade I met a fellow traveller, Hernandez. Our first adventure occurred in the library behind the tall bookracks during freshman year study hall. We decided we could slip out, through the large jalousie windows, fool around and then slip back in without being missed. Everything was good to go on the inside. We climbed up and tried to squeeze out backwards through the narrow windows. Our butts were too big. Unfortunately, at that moment, while we suffered severe embarrassment and world-class wedgies, a counsellor pulled into the parking lot behind us. He took offensive action.

Mrs. Greer, the ancient librarian with a face like *papier maché*, was also a little peeved as she cranked the windows down on us, "Gotta capture these boys and protect the students," she said to the counsellor through the jalousie as he pulled one direction and she pulled the other. It was a bad and elongating day.

Chapter 3

Family Daze

The family name Perkins is one of the most distinguished of the ancient world during a time of Kingdoms, Kings and Knights. If we are to believe Bede, the Chronicler of the Saxons, this founding race of England was led by the Saxon General/Commanders Hengist and Horsa and was an Anglo/Saxon race, settled in Kent during this time. However, there is evidence to support the claim that the name is of Celtic/Welsh origin.

By the 13th century the family name Perkins emerged as a notable English family in the county of Leicester, where they were recorded as a family of great antiquity seated as Lords of the manor and estates in that shire. Notable amongst the family at this time was Perkins of Leicester. For the next two or three centuries, bearers of the surname Perkins flourished and played a significant role in the political development of England.

My dad's family was of English descent with typical bad teeth, a fondness for booze and certain distaste for other cultures. According to family legend the Perkins men were scribes, horse thieves, geniuses or drunks and mostly Episcopalians. Bob once told me that wherever you find four Episcopalians, you'll probably find a fifth."

From the age of fourteen to sixteen I attended St. Paul's Episcopal Church in downtown Milford. I was a "stink slinger" (I carried the incense) an altar boy, rode out Bible school and took Holy Communion. But the worst came during confirmation when we ate the "Holy Wafer." We didn't get any wine and the wafer stuck to my upper palate. I walked back down the aisle with my finger in my mouth. It looked like I was trying to puke so I could leave, but I was just fighting to get the wafer unstuck.

According to my dad, my Great Uncle Frank designed the first moving sidewalk system, some said inspired by his own drunken meanderings. He spent many years in a mental institution from which, in 1932, he corresponded with my grandfather explaining in handwritten detail the workings of the atom and how it could be harnessed. The working model of his moving sidewalk is still in the museum in Deerfield Village in Detroit, I think.

Families are fragile affairs. There are the aunts: the one with hairy nipples who always wears a bathing suit that is too large, making it hard not to notice, the one nobody talks to, the one that talks to no one and the one that hugs everybody and starts to cry. And of course uncles, cousins, nieces, nephews and other relations, all of whom brought something to the table - usually a bottle of booze, a bad cough or a dead frog. Members of the Perkins/Soule clan have been in the States since 1620. I am a Mayflower descendant

The Pimple Years

By 1960, I was so eager to get on with life that my parents' divorce didn't sink in and Bob was not one to encourage depression or despair. I've had a couple wives of my own since then and now know it must have been tough on Bob, not to mention the wives.

One night, when I was fourteen, my dad, without consulting his newest wife, Ruth, decided to have a hayride to celebrate Christmas Eve. My Swiss stepmother, Ruth Ruckstuhl, had moved in a few years earlier. This was her first hayride. The America she found at Oxbow Lake was not the America she had dreamed about or seen in magazines and it came as a surprise to her. Bob invited all his friends. Just at dark it started to snow and rain, freezing rain, so the hayride was screwed. There were fifteen or twenty people at the house. What did Ol' Bob do? He went outside and hollered, "Come on everybody, give me a hand."

The guests brought the hay into the house as I helped Bob push the furniture out of the way. It was a big living room. They dumped the hay in the middle of the floor then brought two of the sleigh team horses inside the house! Two big guys had to squeeze one of the horse's butt cheeks together to get it through the door. The horse made a funny back end sound and everyone laughed. "Wodka, anyone?" Bob boomed. (*Wodka* is how Ruth pronounced Vodka).

"Vhat are you peoples doink?" Ruth muttered. She was standing in the kitchen unable to move. There were horses in her house and the living room was full of hay. Everybody was drunk or well on the way and everyone, except my stepmom, thought this was the funniest thing they had ever seen.

The guests were starting to get raucous when some of the hay near the fireplace caught fire. The living room filled with smoke. The horses smelled the smoke and got spooked. They took a dump, snorted and kicked out the front door trying to make their escape. The horse with the big butt got out without any assistance this time, taking part of the doorframe with him. Sleet and snow were blowing into the house as the horses bolted for safety, a few men peed on the fire trying to put it out and Bob poured another *Wodka*.

Ruth was a solid Swiss lady who had never seen much of anything, at least like this, in her life. "In Switzerland, they don't do this ... *thing*," she said to Bob through the smoke.

"That's tough," Bob said as he went to light a cigarette that wasn't there, burning his nose hairs and dropping his drink on the flaming straw. Mr. Hooper, our neighbor, raced through the front door and threw a bucket of frozen horse turds mixed with snow on the fire to smother it. Merry Christmas!

Ruth looked skyward amid the smoke and then down at the burning hay, spilled drinks and steaming horse droppings on the floor. "America," she said and shook her head, the dream beginning to fade.

The action got everyone excited so of course they got drunker and later helped Bob drag the hay out and sweep the living room floor. Some people stayed over, sleeping on the floor or in the hay outside the door. They were too drunk to go anywhere, especially with icy roads. Most of them were so loaded they couldn't find their cars anyway.

One woman was invited to all the parties. She was a serious businessperson, Bob said. Bob liked her. Her name was Clara and she was not a gypsy or a cowboy. She was a big, voluptuous Greek lady and nobody wanted to mess with Clara, except me. I was fourteen. She was very vivacious and strong. Her abundant, oily, black hair smelled like martini olives. Clara loved people, *"Peoples must make to be happy!"* she sang loudly as she whirled around the room. After deciding that someone had sat on their "Patootie" too long, she came over, picked her victim up, squeezed the chosen one between her colossal Greek bosoms and danced until she was tired of him.

Clara always led. Then she plopped her stunned and weary partner back down on a chair and looked for her next partner in the "Bosom Ballet."

All the guys looked at the floor when she came around, hoping they wouldn't get picked. I looked up with hope, actually two hopes, in my eyes. Clara had a nice set of castanets. She snapped one near my butt to get me out of the chair. I stood up as she tucked me into her significant cleavage and took me to the dance floor. It was my first dance, during which a lifelong faith in random miracles was born! My feet were hardly touching the ground, but it was okay, I could live with them, ah...it. We twirled around the floor. Clara snapped her castanets with wild abandon and loudly proclaimed *"Peoples must make to be happy!"* I was happy.

Bob found his odd friends interesting; he said some of these folks "had gotten pushed to the curb of life." I think he realized that life was not going to be the cakewalk he had envisioned. He was forced to start busting ass and eating dreams early on and I know he wanted me to be prepared for the possibility that my life would not be perfect, either. He set the example; I ignored it. It never occurred to me that I wouldn't make it. Bob gave me work that made me angry, sore and tired but in the process I learned one important lesson: all jobs do come to an end, so hang in there. Bob didn't say too much, but one of his favorite remarks, when he did opine, was "That's tough." No matter what the problem was he'd always say, "That's tough."

My first job, at age sixteen, was working weekends for Mr. Miley on his farm. For fifty cents an hour, I baled hay in the summer and mucked out the horse stalls the rest of the time. It was a winter morning just at daylight when Miley called me into the barn. "We gonna de-ball some lambs today, son."

A dozen lambs with frosty breath milled around the pen. Occasionally, their sad bleating created a perfect harmony. It sounded nice until I grabbed one and flipped it upside down into a Y shaped yoke. Miley took a knife, made a slice, dove in and removed the testicles with his teeth. Bleating, steaming, screaming sheep and a vision of Miley standing like a band director with a sheep ball hanging out each side of his mouth gave me pause. "Wanna try it son?" I declined and quit in the same sentence. I went home and told Bob why. "That's tough," he said.

Almost every evening during "cocktail hour" Bob sat by the front window overlooking the lake, having a sip of *Wodka* and smoking a cigarette. On my bad days I would cautiously approach him and, after listening to my current tale of woe (I was allowed five minutes per woe), he would contemplate my pleadings, then render his consistent fatherly wisdom, "That's tough."

In a way it was nice for me to always know, in advance, the answer to my pleas for help, and oddly enough, with his benign neglect about eighty percent of whatever the trouble was went away. Some stuff just goes away.

Some stuff doesn't. Like the day I broke my leg soaring off a homemade ski jump I'd built in the front yard. I was sixteen and had a set of old wooden skis with the infamous "Bear Trap" bindings, bindings that were guaranteed not to release for any reason. It was my first jump. I poled down the slope to gain speed and jumped with a wing and a prayer but without a clue. I augured into the mud and snow about ten feet off the end of the ramp. The skis were too big and heavy for me. I couldn't get the tips up. Not only would more jump technique study be required but I had twisted the bone apart in my lower right leg. I was about to call for help when Bob came out of the house and yelled, "It's time for dinner!"

I yelled back, "Bob, I think I broke my leg."

He ran toward me, fell on his ass, slid down the hill and clawed to a stop near me. "Yup, you sure did Kid…probably best to leave you here in the snow, it will keep the swelling down, 'til I finish dinner." He kicked some snow on my leg. The wrong leg.

"But, Bob, it hurts! I can't walk," I half shouted through the rapidly freezing, pain induced, mucus running out my nose.

"That's tough," he said over his shoulder as he crabbed back up the hill on all fours. I lived through it; I guess that was the point. However, that knowledge did not change the fact I had crashed, couldn't get up and was lying there, dying. Bob went back in and closed the door so he wouldn't have to listen to me whine. Our dog Laddy came by, licked me with his warm tongue and peed on my skis. I tried to take comfort knowing that the now yellow snow would "slow the swelling" as Bob later reiterated again as we drove to Ol' Doc Bullard's house.

"Looks like you been rode hard and put away wet, son," Doc Bullard laughed as he 'grabbed holt' and twisted my right leg back to a near normal position. It happened so fast I didn't have time to scream. Pushing and pulling, he molded a plaster cast that went from my hip to my ankle. "That outta do her," Doc said. He and my Bob went outside to smoke a Lucky Strike while the plaster cured.

I was sixteen years old. I had one good leg and a cast up to my crotch on the other. For the six months I was in that cast my knee was straight and my foot stuck out in front of me. Finally, I healed and Doc Bullard cut the cast off. He didn't warn me it might hurt to bend my knee. Hurt? The pain was unreal.

For weeks afterward, my cast-free leg would magically lift off the floor, sometimes accidently catching the hem of a girl's dress. It turned out that that leg never did grow proper, but I'm hell in a right hand turn.

As I approached seventeen, my stepmother seemed to develop a temper and it was often directed at me in particular. Was I obnoxious? It's possible. Ruth had a Swiss temper, perhaps caused by too much cheese at an early age. But she only really "lost it" once. She got mad at me, Matterhorn Mad, and looked for a weapon in the kitchen with which to attack me. We had a large dining table. It was the size of a ping-pong table, big enough for five kids and two people (kids weren't people until they were at least sixteen). In her fury and Swiss fashion she grabbed a snow-caked ski boot near the mudroom door and looked at me wildly. Out of all the possible weapons, she picked a ski boot and came after me. We went back and forth around the table, which was too wide for her to get a good lick in. But I was in good shape and ran her into the linoleum. Finally, she got tired. She set the boot down and went outside for a smoke. On the way she said to my dad, who had calmly been observing my fight for survival, "Your son, I don't know vhy I ever married you!"

"That's tough," Bob said.

That was high drama and I loved it. One night we sat at the dinner table; there were seven of us and usually seven glasses and seven plates. This night however Ruth hadn't put out the right number of plates and eventually Bob tapped his fork on the table, *toonk, toonk, toonk*.

"Vhat are you doink, you?" she said.

"No plate," *tooonk tooonk* Bob responded.

"I can't stand to see you people, you're all crazy over here."

"That's tough," he said as he dished the food onto the table.

That only happened once; Ruth learned to count. It was tough but

Ruth was also lucky. One day, she marched into the kitchen and proudly announced that she had found a "four loaf cleaver" in the lawn, and another time she spotted a "Wood Headed Red Pecker" in a tree. How lucky can you get? Between Ruth's stoic approach to life and Bob's variable moods there was always something funny, at least to me, going on in our house.

I learned to drive on an old farm tractor, a Farmall-A series. You had to crank it by hand to start it. If it backfired, it could break your arm or knock you on your ass. It smoked, buckled and belched as I mowed the lawn, ploughed snow and raced the neighbor kids on their bikes. It was a tough piece of equipment.

For a few winters Bob rigged up a rope ski lift on one of our hills. He found two old truck axles in a junkyard. He took the rim off one end, stood it upright and buried one hub in the ground, leaving the drive shaft exposed. Then he put the other axle on an 'H' beam assembly at the top of the hill. He took the drive shaft from the lower axle, hooked it to the Farmall's power take off, put a one-hundred foot manila rope loop around the upper steel truck rim and put her in gear. Off we'd go faster uphill than down, the towline tightened and twisted. It grabbed our mittens and we had to ski over and grab them off the rope on the way down hill.

One day my six-year old brother Carl came down the ski slope on a sled. He was a small kid, a nice little guy, lying on a sled, having fun coming down the mud and snow covered hill. Carl's nose was usually running and I always pointed at it and said, "That's a booger!"

"No, it's snot!" he replied and we laughed like idiots.

Unfortunately, Carl didn't know how to steer the sled. Very slowly the sled curved toward me. I just watched him.

I saw what was going to happen but I couldn't react. I didn't move to save him. He curled across, in slow motion, and hit the three-inch steel drive shaft with his face. He wasn't hurt bad, I guess the boogers helped lubricate the impact. I knew I had had enough time to jump off the tractor and save him, but I froze, I hadn't moved. I had not yet realized you have to be able to think and react quickly if you want to survive.

Carl survived and I decided to get better at reacting.

My stepmother Ruth was thrifty. When it came time for my Junior Prom, I didn't have a suit or a jacket. Ruth decided that we couldn't afford to buy one. I had never been to a prom but I had to go. I had already asked one of our Milford Redskins cheerleaders to be my date and she reluctantly agreed. I was nervous. Ruth loaned me her small, baby blue angora sweater to wear along with my speckled dark blue corduroy pants, white socks and a pair of Bob's wingtips. Ruth had never been to a prom either. I looked like a large baby bird that had prematurely fallen out of the nest. Not only that, but I pissed Bob off by arguing with Ruth and he wouldn't let me take the car, so I had to take my date, the lovely Nancy Partridge to the prom on the back of our Farmall-A tractor. Ruth, still having problems with our vocabulary, was none the less concerned for my personal safety. As I climbed onto the tractor her parting words were, "Mark, do not forget to wear a conundrum!"

My date, the lovely Nancy Partridge never got the oil off her shoes or forgave me, but she did squeeze me tight during the ride, her passion most likely induced by fear. However, my embarrassment was soon replaced with a new confidence when I realized that people, except moms, have a short memory and life goes on.

There are many good memories of my time with my stepmother. She insisted that we follow the Swiss Army-inspired "hot potato safety protocol."

Before dawn, as we left for the school bus stop, she gave us each a freshly baked potato for warmth and lunch. We held it against our stomachs so our hands wouldn't freeze. We looked like a squad of tiny football players carrying the ball to victory as we headed for the bus stop with a small Episcopalian prayer frozen on our young blue lips. The potato also became our lunch, a cold baked potato and a bologna sandwich to go with it. A baked potato was her way of protecting us. Swiss efficiency.

If it was clear and the roads weren't too bad, we could see the bus from the front window of our house and we could get to the bus stop without having to wait. We used Bob's nicotine-stained binoculars. The snow looked yellow in the dawn light and the whistling wind made me feel small.

A few years ago, I went back to Michigan and drove past our house on Hilltop. Arabs had bought it and put a statue of a small Greek God taking a leak in the front yard right over the septic tank. A whizzing God with a concrete dick, day and night, all through the summer. Someone had painted the statue's dick black like Hitler's moustache and the remnant of a leaf was duct-taped across the remaining private parts-which appeared unusually small.

Chapter 4

The Loaner

I spent several high school summers with my Aunt Esther and Uncle Jim who, because it was my vacation and they didn't have any kids at that time, took me for a few weeks. I was a Loaner. I learned about the sea (Great Lakes) and boats. Those days were the most exciting days of my young life.

They had a home near Lake Michigan. Uncle Jim was a businessman and a member of the St. Joseph Yacht Club, where he kept his thirty-foot sailing sloop, the *Escape*. We drove to the Yacht Club almost every day after he got home from work. Uncle Jim wore a blue blazer with the yacht club emblem and a yacht club tie and casually manoeuvred his swanky, new, red Triumph TR-4 through traffic with a pair of purebred Irish Setters in the luggage space behind. Uncle Jim talked about sailing the lakes as the dogs barked wildly. The sparking smoke from his custom Meerschaum pipe, packed with *Borkum Riff* tobacco, billowed out the back. It was true joy, until one of the dogs caught fire. There were no serious injuries, but there was one ugly and smelly dog.

During those summers we sailed in yacht club regattas and races every weekend and even sailed across Lake Michigan to Chicago and up to Mackinaw Island. Uncle Jim was my dad's younger brother and had attended military school. He was a frustrated Captain who felt compelled to live up to my great-great grandfather Capt. Josiah Creesy Perkins legacy. To compensate, he ran a tight ship out on the Great Lakes. The Lakes can be nasty.

"Hear me boy... don't sail her out, if you can't sail her in..." he said, " I've got an engine in this boat, but that's just to help her sail better... it's the weight, don't ye know."

Uncle Jim never used the engine. He sailed in up-wind of a dock, dropped the main sail, and backed into the slip under a back-winded jib. Fabulous! People always clapped and I felt great.

Uncle Jim knew all the sailor's knots and the right knot for every situation. He made me learn a new knot every week and required me to squeeze a rubber ball every day for two hours, to strengthen my grip. "One hand for you, one hand for the ship!" he bellowed on almost any occasion, usually at the bar. He tested me weekly by blowing *Borkum Riff* smoke in my face and crushing my hand in his grip. He was the consummate mariner and I have a deformed, and sometimes uncontrollable, middle finger on my right hand.

Uncle Jim loved to tell the story of my possible great-great-grandfather, Captain Joshia Cressy Perkins, who with his wife Eleanor as navigator, set the "Around the Horn" sailing record in 1854 aboard the "Flying Cloud," a 208-foot clipper ship From New York to San Francisco: 89 days and 8 hours. She was the newest and largest clipper ship the world had seen.

The record stood until 1989. From an account of their journey I read-

"Perkins was the son of a New Hampshire carpenter. In his youth, Perkins had been a big strapping freckle-faced boy from Marblehead who spent his summer vacations frequently sailing over to Salem on a dory and hanging about the docks. The sight of an Indiaman sailing into port from halfway around the world with monkeys in the rigging and the rich aroma of spices wafting in the salt sea air intrigued him. The amazing variety of ships' figureheads, especially those of wild animals and warriors, fired up his imagination and he held the sea Captains of the Indiaman fleet in his highest esteem. There was no way to keep young Perkins away from his heart's desire and his parents permitted their son to sign aboard a sailing ship. He sailed "before the mast" for several years. He quickly advanced through all the grades, and at twenty-three became a Captain and went on to a long, illustrious career at sea. By 1854, he was Captain of the *Flying Cloud.*"

I imagined myself at the helm of the magnificent clipper ship whenever Uncle Jim re-told the story.

My first taste of open water came during cruises up and down the coastline of Lake Michigan. Unfortunately, on my first voyage, someone hadn't drunk enough water at a cocktail party the night before and one of the crew fired off a rock-hard turd into the head, the marine toilet. It was jammed in there and no one else could use it. There were women onboard! Hence my first task aboard the sailing vessel *Escape* was to dig this seagoing butt meteorite out of the "marine" toilet. Down in the bilge I took the head (toilet) apart. I tried to "remove the obstruction" and put the pieces back together as the *Escape* rolled back and forth in an oily sea.

Uncle Jim called out, "How goes it down below, Young Mark?" He was braced against the deck, holding the wheel like we were in a storm. There was no wind.

I was puking into the un-flushable bowl.

"Speak up, Lad, I can't hear you!"

"I need help!"

"You say, PUT ON MORE SAIL? Good Lad!"

The smell of warm scotch and pipe tobacco wafted into the bilge. It was my first bout with seasickness. Still I began to notice that sometimes, the harder things got physically, the better I liked it. I was young.

The Power of a Woman's Attention

I had an Aunt who read to me
Sagas of pirates who scoured the sea
Cutlasses clenched in their yellow teeth;
"Blackbirds" stowed in the hold beneath
I had an Aunt who read me lays
Of ancient and gallant and golden days;
Stories of Marmion and Ivanhoe,
Which every boy has a right to know.
I had an Aunt who read me tales
Of Gelert the hound of the hills of Wales
True to his trust till his tragic death,
Faithfulness lent with his final breath.
I had an Aunt who read me things
That wholesome life to the boy heart brings—
Stories that stir with an upward touch.
Oh, that each Aunt of boys were such!
You may have tangible wealth untold;
Caskets of jewels and coffers of gold.
Richer than I you can never be—
I had an Aunt who read to me.

Adapted—S. Gilliam

We ghosted along Lake Michigan's coast with an offshore evening, breeze. Aunt Esther read to me. I imagined myself being in the jungle or the Arctic as she read Rudyard Kipling's "The Jungle Book," and Robert Service's "Dangerous Dan McGrew."

"There are strange thing done in the midnight sun where men moil for gold." she read with gusto.

"A bunch of the boys were whooping it up in the Malamute Saloon,
The kid that handles the music box was hitting a jag-time tune;
Back of the bar, in a solo game, sat Dangerous Dan McGrew,
And watching his luck was his light-o'-love, the lady that's known as Lou.
When out of the night, which was fifty below, and into the din and the glare,
There stumbled a miner fresh from the creeks, dog-dirty, and loaded for bear.
He looked like a man with a foot in the grave and scarcely the strength of a louse,
Yet he tilted a poke of dust on the bar, and he called for drinks for the house.
There was none could place the stranger's face, though we searched ourselves for a clue;
But we drank his health, and the last to drink was Dangerous Dan McGrew."

When she read "The Jungle Book," by Rudyard Kipling, I became Mowgli, the Jungle Boy with my animal friends Riki Tiki Tavi the mongoose, Baloo the bear and Kaa the python. Together we fought Dhole, the Red Dog.

She was my introduction to the world of words and imagination. Uncle Jim said Esther's readings put him to sleep; he called her "Aunt Ether."

Aunt Esther was a first class sailor, a sturdy woman with a friendly laugh that made everyone smile, a welcome trait in any sailor. I thought she made the world exciting and, I learned the power of a woman's attention.

I spent several summers in the hot sand dunes near the St. Joseph Yacht Club in Benton Harbor, Michigan with Betsy, a girl my age, who lived on the beach nearby. We met while crashing into each other as we sailed dinghies around the Yacht Club basin. Her thick, sweet-smelling blond hair was full of sand and sweat; we swam in the cold Lake Michigan water, then rolled through the hot sand and dune grass to get warm, laughing and accidently bumping into each other. It was before I found out about sex, but I saw it coming.

Jim, Esther and I sailed from port to port, up and down Lake Michigan. During one voyage, our idyllic adventure was interrupted by thousands of black flies that settled on our leeward side. Out of sight of land and some leagues off shore the black flies arrived and within minutes we were coated with them. The unwelcome bugs stayed on the low side where the wind couldn't reach them. The flies, blown out to sea, didn't know where they were. The first thing they could land on, they did. They also bite. Uncle Jim brought the sailboat about and pissed into the wind to drive them away, an "old Indian trick" he said. The flies stayed. With disgust Jim cranked up the iron jenny (motor), "It's all this thing is good for ... getting rid of flies," and motored into the wind. My aunt went below to read.

We'd plan a trip, fit out the boat and sail to the out islands populated with strange, (everybody was strange to me as a teenager), and remote Michiganders. Those days encouraged my dreams of adventure. We were out in the bush, sailing into ports after dark and going ashore to meet the natives. One summer, we sailed aboard Uncle Jim's Chinese junk, the *Mandarin*. The *Mandarin* was a forty-five foot, wooden, double-masted, Chinese junk. She had been abandoned in a freight yard in New York. When Jim found out about the junk, he went to look her over. It was love at first sight. He paid the hobos who were living in it a reasonable amount to move out, then shipped his new love to Michigan on a semi-trailer.

Everyone we met on the lake wanted to hear the story of how my uncle came to own a Chinese junk on Lake Michigan! Uncle Jim would pause, draw on his stinky pipe (he liked an audience when it came to sea stories) and tell the tale of the sailing vessel *Mandarin*.

When the Chinese build a junk they use two teams, one builds the port side and one builds the starboard side. Each side has a separate crew and a separate foreman. A Yin and Yang team. They start together by laying the main timber, the keel, the backbone of the ship. After the keel is laid, two foremen, one on each side, measure out timbers, beams, frames, ribs and other private parts in finger, hand and arm lengths. The two crews work from stem to stern. Each foreman's fingers, hands and arms were different sizes. When the vessel was finished it appeared to be symmetrical but the two sides were different in specific dimensions.

Most junks were built for one trip down the river. When they arrived at their destination, the cargo was unloaded and the junks dismantled and used to build houses and furniture.

Junks have a big main cabin and a smaller one underneath the back deck, for the cabin boy-slave-me. Two holes, cut in the afterdeck that hangs over the water at the stern, are traditionally used for cooking/pooping. Unfortunately, this "poop deck" hangs out over the cabin boy's windows. The poop deck on ship is not actually for pooping, although in this case it was. Normally the poop deck is the deck farthest aft that may be overtaken by a following sea. Getting smashed by tons of water from above is called "getting pooped" at sea. Thankfully, I never got up early enough to watch a sunrise and accidently catch a mooning at the same time. It was indeed, a room with a view. It was a well thought out vessel until you hit that one little design flaw. The other hole was for the hibachi, the charcoal cooker. It was best not to get the holes mixed up.

When we cooked, the ashes fell out behind the boat leaving a chicken scented wake. Convenient, except for the ashes that blew into my cabin, but "Only," as my uncle explained, "when the boat was anchored, not anchored, facing into the wind or not facing into the wind or anytime the Hibachi was in use." Sometimes I came up in the morning looking like a small seagoing Al Jolson but it was efficient and easy for them. No mess or stinkies in the boat. I've sailed on a lot of junk in my life and it is my distinct pleasure to say *Mandarin* was the only real one.

For a few golden summers the *Mandarin* was famous as she the sailed the Great Lakes, from the Chicago skyline to the uncharted reefs of Skillagalee. It was freedom at its best, only nature to contend with and the feeling of motion, of velocity, of moving, where time felt like wind.

Coulda, Woulda, Shoulda

Time rolled by.

During my teenage years my father loved being as crazy as he could be, in those days. He was good to us kids and our animals, including the six horses. He stayed in the game and got all five kids through school. He was an engineer; he did what was needed to do to keep things working.

One evening I had nothing to do. I went with my dad down to our neighbor's house. There was a travel agent, an attorney and someone who owned a car dealership sitting at the card table. They all had riding lawn mowers, garage door openers, and color TVs, all the stuff you were supposed to have in that community. They had money and were upper middle class. I remember looking at them and thinking, *so this is where I'm headed.* Not bad.

Left alone, sitting in the kitchen I spied a smelly Brittany spaniel. "His name is Spud," Mr. Gustafson told me.

Spud was dumber than a rock. I sat on the kitchen floor and threw pieces of dry dog food across the linoleum. Spud the spaniel went for them. The dog had no traction on the slippery surface but still ran like mad to get that nibblet. He couldn't stop on the linoleum and slammed head first into the counter across the kitchen. Spud shook his head, found the nibblet, ate it and came back wagging his tail to do it all over again. Head first, straight into the counter, dumb as a post. I was having a great time but the enjoyment appeared to be wearing thin as Spud staggered back towards me. Bob shouted, "Hey Mark…Stop making all that goddamn noise in there!"

The night wore on and, with nothing else to do, I sat and listened to my dad and his friends. I heard many of the same words repeated throughout the course of the night, the words many of us have heard. Drunker and drunker, they kept echoing, "Could have- would have- should have." That stuck. If these old guys were saying it, it must be true, I thought. Later, we got into the car and drove back up the hill. I said to my dad, "Bob, I'm never going to do that."

"Do what?"

"I'm never going to sit around when I'm old and say I should have done something."

"That's tough," he said.

I didn't think he got it. He didn't think I got it. Who did get it?

That was the first thing I ever told my dad, the first real thought about my life I was sure of. I think.

Bob was good with horses and took a job breaking ponies for an old "glue merchant," a guy who bought ornery horses nobody wanted. He hired Bob to break them so they could be sold to a livery, a riding stable or, failing that, he'd sell off their body parts. The hoofs were used to make glue and Jell-O, Bob told me. One winter night we were in the indoor corral at the Four Q Ranch. Bob was trying to get a saddle on a spooked horse. It was genuinely cold. My dad and the horse were both steaming at the mouth, the horse turds seemed to freeze in mid-air and bounced when they hit the ground. As Bob was talking to the horse, so it would know his voice, the animal leaned over and bit Bob on the shoulder so he would know its bite. Horse bites are not pleasant. Bob cursed, then got mad and stuck his left hand up the horse's left nostril, but not on purpose; he was reaching for the bridle and missed. The horse seemed surprised by Bob's action; he'd never had anyone try this move before! With his left hand stuck in the horse's nose Bob smacked the animal on the side of the head with his right hand. The horse quivered and went down in a heap. My dad couldn't get his hand out of the horse's nose so he went down too. They laid peacefully together on a frozen pile of manure for a minute or so. Then the horse shook, got up and snorted which helped get my dad's fist out of its nose. It stood up, still a little wobbly, and waited for the saddle. I had never seen anyone hit something so hard. The horse looked at me cross-eyed and snorted in agreement. I learned that when it came to the relationship between man and animal, somebody had to be in charge.

Chapter 5

Leaving Milford

It was 1964; the Milford Redskins won a football game. It was a good year, my junior year.

Hernandez and I were in the cafeteria. A student had died. An assembly was held. Dying was rare in those days. The cafeteria smelled like doughnuts, girls, hair spray, hormones, girls and institutional discipline. Everyone was quiet, some were even serious. Except, Maurice Peasley, who of course, farted succinctly, then pointed at the unsuspecting person next to him. In the same instant of fartage, Maurice turned his head and lofted his nose in utter disdain. We all had suffered Maurice's cruel joke. The faculty members frowned at Maurice and said memorable things about the kid who died. The teachers opened the windows to get some fresh air and attempted to get students to speak so they, themselves, wouldn't have to. Unfortunately Hernandez was near the front of the resistant speaker line and, Hernandez loved to volunteer. "Well... it's a shame the guy died, but I guess that means... more food for me," Hernandez puffed. He glanced toward the food line, pretending to do the math.

Everyone reacted. Some yelled at Hernandez, some yelled for Hernandez. Soon, the classic adolescent, "Huh?" a common and frequent inquiry amongst my peers, was intoned.

We were teens, didn't know anything about life and less about death. The learning came when the teachers and students, made equal by grief, started joking.

The kid who died got a good send off and I took notice of Hernandez. He was a potential candidate for future adventure.

My girlfriend, for a while, Karen was a dark-haired beauty. She smelled rich and looked like Wonder Woman. We "went steady" for awhile. That surprised everybody, including me. Karen was a good bad girl with a Revlon, Lip-Luster, smile and perfect diction. She was excited by boys willing to take risks for her. The bigger the risk, the bigger the kiss was my hope.

She was the only beautiful girl I remember in high school. It took all my courage to approach her during a church-sponsored hayride. I introduced myself shortly after she and I were pushed off the hay wagon by more "classically trained" chortlers, for singing Christmas carols too loud at "inappropriate moments."

I clawed through the frozen mud to help her. Her perfect ass was driven 5/8ths of the way into the mire.

She blew condensed breath in my ear. "Milford's a shit-bird hole in the wall." Karen breathed eight words and I was only up to the "shit-bird" line, when her steaming red lips and sorbet sounds encouraged a well-known passion. I grabbed her armpits and pulled. We crabbed out of the damp ruts. The wagon stopped. Chastised, we silently climbed onboard and covered ourselves with hay to hide our make out session.

Karen cultured her words, like an oyster making a pearl. She could enunciate and words loved her for it. They blissfully became oral fossils and seemed to fall to the ground when she finished with them. Her lips left an articulate trail. She was an old soul with a young body. Love is a powerful thing. So is a young body.

Karen's father was an optimistic optometrist, her mother, a sharp-tongued boozer with a sense of humor. They were rich, arrogant and likable. Karen was their only child. I was their only fear. Karen detested almost everyone, especially jocks and vigilantly singled them out for her stunning disregard. Karen made you feel that ... if she chose not to look at you, you didn't exist.

Karen knew all about her powers. In the right mood, she twirled her head around fast. Going eye to eye with her silent admirers, her lascivious black curls wrapped her shoulders in velocity-induced awe and sprung back, in strict obedience to her wishes. She launched her Wonder Woman smile down the linoleum hallway like a bowling ball. Her self-assurance settled all doubt. The pimpled pins scattered. I got to see her lips when she turned back around. "Let's fuck," she said.

I thought she was kidding; I didn't believe her and went to the library. It was a bad mistake. But, she was untouchable anyway, she wanted more. Now.

One day she didn't look at me. I disappeared.

Hernandez and I were in drama club. He had a car; I could get home. In our senior year we almost performed Peter Pan. I was Peter Pan the star of a doomed production; a brilliant interpretation, cut short by tawdry technical hitches.

A wire, from the balcony to the stage, held me. In Pan's green tights I launched and glided across the audience's heads. Hernandez, however, the technical and consummate professional, was not paying attention to the procedures required to STOP me, Peter Pan, at the end of the dramatically short flight. Down the wire flew Peter Pan! PETER PA...! The braking procedure failed during the critical seconds before landing. I punched through the back of the stage. The set went down with me. I was now Peter Pain.

A classic performance, a unique, random failure, but I made it out alive, and that simple fact inspired me further.

"There are many reasons for the possibility of failure, let alone failure itself...We almost made it!" Hernandez, who got an A in philosophy, explained amidst the rubble. *Almost*, is a dangerous word that feels good but can lead to severe and flawed conclusions.

There was no time to rebuild the set. My first acting experience was over, or was it? Would it affect my career? Was it another world?

I was eighteen and hormonally unable to live a life of moderation.

I told my dad I was going to be an actor. "That's tough," he predictably replied and lit a Camel.

After graduation I hitchhiked toward New York for an interview at the Actors Studio. It was winter.

Mr. Rodney Bahn had been my drama coach and even though he was exiled from the New York theatre community for reasons I never knew, but could guess, he still had *"bonified connections,"* he said, to get me an audition at the Actor's Studio and he did. Bahn wrote a letter to a friend lisping my talents. "Young Perkins may have some potential," he wrote.

I may have had potential but only hitchhiked as far as Pennsylvania. I was freezing my 'nads' off on the side of a winter road. A guy in a convertible, the top up and the back seat full of luggage, stopped. "Where ya going kid?" he asked.

To impress him with my importance I shivered the words, "I'm g, g, g, oing to New Yuh, Y, Y, ork to become a, ah, a, a, ac ..."

"Too bad kid, I'm going to Florida where it's fuckin' hot." He gunned the engine.

"Me tttt, t, t, ooo," I said quickly, diving into the warm car.

The driver dropped me in Delray Beach near my grandmother's house. I remembered she used to love me. I walked into her house, gave my surprised Grandmo a hug and called my dad for money.

"Bob, It's me, your son, Mar..."

"I know who the fuck it is."

"Ah, I'm broke, I nee..."

"That's tough ... I know what you need, it's a good kick in the a ...!"

Click. He was tired of my bumming around

Grandmo and I had lunch, but we didn't have much in common anymore. I was starting to live; she was starting to die. After lunch she got up. Oh boy! I wanted to see my room. Instead she turned, gave me $50.00 and pointed at the door. It closed behind me without a sound. Guess she didn't need a hero anymore.

I hitchhiked back to Milford, very hungry. I finally realized I had to have money to live.

I was embarrassed by my lack of understanding of the real world and already, without much effort, I was a disappointment to my dad.

I walked into our house and, after initial greetings, started the conversation casually with, "Ah Bob..." I smiled, "can I borrow ... ?"

He finished the sentence, "Get the hell out of this house!"

He put down his Camel and raced toward me with remarkable speed, his comb-over causing him to veer off course as he picked up momentum. I guess he had good reason; he certainly appeared convinced of it. With the instincts of a scared cat I headed for the front door, Bob was in close pursuit. He closed in fast. My notion that Bob was old didn't seem to matter to him, it was his home turf. I thought he was going to hit me. He didn't. Instead he tried to kick me. Martini glass in hand he planted his left foot and gave it his best shot. He missed. "I'm gonna kick your ass!" he foamed.

He sounded like he meant it. A piece of olive ejected from his lips and flew at me, like a tiny rocket. I beat him to the screen door, threw it open and, as I had been taught, closed it behind me. Bob took his second kick, missed and drove his scrawny leg through the copper screen. The door swung open. Badly tangled and clutching his groin, Bob bounced face first into the wall he'd built so well. I watched him hang onto the screen door as it slowly ripped from its hinges. He may have called my name, but I don't think so.

"That's tough," I screamed back.

He weakly threw his empty Martini glass at me.

I was gone. I stayed gone. It felt good, until the adrenalin wore off.

Chapter 6

California or Bust

After the previous incident I didn't feel comfortable going home. It would be tough so I told Mom Hernandez some lies. She let me move in with them. It got old for her, me and us. Hern and I decided to set out on our own. See the world before the draft could take us. Our plan was to formulate a plan, later.

Hernandez always parked himself near the intersection of unacceptable behaviour and uncontrollable hilarity. Everything was funny to Hernandez. He'd never been in a box, his thinking was already outside.

Milford was not near the Interstate highway. We got to the freeway on a dirt road. Mom Hernandez drove us to a truck stop and, after a tearful goodbye, dropped us off. Once she arrived back home, we called her from a pay phone and told her we had forgotten our money. She brought it to us with fewer tears accompanying the second farewell. The first person who stopped to pick us up asked, "Where are you boys going?" We grinned at each other, "We're going to California!"

With the sincere faith that only fools possess and our duffel bags stuffed full of young dreams we set out hitchhiking, from Michigan to California. It was an adventure. Our first day took us as far as Toledo, Ohio where it was colder than a well-digger's ass. It was late, dark and there was no traffic. We were tired and decided to climb up a nearby hill to get away from the piled-up grey snow with our yellow initials written in it. Before we left Michigan we got our hands on a used tent from the Salvation Army, a two man, state-of-the-art (in 1940), Vulcanized rubber tent. It had an outside tent and an inside tent so you didn't get condensation. One tent inside another, cool. Without much forethought we managed to put up the tent for the first time. But, being idiots (not a calling for the weak), we didn't know that a double-sided tent needs ventilation. Condensation, the enemy, occurs in a hurry without it.

We woke up in the dark at six the next morning. There was frost on the inside of the tent and we were freezing our butts off. We tried to get out of the stiff, frozen tent but it broke loose and started to slide down the hill; a couple of tent pegs held for awhile, slowing our descent. Struggling to escape, we only managed to twist the tent into a frosty ball as we hit the edge of the hill and slid down en masse. It was like being in a big, cold Chinese finger trap. The more we struggled the worse it got, the outer tent wrapping around the inner tent. There was a brand new motel near the bottom of the hill. We were wrapped and trapped inside the tent. We clawed around like morons, laughed like fools and managed to wiggle right up to the side door of the motel. I could smell coffee. We pounded on the glass with our heads and begged the lady in reception to let us in.

Her nametag said "Hi! I'm Elaine." She looked us over and finally said we could come in, "Just inside the foyer,"… neither of us knew what a foyer was, "just long enough to warm up," but, at first, we weren't allowed to get out of the tent. Perhaps she thought we were escaped towel thieves, our tent full of little shampoo bottles. The security guard pulled us, still in the tent, into the lobby and helped unwrap us. I didn't pretend to understand the logic, I was just happy to be warm. We loved Elaine. She was very cool. The guard determined we were no threat, "Don't worry about these fools," he said. Elaine gave us coffee. Midwestern hospitality at its best.

The next day, Hernandez and I were hitchhiking through Hinckley, Ohio, home to a tribe of buzzards that migrate to Key West every year. We had plotted an erratic course to California. We should have followed the buzzards. But instead we stood near a new looking on ramp for hours trying to get a ride to the Interstate. Nobody would pick us up, even though we were clean and presentable. All day we stood beside the on ramp getting madder and madder, commenting to each other, "What the hell is wrong with these Hinckley people? Why won't they pick us up? I hate these Hinckleys." Finally, later that afternoon, one of the cars that passed us earlier that morning and again at lunch came back. A guy stopped, rolled down his window and said, "You boys looking for the interstate?"

"Ah … yeah."

"Well it ain't done yet."

There was no freeway and if we had walked half a mile down the road we would have seen the sign-ROAD CLOSED. We didn't have a clue; just two fools standing near a dirt pile on an unfinished road.

Hernandez and I eventually made it to Los Angeles and met his Aunt Margarita who resembled ageing *femme fatale* out of film noir. Cigarette smoke curled around her as she gestured with long, blood red fingernails. She had the classic two-tone, dyed red hair, a gravelly grit voice and a gunshot attitude. She carried a small .22 calibre pistol in her purse. She liked showing it to us. "I'll blow the dick off any jerk who messes with me!" she advised. I tried not to be a jerk.

During the month we were in Los Angeles Aunt Margarita dragged us around like a couple of studs, young, naïve studs, she'd picked up somewhere. We became members of the union of souls known as BITOA, a group of like-minded people whose motto was "Booze Is the Only Answer"-hence BITOA. We also became Turtles while in LA. Turtles were another group of like-minded individuals. If you met someone in a bar and asked them, "Are you a Turtle" The secret reply, if they were, was "You bet your sweet ass I am!" Drinks were poured.

About this time, things started to get more serious on the Vietnam front. Hernandez decided to enlist in the Marines and got his orders to ship out which meant he had to head home early from our grand world tour. After we parted ways, I didn't see Hernandez again for thirty years. I was in the draft lottery but wasn't very concerned about it. It seemed unlikely to happen to me, I thought.

***

After leaving California, I hitchhiked to Miami and caught a flight to Nassau in the Bahamas. Islands fascinated me and they were warm. I landed with a hundred dollars in my pocket and ended up living in a fish trap out on the West End of the island for a few months. The trap, made out of semi-rotten palm fronds, bamboo and rusted chicken wire was L-shaped and designed to catch large groupers. The trap was sitting on the beach, apparently abandoned. So I moved in. I was a grouper groupie! I wriggled my way in one end at night and wriggled my way out the other at daylight. No first or last and the only deposits were from sea gulls and snails. I called my beachfront condo Roach Royale. It was not your typical tourist trap.

I slept in the fish trap at night and trolled the beach for Canadian lovelies during the day. Bahamian law prevented me from working. Not that I wanted to or tried. I knew I would run out of money soon. It always came down to money. I'd have to find a way to get others to pay for my fun.

One afternoon, in the bar at the British Colonial Hotel, referred to as the BC by the locals; I met an older aristocratic chap named Nigel. He was of noble blood, at least the family crest on his crisp blazer indicated such, and had been exiled to Nassau for reasons not explained. Nigel appeared wealthy and owned an estate out on the West End. He and some fellow Brits were drinking gin and tonics and watching the Bahamian Independence Parade on TV. The proud Bahamians were granted "limited self-government" in 1964 but would not be formally recognized as an independent nation until 1973. This caveat did not deter the happy Bahamians, who had thrown off the yoke of British oppression and the Brits organizational skills, from wanting to party. They finally controlled their own destiny.

We watched the parade on TV. The Royal Bahamian marching band passed in front of the single, now government-controlled, TV camera. In full Goombay regalia with feathers flying, butts bouncing and drums fighting whistles for attention, the colorful revellers crossed the Fox Hill Prison parade grounds. A third round of gin and tonics was poured at the BC. After thirty minutes or so, the parade crowd began to thin. A few drunks and dancing stragglers weaved by. A scraggly dog staggered into the frame and sought relief on a fallen feather boa. A Bahamian carrying a stick with a nail in the end passed by picking up discarded beer cans and a wide variety of colored feathers. The cameraman had gone off with the parade!

One of the Colonial chaps raised his gin and tonic; "To Independence!" he said shaking his white-manned head sadly. "Stiff upper lip and all that rot ... Civilization, old chap, was rather fond of it myself, don't you know ... what?"

Because I said nothing amidst the passionate outcry of distraught Colonials, Nigel may have mistaken my silence for wisdom and occasionally sent his chauffer to pick me up at the trap and bring me to his estate. On those mornings, I crawled out of the discarded fish trap, dusted myself off with a palm frond and got into a Cadillac limousine for a ride to Nigel's estate where I enjoyed Jamaican Blue Mountain coffee and English crumpets. I loved the balance of nature.

Nigel spoke about the less than appealing aspects of getting old while in exile. I listened to the aging expatriate. I did not have a clue what he was talking about, but I listened and didn't say much, which seemed to give him some comfort. "It does one good to get a different perspective from the young, wouldn't you agree?" he said tugging at his perfect handle bar moustache. There was something odd about this British aristocrat. He was straight, and he must have seen straight away that I was too, because I ogled his beautiful daughter each time she passed the table. She was gorgeous, but I couldn't get near her. I was not in her league and I knew it. I tried everything, short of going up and talking to her.

Nigel was good to me but I didn't thank him, or even tell him when I left. You know how you are when you're young.

While in Nassau my limited resources sometimes forced me to go "over the hill," where I learned to live in peace with the poorer Bahamians, they were poorer than me. That was poor!

The main street in Nassau is named Bay Street and runs along the waterfront speckled with cruise ships, straw markets, piles of conch shells and bars. On the other side of Bay Street the town moves away from the water and up a hill. When you go over the hill you enter another world. I went back in time with each step ... campfires, smoke, barking dogs and a night black as pitch. There was very little electricity; cooking fires were built outside many of the shantytown dwellings. I liked it and as people danced around half naked I could almost see the cruise ship passengers, dining on *fois gras and Boeuf Wellington* half a mile as the crow flies, away.

Kids were playing, yelling in singsong Bahamian and leaping over the fire. Someone gave me a plate of fire-cooked food. I ate the dark smoky substance, tapped off some rum and played my guitar. But no one could hear me. That's probably why I survived.

Anointed with cheap warm rum and heated by the fire, all humanity melted together in a puddle of collective consciousness- black, white, white, black. It was a grey area.

Near a sparking fire I met Winston Hercules, a Bahamian about my age. After a few minutes of jaw, he asked if I wanted to go to a "different" party. Winston, dressed in skin-tight red pants and a tank top, appeared to be a person of debatable character and inclination, so of course I went. It was about two in the morning. I walked into a house party and everyone was naked. I was a white guy in flip-flops. In the dark room I must have looked like the "light at the end of the tunnel." Everybody was doing something to everybody else. It was gay and straight, lots of girls, everybody balled up in an Ethiopian cluster fuck, looking like giant clasped hands.

Winston looked askance at me, "This might be a little loose for you. You look a bit too straight, Mon." I noticed Winston's words became softer and his tongue slipped around in his mouth when he spoke with half closed eyes. *No! Oh God No! Oh hell no! ... Oh well.*

"Okay, Herc, I'll fix that. Give me your bag," I said. Adapt and survive.

Winston handed me his straw purse with a queenly flourish. I took his powder puff and powered myself pink and, with a touch of lipstick in my moustache and nose hair for effect, turned back to Winston, "How's dat, Mon?"

He looked at me, and smiled broadly, "Oh Mon, I'm worry 'bout you." He paused, "But you don't have to worry 'bout me."

I followed Winston into the maze, drank some rum, found a set of tits, safe ground, and settled in. I was only eighteen and already I was "over the hill."

During that shantytown night I learned that no one can tell you are not crazy quicker than a person who is. It takes practice to make the team. I was a contender.

I occasionally hung out with a "counter jumper," excuse me, "ex-counter jumper." We met in the British Colonial bar, his name was Lucas, and after we swapped conventional lies I asked, "What do you do, Luke?"

"I'm an ex-counter jumper," he said quietly with emphasis on the "ex." He was buying the drinks, so I listened further. "I like to rob banks. Love to jump over the counter and take the money myself. I just get in there and grab it because I don't want to fuck around with the girls behind the counter. They're deliberately slow, and they take too much time bagging it up. Then I jump back over and haul ass. You gotta do it fast, man, you don't hesitate. You jump over the counter and scream and wave your arms around and don't forget to take your own bag. Damn, that money smells so good, man!"

"Sounds like fun." I said but didn't intend to try.

Around the same time I met another expatriate named Gil. Gil was an aging Golden Gloves champion from New Jersey. He was a drifter. We met while trolling for girls on the beach in Nassau. Apparently Gil never got over the urge to beat the shit out of someone. He usually picked on the biggest guy in the bar; he was courteous that way. He didn't pick on him exactly, but when he found himself in "that mood" it didn't take him long to piss someone off. He'd insult a guy and let him get angry. "I always let the other guy get his ass up on his shoulders, first. It's not good for balance, ha ha." Gil said. He waited until the "chosen one" threatened him then made a funny face or a distracting noise and swung.

Gil said, "Kid, if you have to hit someone more than once you're liable to get your own ass kicked and that hurts." No past, no future, just kick ass and move on. I was part of that world then, the moving on part. After a few months my visa expired.

Chapter 7

Un Frijole Malo

    Back in the States, I hitchhiked through Texas on my way back to California. I liked California. In east Texas I got a ride from a trucker driving a big White Motor Company Freightliner with a load of hogs bound for El Paso in an open sided trailer. He was a scrawny little trucker. A skinny cowboy with stringy arm muscles, and a big Adam's apple, he introduced himself as "Ticks."
    "Tex?"
    "No, Ticks, they call me Ticks son cause, gol'darnit ... I'm a little fella, but I get rained on last, an ...I got me a bad bite!" he informed as I climbed up and into the right front seat. The driver's seat was worn out; so Ticks had installed two lounge chair cushions on top of the seat to prevent "hissef" from falling into the springs. He sat about six inches up off the main seat, his legs were so short that he had custom high-heeled cowboy boots made to his specifications. Ticks could clutch, brake and throttle with his heels. Walking was more difficult and gave him an unusual gait. I made the mistake of saying that I thought it was pretty cool how he drove the truck and shifted gears. The White had an old style twelve-speed transmission. Ticks shifted through one set of six gears, then pulled a lever and switched to a second set of six gears. It was a lot of work and every time he shifted, he looked over to make sure I was watching. Every damn time he shifted I had to watch him. If I didn't look, he didn't shift. He'd run it up in gear until the RPM redlined and black smoke was pouring out of the stack. He wanted me to see the muscles ball up in his arm, muscles the size of a chicken leg. He also had a tonnage load of hogs in the trailer, a stinking, squealing pile of porkers that swayed the rig when they started (it seemed they never stopped) mating. Yeah, it was weird.
    During the first few hours I noticed that Ticks constantly pushed his cowboy hat up. It was too big and kept sliding down over his ears. He kept saying his ears hurt.
    Finally I said, "Well hell Ticks, why don't you get a smaller hat?"

Ticks looked puzzled.

Having nothing better to do I contemplated the hat situation and the next morning outside of Abilene I got him to put a pair of his jockey shorts on his head, underneath the hat, to keep it from falling down and affecting his ability to see the road. His waist size and hat size were about the same and the jockey shorts looked like a nasty beret when he put them on. He looked in the rear view mirror, adjusted his cowboy hat just so then said I was "one smart sumbitch!" He down shifted and looked over at me. I turned to watch him shift the big rig as we headed through the desert with a yellowed Jockey label visible just below Ticks' hatband.

We pulled into a truck stop somewhere deep in Texas and went in to eat.

Let's "bean up" Ticks said as we entered the diner. With a cowboy flourish Ticks took off his ten-gallon hat and started chatting up the waitress. Her nametag said *Rosa*. She was a nice looking Mexican woman with long black hair, a big butt and a gold tooth in the front of her mouth. Rosa started laughing and I knew why, but Ticks missed it and winked at me. Ticks prided himself on being a 'swordsman' and had graphically shared some of his exploits during the trip. He said women were always "drawed" to him.

"Man she sure is friendly," the words slipped out the side of Ticks mouth as Rosa picked the Jockey shorts off his head with a fork and set them on his hat. Ticks' face turned red as a Texas sunrise. Rosa laughed again.

We sat there eating for quite a while, Ticks was laughing, Rosa was laughing. All I thought about was sleeping for the next few hours. We were close to heading out when three Mexicans came in and started after Ticks. , "Hey Gringo," one of the Mexicans chirped, "that's my girlfriend, what are you doing talking to her? *Porque* asshole?"

Ticks changed from lover boy to a ball of meanness in a nano-second and said, "I ain't doing nothing, I'm eatin' a danged cheeseburger, she's the waitress, Fuck Off! Comprendo?"

The Mexicans started to get abusive and it wasn't looking good. Finally, the owner of the restaurant came out of the kitchen holding a baseball bat, he looked like a right-hander.

"Get the fuck out of here, all of you," he said to the Mexicans in English. He looked at Ticks, "Sorry about that, boys."

"Hey, no problem pardner', we all got a little asshole in us," Ticks replied.

The owner, not sure how to reply, faked a bunt to Rosa's ass, shook his head and returned to the kitchen.

We finished our meal. Ticks went into the bathroom to adjust his hat and then we went outside. The truck was parked near some scrub pine and suddenly out of the bushes came the "Three Amigos." They came right up to us, the lead beaner walked with jerky little rooster steps. They had their asses on their shoulders. I wished Gil was there. Ticks was looking at them but said to me out the side of his mouth, "You take the two on the outside; I'll take the guy in the middle with the knife."

"Knife?"

Ticks never blinked while he talked; he had bowlegs, a funny gait because of his boots, a big hat with undershorts sticking out the side and an unusual tone in his voice. The Mexican with the knife was listening intently to Ticks, too intently. Ticks spoke calm and low, it didn't make sense for the circumstance, to the Mexicans or me. He was mesmerizing.

"OK, I'll take the outside two." Standing at the intellectual confluence of ignorance and stupidity I pulled off my belt and wrapped it around my left hand. I didn't know what I was going to do with it but I had seen it done in a movie. My pants would make their own decision. "OK," I thought, "I'm not going to be much use here, but it should be quick."

Ticks talked softly, mesmerizing Mexicans. El Knifo leaned forward to hear him. Ticks had him off balance. Mexican mistake number one.

"Neenee, nawnee, nooney..." said Ticks it was an old Jonathan Winter schtick. El Knifo couldn't stop listening to this high-heeled trucker talking complete nonsense. Ticks eased up in front of El Knifo. Knifo was a little bigger than Ticks. Ticks winked evilly at his buddies to distract them and ZOT! He reached in toward the Mexican's belly button. "Coochee Coochee" he whispered. El Knifo looked down. Mexican mistake number two.

Ticks instantly stepped forward, head butted Knifo's chin, slapped his arms apart, grabbed his head, held the hombre's knife arm back with his own elbow and locked his hands behind the uncomprehending brown neck. Using the Mex's neck for leverage he jumped up, wrapped his legs around the Mex's waist, pulled his head toward him and, riding the staggering antagonist for a few feet, quickly bit off the Mexican's nose. I had not seen that in a movie.

It happened in less time than it takes to tell.

Ticks spit the nose out underneath his armpit. PHOOWEE! The Mexican's nose was skittering through the dirt when Ticks jumped off him. El Knifo freaked, dropped the blade and watched blood blowing out of the hole where his nose used to be. He dropped to his knees in the gravel trying to find his beak.

One of the men puked. The third guy screamed and ran. I checked my trousers for stains and tried to figure out what happened.

Ticks looked at me, "You know Red, that always leaves me a baaad taste in my mouth, let's go have us another coffee."

I casually pulled my pants up and put my belt back on. We walked back into the restaurant where Ticks started talking to Rosa again. He even told Rosa that he just bit her boyfriend's nose off. "Talk about blood, man! Holy Jesus!" He slapped the counter, "There's some big fucking vessels in your nose, you know."

Rosa just laughed.

Ticks had a glob of blood in his armpit where the nose had passed by. "Dang Beaner winged me," he laughed while trying to clean it off with a napkin. Rosa thought it was funny and poured salt on his shirt. They were both laughing. Their faces got closer together, Ticks winked at Rosa, "Fucking Mexicans, I'd sure hate to eat a whole one ... wheweeee!" Rosa laughed. "Leaves me a baaad taste," scrunching up his face. Rosa laughed again, she must have seen a lot of crazy things in her day and found the best response was laughter plus, she liked Ticks' style.

"I bet it does," I, the grizzled road veteran chimed in, "biting off a Mexican nose."

Rosa didn't laugh and looked away.

After we got back in the truck, the first thing Ticks did was look over to make sure I was watching. His little muscles balled up tight while he got ready to shift gears. The big White Freightliner coughed to life and we drove out of the parking lot. I saw that the nose-less Mexican had put a rag on his face. He was still looking for his nose in the dirt. It would probably be even harder to find after Ticks drove over it on the way out.

50

I had to give that trucker credit; it was a cool move and the only thing he could have done to save our/his /my asses.

An hour or so down the road the adrenalin wore off, I said, "You know Tick, I'm really not going a lot farther than here, so the next the town is good."

"You got it, Red."

He dropped me off without a word. Twelve gears and gone.

I went on to California. After a few days I returned to Michigan with a bruised face from a poorly executed body surfing manoeuvre and a growing realization that I could not hang out forever.

On the way back I got a cross-country ride to Atlanta where I almost got arrested for vagrancy in the Grey Hound bus station. I was trying to talk my way onto a bus without paying. I was tired of hitchhiking and my face hurt where I had augured into the golden California beach sand. A transit cop appeared. "Tell me, son, how much money do you got? You gotta have ten dollars in your pocket or else you're considered a vagrant."

I pretended to search my pockets but I didn't have ten dollars. I stood in line wondering what the hell to do, certain I was going to get thrown in jail, when a very well dressed, cool-looking black guy glided over. He'd overheard the conversation.

"What's the problem heahh, officer?"

"This kid's a vagrant, he's a bum, and we don't want his type in our town."

"Really," said the black man. "Is that right?" He glanced at me, "Are you a bum?"

"No sir, not really, I, mean ..."

"Shut up kid." Then to the cop, "What does it take to make someone not a bum in Hot Lanta?"

"Ten bucks," said the cop's mouth, "He's got to have ten bucks in his pocket."

Mr. Smooth reached in his pocket and pulled out a wad of money as thick as a hamburger, peeled off two hundred dollar bills and handed them to me. "Now you're not a bum."

"Who the heck are you?" the cop and I asked in unison.

"I'm Junior Walker, ya'll know... Juuuuuunior Walker and the All Stars- Rhythm and Blue Band... man everybody know me in Hot Lanta!"

He made a couple dance moves and spun away with a two-step. The cop's mouth dropped open. Junior had more money in his pocket than the cop would make all month. When he flipped the wad open it was all $100's. The cop couldn't understand why a wealthy black man would help a young white drifter, neither could I. It didn't register with the cop and by the time it did, if it did, I was gone, headed for the ticket counter inside the building.

"Thank you, Mr. Walker," I yelled as the doors closed behind me with a hiss.

In that Greyhound bus station in Atlanta I found my faith in random miracles had not been misplaced.

Chapter 8

The Dude Ranch

With the last of Junior Walker's two hundred bucks I returned to my patch in Michigan. It was 1966, the summer before I enlisted in the Army. Junior's two Franklins got me home in style, but I was tired of travel, not to mention broke. I thought being a hobo or a drifter would be exciting and romantic and it had been, for a while, a short while. During the last few months on the road the excitement began to fade. I was tired of shaving in public restrooms and sleeping in the bushes. I wanted something more. I wanted life to be exciting like when I was young, not a series of truck stops, bad food and weirdoes.

DUDE RANCH

I got a job at The Jack and Jill Dude Ranch in Rothbury, Michigan. The ranch was managed by a man named Bill who resembled a clown; he had naturally big ears and an engorged red nose that looked like a road map of Atlanta. He tried to come off as affable but didn't make it.

When I arrived at the fifty-acre ranch, Bill looked at my application, "Well (he didn't use my name, just the word well) ... All right, what can you do?" "Well," seemed to be the operative word so I ran with it.

"Well, what do you need done?"

"Well, we need trail guides and we need musicians."

"Well," I said, "that's me."

"Well, are you sure you can ride?"

"Well," I said, "what horse do you have here that nobody else wants to ride?" A possible adventure loomed.

"Well, we got a spooky mare called Chinook, oh and incidentally everybody here has a nickname. What's yours?"

I hadn't thought about it. I looked around at all the guys in jeans and said, "My nickname is Levi."

"Levi, huh?"

Well, that's when he showed me Chinook. The head wrangler said she was being shipped off the following week because she was too easily spooked. Even the trail guides wouldn't ride her. Chinook was a beautiful horse, a Morgan about fifteen hands high.

"Well, how about giving me a day or two," I said.

"Well, OK, but we're short on horses; she's being shipped off next week."

"Well, thanks."

I went into the horse barn, rich in hay and its aftermath, as often as I could that day and stayed into the night getting to know Chinook, I even gave up the chance to corral a "split tail" (cowboy term for a girl) after our evening musical show. The next morning I saddled up. Chinook was a high-spirited quarter horse that liked loose reins and didn't like to stand in line. "If you're not the lead horse the view never changes," she would have said. I agreed with her and she knew it. She let me ride her. I led trail rides five days a week

Sometimes, after a trail ride, Chinook needed to blow off steam and that could be a problem for the untried rider. Chinook wanted to run until her heart exploded.

I was nineteen and knew the feeling as I led her out of the corral, kicked the gate shut, mounted and leaned forward. I put my arms around her neck, wrapped the reins loosely around the western saddle horn and hung on.

Stay below the top of her head, I repeated to myself hoping that she, like most horses, would run with her head up.

Chinook didn't like to be distracted while in the middle of her full on, frothy-mouthed, mad dash through the underbrush. If I had been sitting up I would have been killed. When she tired she stopped on her own, her mouth speckled with white foam, her body heaving and covered in sweat and burrs. For her it was like getting out of prison. She turned her head, looked at me with one wild eye and snorted a fine mist of horse snot into the air. "Love is a powerful thing," was the trail guides motto, and Chinook loved me. We walked back to the barn, both breathing heavily. They kept Chinook, at least for that summer. The wild ones are the most fun to ride.

My other job was to play the guitar and lead the "Hootenannies." I started doing my act, I was "Levi" the folk singer and trail guide. Damn I was good. I was a dude's dude, Dude.

Every week, a new group of guests arrived at the Ranch, mostly youthful types from high school or first year college. Seventy-five percent were girls, good strapping Midwest girls with healthy hormone filled minds. The ranch staff was required to say, "Howdy, Pardner!" to all new guests upon their arrival and all during their stay. We were taught to "Set the Dude Mood."

"Powdy, Hardener!" we would exclaim to select girls, acting surprised at our cleverness.

One night after a good evening's fun with a new arrival I gasped something like, "We'll have to get together again."

"Don't worry about that, cowboy. I'll be dead before you call me," she said.

"You're kidding, right?"

"No, I have leukemia." I still thought she was kidding.

"Nah!"

She liked me because I refused to accept the fact. She didn't want to get into it. The last thing she wanted was sympathy, but she did have other, more personal, demands. I still like to think she was making it up to inspire me.

Most girls were dropped off by their parents and, after they settled in, I'd take them on a trail ride. Young women bouncing up and down on the Western saddles; Ride Em' Cowgirl, Yee Haw! They smiled and giggled a lot. That was the summer when black stretch ski pants were in, fitted with the ankle straps to hold them tight. That was the style and it was a good style. Some girls were in the "mood" by the time they got off the horses and even more so by the time we were done with our show later that night. I looked out at the audience and thought, "Oh yeah! - the Horn of Plenty meets the Plenty Horny."

It was every man's dream, or at least every young man's dream, or at least this young man's dream! The guests were only at the ranch for a week and then they were gone. We walked through the dunes, built campfires, got sand in the wrong places and tried to remember each other's names.

One night our saxophone player, Bud, and I were doing laundry in town and, because we were cool, we developed the habit of raising our right hand with the index finger up as a kind of "in crowd" greeting.

Two local red necks in a pickup truck pulled into the parking lot outside the Laundromat. They were leaning out the windows, drinking beer and being obnoxious. Bud and I didn't do anything, but when they drove away we raised our right hands, index finger up, in a farewell salute. Apparently, in their nicotine-fogged rear view mirror, it looked like we offered them a different finger.

Back they came. I was near a washing machine and Bud was near the door as the two necks came in. One walked up to Bud, said something, and then punched him in the mouth. I got pissed. The other guy swaggered over and leaned on the empty washing machine next to me. I knew he was going to say something stupid and then hit me. I grabbed the lid of the machine and slammed it down on his fingers; he screamed and looked for his fingertips. I ran to the pay phone to call the police, but the other guy came after me. He grabbed me by shoulder. I spun with the pull, grabbed him by his shirt and whacked him in the mouth with the receiver, wrapped the cord around his neck, kicked his legs out from under him and ran to help Bud.

I had never hit anyone before. I felt bad. I felt good. We grabbed our wet laundry and got into the car, Bud was crying, his summer was over. You can't play a reed instrument with a busted lip. I still felt good and spent the rest of the summer living a young man's dream, girls, horses and beer. The dream was about to end.

Chapter 9

Gullible's Travels

After the dude ranch experience I came home and tried to fit in, to find a job and make my dad proud of me. I enrolled in college, twice. I tried but just couldn't stay awake. The fluorescent lights, institutional smells and endless droning of tedious professors, who got all the girls, only increased my desire for "real life." I didn't flunk out; I quit.

By this time the Vietnam draft was getting close, I was 19. I had no legitimate deferment and wasn't inclined to hide. The Vietnam War was going full bore. Balls to the wall, turn and burn, lock and load, high speed, low drag, flaps up, gear up! I didn't have any idea what the hell was going on. I was gullible. I went to the draft board and cleverly asked the Army recruiter, "Excuse me, sir, do you think I'm going to get drafted?"

The recruiter opened his desk drawer, pulled out what was probably a Playboy magazine with a fake cover and started thumbing through it. He said, "Yeah, you'll probably get shafted, ah, drafted." I did know that if you enlisted you got to choose what you wanted to be. I thought he was bluffing. He thought I was stupid. We were both right. So I stupidly bluffed back, "Well, then, I guess I might as well join up and save them the trouble."

"That would probably be breast, ah... best," he said without smiling.

I sat in the Army recruiting office and looked through the pamphlets on the rack.

If I had fully understood the level of my incompetence and played it up, I wouldn't have feared the draft. I figured it out, too late. If you went in for a screening and acted like you had "strayed a little too far from the herd," there was no way you were going into combat. Political office maybe, but not combat. As a young man I was ignorant of history. All I knew was that America always won. So I'd be part of the winning team. I'd do my duty, it'd be over and then I'd come home, a real hero at last. Grandmo would be proud.

"I guess I want to be a helicopter pilot," I finally said to the recruiter.

"Great," he mumbled. "We'll put you down for Airborne."

That sounds like flying ... doesn't it? It's not. I didn't know anything.

Second Lieutenant US Army

It was 1966 America was changing. Lyndon Johnson was president. The Sound of Music won the Oscar. Walt Disney died. The first Star Trek episode premiered. Anti-Vietnam sentiment was running high, the US bombed Hanoi and rolling papers were on a roll.

I hadn't bothered to consult my parents and, after a less than tearful goodbye, my stepmother Ruth dropped me off in downtown Detroit at the Armory Building. I walked into the designated office and "POOF!" I was in the Army, now. I called Bob after he got home from work and proudly told him I'd enlisted. "That's tough," he said and hung up.

I got to Fort Knox and after eight weeks of basic training and a severe hair styling I, along some other recruits, were gathered in an old

Quonset hut next to the hand-to-hand combat course and within bayonet distance of the latrines. The hard-ass drill sergeant barked, "OK Paratroopers, listen up, here's how you pack your parachutes. Learn or DIE."

It was a catchy phrase. I stopped packing before I started and said "Ahhhh, excuse me Sarge, I'm here to fly helicopters."

"No you're not, Dickbrain. Does this fucking piece of silk look like a helicopter to you? You're Airborne, you're here to jump out of planes and love it ... hoo-rah!"

"GERONIMO!" the others all cheered.

"No, actually I'm a helicopter guy, that's what I signed up for," I insisted. Soon I found I had been "shat on" by the recruiter. Leaping out of a plane, being a floating target to a disgruntled enemy below was not my style. Getting shot in the ass is considered poor form in my family.

The Army Life

In the service you decided where you wanted to be by how you behaved. I didn't know that. I acted like I knew what I was doing, a dangerous ploy at best. I didn't learn until years later that my eight weeks of basic training had been an aptitude test.

Every new recruit is given a battery of psychological, physical and emotional tests, the Army General Classification Test. I hadn't studied. They were looking for, well, whatever they wanted. I had no idea what they were doing. I took the tests, hoping my brilliance would become evident.

Some days later, an NCO (non-commissioned officer) came into the barracks and said with apparent pride, "Okay you grunts, now listen up!" He called out several names, "You boys have qualified for OCS!" I was on the list! No one cheered.

I didn't know what OCS meant. "That means you get to die first!" one wiseass cracked. We always send our best to die first.

I laughed, looked at the guy next to me and asked, "What's OCS?"

"Overnight Cook School," he said, not smiling an inch.

Okay, that sounds all right, cooking, I'll be safe wherever I go, I'll be a cook and be in a mess hall on a secure base. I'd rather be fat than dead. Adventure is one thing, dying is another.

"Who wants to go?"

Up went my hand. Down went my chances.

An Officer and a Gentleman

OCS is Officer's Candidate School, typically a six-month ordeal. Candidates were supposed to have a college degree, but at the rate we were burning through second lieutenants, they lifted the requirement. How thoughtful, my lucky day and I got to spend an extra year in the Army. It was 1968.

I transferred from Fort Knox to the Engineer Officer Candidate School at Fort Belvoir, Virginia. Initially it didn't seem too bad. During the first hour we got screamed at by Tactical Officer Loudermilk, got our heads shaved, were issued ill-fitting stiff green jungle fatigues, ill-fitting stiff green jungle underwear, boots from WWII, stiff green toilet articles, a Bible (optional) and were informed that we were a bunch of no good military turds. One hundred push-ups later we marched to the barracks. Things were looking up.

Every morning at 0500 hours the barracks doors slammed open, lights flashed on and the TAC (training, advising, and counseling) officers screamed, "Drop your cocks and grab your socks! Reveille, Reveille, Reveille!" It was the way we started every day for the first one-hundred-twenty days.

At the command "Reveille!" we jumped off our already made bunks, pulled the blanky tight and within minutes were standing at attention, fully dressed, polished up and STRAC (Standing Tall, Ready for Action) ready for inspection. Among other things the TAC Officer's had to be able to bounce a quarter off your bunk blanket in order for you to pass muster. Over the years, other Candidates had figured how to twist and pound the thirty-year-old mattresses in a way that made them look flat and full and how to tuck the sheets to hold the tension. It was a secret passed down from one class to another.

I was training to be an Officer and a Gentleman and I would have been one sooner except three months into the scheduled six months of OCS I got caught smuggling McDonald's hamburgers. They never gave us enough to eat.

Hamburger smuggling had to be done. We stayed up almost all night, every night, and we were starving. Lights were out at ten o'clock, but that only meant it was time to polish your boots, your belt buckle, every military thing you owned, in the dark, because they didn't give us time to do it during the day, yet it had to be done for morning inspection.

We were told not to deprive ourselves of sleep but the TAC officers knew everybody was staying up most of the night studying tactics, combat engineering, high explosives, demolition, construction and whacking off.

We didn't have a choice about the first but at least didn't have to study for the latter.

I decided, with encouragement from my fellow "bean heads," to smuggle in some burgers. I collected the money, went to a pay phone and made the call.

It was 0200 hours when I lowered the money to the delivery guy. I had 150 hamburger units in a bed sheet. I hoisted them up the side of the barracks via a second story window when a TAC Officer spotted me. I was captured at the start line and would face a review board. Damn.

I had thinned my own herd. I was the guy who took the risk, I was the one who got caught and stood alone in front of the HIC (Hamburger Inquiry Commission) near the end of my third month. I was one week away from becoming an Upper Classman.

As punishment for my infraction and "copious neglect of protocol unbecoming an officer," I was given the reasonable choice of starting OCS over or being sent to Vietnam as an infantry grunt-MOS 11 Bravo, private first class Perkins. I didn't know what to do. I was confused, I didn't know if I could hack another six months of OCS, if I could hack going to Vietnam as a grunt and get killed, or if I could hack-period.

I called Bob, and told him my situation. It was the first time I'd asked for his advice.

"That's tough," he said and then, in a moment of unusual lucidity, continued. "Look, Kid, it doesn't matter what you do. What matters is how well you do it. Do the best you can and you'll be okay ... Oh, and if you have athlete's foot leave soap between your toes, hold your stomach in and keep your own teeth as long as you can ... oh and Ruth says try not to die." Click.

My dad gave me a life and let me live it the way I wanted. Thanks, Bob.

I decided to start over, secure in my ability to bounce a quarter off a bunk blanket. It would be another six months of hell. I did nine months of

OCS all together. I started over as a Bean Head. Bean Heads was what the Upper Classmen called us. The sadistic barbers shaved our heads to the scalp on day one and once a week thereafter for three months. But the upper classmen got to have one-quarter inch of hair. Our heads look like big white, pinto, Boston or black beans.

I started at the bottom of the pack, again. I had almost been an "Upper Classman" and overnight I was a "bean head," again. The guys in the barracks had a party for me when I left. We had "government authorized" hamburgers!

The next day I would be at the mercy of my old classmates.

When an upper classman stopped me and screamed, "Bean Head, LAY HOLD!" I stood at attention with my back ramrod straight and stuck my chin out as far as possible. On the command "HEAVE!" I sucked and tucked my chin back into my neck and chest creating as many wrinkles under said chin as possible. The upper classman counted the wrinkles. This exercise was designed to help new officers develop the proper military posture, to react to orders immediately and had the practical effect of protecting your neck in a fight. Good habits to get into.

At other times, when an Upper Classman had nothing better to do, he might decide he didn't care for your attitude or, lack of attitude. "Drop down, BEAN HEAD and give me twenty!" He meant push-ups. They couldn't order more than twenty at time. I averaged about 100 per day. When I came out nine months later I was highly motivated (by the idea of getting out of this nightmare) and in great shape, except for a sore neck. Lay hold ... Heave!

There was a black guy in OCS with me named Webster. He had been training for the ten-thousand-meter Olympic event before he got drafted. He could run and so could I, but not like him.

One night Webster, two other guys and I set off on a timed five-mile cross-country night infiltration course in the swamps of northern Virginia. It was winter, midnight, wet and cold. We had to find our way through the forest in the dark, trying not to get "captured" by the TAC officers. The final treat was a swamp. You could go around it, but we were judged on our times and figured that the "aggressors" were not standing around in the swamp waiting to catch us; they'd be on the edges.

No one else went through the swamp. We did.

One guy named Lemieux got tired early and we dragged him along when we needed to. When we got to the swamp we lashed Lemieux to a couple of logs to float him across. He loved it and laughed out loud.

'Shut the fuck up Lemieux, you'll get us caught!" Webster hissed.

"But it's so fucking fu..." laughed Lemieux as I rolled the logs and pinned his face in the mud.

The TAC Officers sent out timers to the endpoints around 0400 hours because the best runners took five hours to finish the course. We got back to the rendezvous point before they sent out the advance forces that would try to ambush and capture us. The TAC officers were sitting in their tent, staying warm, scratching themselves and joking when we walked in soaking wet and steaming at the mouth. They immediately accused us of cheating.

"We didn't cheat, we're just good, man, ah ...Sir."

We were encouraged to be cocky. It helped develop the required attitude.

I don't know how they thought we cheated, but they did. TAC #1 said, "No one has ever done that course this fast. What did you do?"

"We didn't do anything, we just hauled ass, Sir."

"You had to be cheating," TAC #1 said. "There is no way you could do this course that fast. We weren't even out of the tents yet."

"I know, we could have captured YOU-SIR! You'd be OUR prisoners, Sir. How would that look on your permanent record, Sir? We decided to let you live, Sir." Obviously, I was high on adrenalin and short on common sense. In my case they seem to go together.

"You're a wiseass, aren't you Perkins?" said one of the TACs.

"Sir, No Sir, but I could be with the right training, Sir."

"I'm worried about you, Perkins," TAC #1 stopped a smile.

We went back and forth under interrogation. Finally they said, "Look, just tell us how the hell you did this?"

"We'll show you tomorrow," Webster said.

The next day, we went out to the quarter mile track where the TAC officers would time us in a mile run, four laps. Webster and I weren't worried about the other two soldiers; they'd told the TACs that we carried them and that we weren't lying, that we had pushed them through the swamp.

Standing on the track, running in place, I winked at the TAC Officer. "Okay, here we go... Sir!" I, the cocky bean head, said as Webster grimaced and looked away.

We'd made our time the night before by cutting through the swamp, but there were no short cuts on the oval track. Under my breath I said to Webster, "How are we going to do this? I don't know how to run like this."

"Don't worry Perk, just follow me. Get behind me and listen to me breathe."

We started to run. I slipstreamed behind Webster, I could hear him breathing and forced myself to breathe the way he did, slowly at first, in time with my pace. Interesting. We started, first lap-good, the next lap we were going faster. On the third lap we went even faster, making weird sounds and snorting. I had come to count on my adrenalin and it kicked in right on time. On the fourth lap we kicked it out and finished the mile in five minutes and ten seconds, wearing shorts, jungle boots and vomit.

The TAC officers looked up and said, "Okay, that's all we need to see. Sorry we were accusing you ... LAY HOLD!"

Being stupid and willing to take risks were my only valuable attributes. Maybe that's how I ended up being transferred into special warfare. In the end, prior to being shipped to Vietnam they even re-evaluated the hamburger smuggling incident. And although I didn't get a medal for it, "The Double Mac with the Hold the Cheese Cluster," I was pardoned. Meaning the "indiscretion" would not become part of my permanent record. They chose to think of the incident as part of my training and even called it "unusual initiative" on my part. Even though I got spanked, they looked at me from a different angle by the time I came out the other end. Wait a minute, that doesn't sound right. I wanted to be a Colonel not a Colon.

Night Warfare

I had been in the Army eleven months waiting to attend helicopter school. They'd promised me, it was in my missing contract. "It may have been misfiled," was an explanation that did not suit me. I persisted, and while the Army tried to find my enlistment papers it was decided that I should teach night warfare.

"Why me?" I asked.

"Because you're qualified."

"Hunh?"

I spent my childhood in the woods. I was a Boy Scout, for a short while, but was demoted for throwing my hatchet and quit. Since enlistment I had earned my "stinking badges" for expert marksman, demolitions and hand-to-hand combat in basic and advanced infantry. But still.

After a thorough vetting the "powers" sent me to Indian Town Gap, Pennsylvania. I set up night warfare courses designed to teach soldiers how to move through the woods in the dark, how to rig booby traps and how to avoid them (stay home). It was good fun, for me.

I started out simple, using natural devices, like putting dog turds on the trail. The sergeant private detailed to find them for me was not happy with his assignment. The soldiers were supposed to stay off the obvious trails, but the lazy guys didn't and paid the price. They were easy to pick out when they got back to camp, not that anyone wanted to. Sometimes I would hide on the side of the path and fire off a whoopee cushion to see what would happen. You're not supposed to laugh on patrol but the trainees were so stressed they couldn't contain themselves and fell down trying to choke back their laugher. Not a good thing to do in the bush. Then there were the fire crackers (poppers) rigged to a trip wire, the bags of white flour dropped from a tree and the poison sumac that I tied back then released by a trip wire or hand pull. I even built a Punji stick pit, without Punji sticks, over an old latrine site. It was a short fall but quite unpleasant upon landing, I was told.

It wasn't the traps that hurt them. It was what the fools did afterwards when they panicked. "Close contact with a dog turd or a firecracker is no reason to jump off a cliff in the dark," I counseled them before each exercise. For some it made no difference. For me it was fun. But before long I got called into the Colonel's office.

"Ahhhhh ... Lieutenant Perkins, you may not be aware of this, but we don't actually want to kill these recruits or even scare them to death while in our care. Did you read the manual? This is TRAINING, you savvy? Your booby trap methods are of some concern. Dead or scared soldiers are not properly motivated and of little use on the battlefield!"

"So you want the real thing to be a surprise?" I asked. I **was** getting a high percentage of the trainees, and the laundry people were complaining.

"It's better that way," he replied. "Perkins, you are discouraging some of the troops."

"They might be even more discouraged if they get caught by the gooks and get their nuts cut off, Sir," I said.

"Perkins, I'm worried about you," said the Colonel, shifting uncomfortably in his chair.

So I lightened up. The Colonel, however, was not convinced of my sincerity. I was soon transferred to Camp AP Hill in Virginia to be an XO (executive officer) in a combat engineering company. That was where Navy Salvage School came into the picture.

I was in the mess tent one day. I lived in tents; I smelled like a tent, I made my own small tent occasionally. As I poked through a pile of cold, undercooked hotdogs, a Navy Lieutenant Commander stumbled over an outside tent peg. He fell and grabbed the entrance flaps swinging unintentionally into the mess tent, like Tarzan in a Navy uniform. "Hey! Ahhhh ... any of you grunts want to go to Navy Dive School?" he said, trying to recover his composure.

Our muffled laughter subsided as the Lt. Commander strolled through the mess tent where he gobbled a wilted pickle and talked quietly about the Dive School.

He never stopped walking as he talked and headed for the exit. He wasn't interested in us, he'd been sent to do a job. Navy guys do not like Army guys unless they, the Navy guys, are in trouble. His task was to ask if anybody wanted to go to dive school all the while doing everything he could to not encourage anyone. The Navy only allowed one Army Officer per year to attend the prestigious Navy Salvage Officer's School. I was eating a hot dog and potato chips. But even the crunching of the chips could not stay the message from my ears. *Escape!* I thought. I took one last bite of that hot dog and tossed it like a grenade. With bun filled lips I stood up and ran to catch him. As I slipped into lock step beside him I recalled hearing that the average life span of an infantry lieutenant in a helicopter assault sortie was about one minute, the pilots a little longer. That was an average I didn't like. The leader is the first one off the chopper, another thing that didn't appeal. The pilots don't stop and they don't land. The troops jump five or six feet and roll down flat in the weeds. It might have been worse for the pilots, they got lead hemorrhoids. That's why I decided to go to Navy Deep Sea Diving and Salvage School. It sounded safer.

I thought of myself as brave but I wasn't. Any semblance of bravery displayed or reported herein is purely the result of stupidity, lack of attention and not taking things seriously.

Chapter 10

Deep Sea Diving for Fun and Profit

Marine Salvage: "A science of vague assumptions based on debatable figures taken from inconclusive experiments and performed with instruments of problematic accuracy by persons of doubtful reliability and questionable mentality."

> —Charles "Black Bart Bartholomew" Head of Navy Salvage who did not come up alive from his last qualification dive.

The United States Naval School of Deep Sea Diving and Salvage was located in the old Gun Factory on the banks of the Potomac River where it runs through Washington, DC.

When I arrived in March 1969, there were about fifty candidates; when I graduated in August there were twenty-two. The school was justly recognized as the best in the world for meta-physical training in the art of Deep Sea Diving and Salvage.

It was a wonderfully special school where enlisted instructors could slap the shit out of an officer simply because they didn't like his "attitude" or wanted "to help him grasp the concept."

"The floggings will continue until morale improves," seemed to be the operative slogan.

The instructors were Navy Chiefs, tough. We were young officers, maybe not so tough. The new Navy ensigns and one Army lieutenant (me) knew it was the only time the Chiefs would ever get away with roughing us up and the Chiefs, especially those near retirement, took full advantage of this perk. On day one they took us into the school's hallway that connected to the famous Navy Experimental Diving Unit, the EDU. It was a long linoleum hallway with rows of pictures, pictures of divers…dead divers.

I walked down the hall with our guide, staring at the one-dimensional faces. I noticed a Chief standing by a door: he was missing one leg and was leaning against the wall for support. He was a deep-sea diver. I saw another Chief with a coffee cup in his shaking hands. He didn't have any ears. He was a diver. Farther down the hall another Navy Chief, missing an eye, stood picking his nose with a crooked finger stub. He was a diver too! The old Chiefs were going up and down the hall doing the Diving School business which was trying to stay alive. I stared at the twisted old sailor. With a squeak, a door opened and another mangled Navy Chief came out. His right arm was gimped up behind and he couldn't salute in a proper military manner. When he dutifully did salute, it looked like he was a wounded chicken trying to fly. His tongue kept slipping out of his mouth and he pushed it back in with a gnarled index finger stub. We pretended not to notice.

The EDU survivors were old and their tough faces showed battle scars framed in a countenance of pride. "You boys can start at the top … and work your way down," the arm flapper said. He walked away laughing then stopped, turned and said, "Remember boys, you gotta go down, but you don't gotta come up." Every one of these guys was fucked up! I could be fucked up too, if I tried.

The Chief giving the tour must have seen how impressed we were. He squinted through his remaining eye and pointed a warped finger down the hall and at the rows of photos. He paused, took a deep breath, projected his command voice and proclaimed, "NOW, if you boys work reeeal hard, why, you can be just like them Chiefs down there."

Five guys on our orientation tour turned around and left on the spot.

"You'll miss all the fun!" we teased, then looked worriedly at each other for encouragement, as the quitters scurried down the hallway toward the EXIT sign.

In that hall of mangled survivors, I saw that no matter what your accomplishments, in the end, you must be present to win. I was present, which is a start. It was easy to be tough when I was young. It's getting harder.

**

One, and there was only one, of the great things about Navy Salvage School is they never kicked anyone out. They never broke a man's spirit. You quit honorably. Nobody "failed." You stayed in as long as you could hack it and when you couldn't hack anymore, you could leave, return to your unit and regain your previous position. Maybe, but always dependent on the "needs of the military." You got to "Ring the Bell" on the way out, they let you go gracefully and there was a lot of grace heading for the doors. I liked it; it made me feel like something was happening. I decided to stay for the party.

Unfortunately, there were a few guys who didn't know when to quit. Our Navy invited other countries' Navy Diver *wannabees* to attend the school as a gesture of good will. They would train with the Americans. The training however was not a gesture, although many one-finger salutes were exchanged.

It was Dive School, after all. They were trying to kill you without actually killing you. It's the thought that counts. The Chiefs wanted you to crack, in public if possible, so as to attain the maximum enjoyment from the process, reap a new story and possibly supplement their income with side bets. They wanted to learn when you were going to crack, where you were going to crack and, how long it would take to un-crack you should that become necessary. If you were going to crack it was better to do it in a "controlled environment." Sounds reasonable, but there are some things you can't control.

The Chiefs made us dive thirty-five feet down to the bottom of the Potomac River, during the late winter, where we dredged into the mud, assembled heavy steel pieces of discarded plumbing fixtures and tried not to cry. The suits were thirty years old and leaked bad. The dive-training program took about four-and-a-half months. Still, diving in the Potomac River in the winter was better than summer, there was less toxic waste and it kept our mascot around longer.

Our mascot was a dead beagle. Somebody found the bloated beagle floating down the river, drowned, its expensive leash still attached. We tied him off about ten feet below the surface. You had to pet the beagle on the way down the ladder and, even though it was winter, he only survived a couple of weeks despite our attention. We all missed the beagle; we named him Puffy. (No real beagles were harmed. The beagle is a fictional beagle.)

Occasionally, during the process, the dredge pump would "fail" and six feet of mud slurped in on top of the novice diver. Sometimes the pump actually failed and sometimes the Chiefs did it on purpose. In my case one of the Chiefs that "liked" me turned the pump off to see if I was going to go "claustro" buried in muddy bottom. I didn't. I disappointed the Chief, but he looked for another way to test me.

When a nasty dive project, one that could go either way, was scheduled the Chiefs and other interested parties huddled around the dive station and listened over the two-way communication "COM Box" connected by wire to the helmet. Elbowing each other to get closer to the speaker they listened closely to hear if the diver was going to go nuts, or not. Not much middle ground and, of course, there was some betting.

The Navy Standard MKV (Mark 5) deep-sea diving gear is heavy and we had to endure the stench of a thousand scared boys whose history came wafting up out of the thirty-year-old canvas suits. Additionally, we had to be able to climb up and down the barge ladder with our gear on, two hundred pounds up and down a ladder and, you had to be dumb enough to want to do it. The "deep sea" boots weighed sixty pounds, the helmet fifty-five pounds, the suit twenty pounds and the weight belt sixty pounds. It was right at two hundred pounds not counting the occasional "Brown Trout" down your pant leg. A diver had to climb down the ladder, do a project on the bottom, come to the surface and climb about ten-feet up the ladder. If you didn't make it that far, you didn't have a chance with anything more advanced.

The Ladder

A few guys went nuts while on dry land. One trainee went berserk in the barracks but didn't want to damage his fellow officer's footlocker displays. He climbed inside his wall locker; (you can't open them from the inside,) slammed the door and went nuts. The Chiefs carried him out in the wall locker, banging and screaming, all the way to the infirmary. It appeared that he would rather go nuts in a wall locker than be buried in the mud on the bottom of a dark, polluted river in the middle of winter. Some people aren't cutout to be stupid. To each his own.

Underwater and suddenly buried in six feet of mud, some guys "lost it." When that happened his tender would grudgingly take up some slack as the Chief turned the water pressure back on. Then the Chief hit TALK on the COM box and said to the panicked diver, "Red Diver, Red Diver, calm down, you'll be fine… fine… Just point the hose up … there you go … point the hose up … here we go … easy now … good man, you'll be fine. Translation-"PUSSY!" All of a sudden the mud suction broke and the tender jerked the diver up, out of one mess and into another.

Unclear Motivation

There was one diver who was just not ready to be buried in the mud, his skills were debatable and his motivation unclear.

A student diver was teamed with two men on deck; his tender who dressed the diver and handled the hoses and the COM watch who talked with him over the helmet headset. They helped their diver to the ladder and got him on the bottom where he dredged a hole. Then the Chief turned the pump off. Tons of mud came in around the diver; he called over his helmet radio, "Topside … Red Diver … I've lost pressure in the hose… I'm in the mud … I can't get out. I … Over."

He repeated the message, with increasing urgency. The Chief put his hand on the COM box talk switch and shook his head sideways.

"Topside, Red Diver, I'm stuck in the mud, Over." Still no response.

"Topside, No … pressure … I'm in the mud here! Chief, come on! Over…" No response.

By now Red Diver was thinking that the radio was gone, or that the com wire was broken. He knew he was stuck in the mud. Not hard to figure out. He knew that they knew he was stuck in the mud, so he pretended not to worry. He whistled a stupid ditty for a few seconds. The Chief let it go on a while longer, but lunch time was not far off so, somewhat disappointed that the guy wouldn't crack, the Chief walked to the air hose hanging over the side of the barge. He picked it up and kinked it.

"Topside, Red Diver. My air supply is off. I can't get any air. Over!"

Every diver knew that there was enough air inside the helmet to last for a few minutes, but when you think there's "No More Air," a few minutes doesn't seem like much.

"Topside, (gasp, gasp) I'm out of air. I'm running ou ... of ... air ... hard to breathe ... Gasp! Over. Gasp!"

The grinning Chief looked over at us, put his finger to his lips for silence, "Watch this boys... he's going to shit."

The Chief knew his business. The guy did shit. Finally the Chief let air back into the suit ... the final punishment. You could hear everything that was going on inside the helmet. Red Diver is now Brown Diver. After we got Brownie up, he sat on his bench shaking his helmeted head saying, "FUCK!" over and over through the headset. The Chief got on the wire and said into the guy's helmet, now open so everyone could hear, "You're a pussy."

That guy quit. The Chief made $20.00. The dive locker smelled bad.

Needless to say, some men, myself included, considered the Chief to be unusually nasty, even for a Chief.

When it came to coiling our hoses, we were supposed to do it in a figure eight to ensure that the hose wouldn't develop a "memory." One time I missed one of the figure eights during the coiling maneuver. The Chief caught it. I stood up and turned around, "gasp," there he was. He slapped me across the back of my head (you can't see bruises there) and knocked me on my ass. He stood over me and said, "What do you think of that, you miserable motherfucking Army puke?"

I was not the only one who got smacked and at that point a diver had choices, although not many. Either you took it, you quit, or you fought back and got your ass kicked anyway. They were tough bastards. There was no way you were going to whip the Chief's ass and I didn't remember to bite his nose off in time to try it. So I said, "Well, I thought that was very instructive and I appreciate the attention."

His nicotine stained lips locked together and he stalked off.

A few days later, he whacked me on the back of the head again. I don't remember why, maybe because I had a concussion from the first whack. He said, "And what do you think about that, you pukey fucking mule-faced Army dip wad?"

Again, a choice. "Well, for a moment I thought my little sister had snuck up behind me, but she hits harder, Chief."

"Oh, you liked it, huh, are you a wiseass? Thought it was a good one, huh, thought it was FUN?"

"Roger that Chief!" I got in his face and stood at full, rigid attention, "It was real fucking good, go ahead and do it again."

He looked at me. "Are you fucking nuts son?"

"Yes Chief, I am."

"I'm worried about you, Perkins" he said and walked away smiling.

He was a success and so was I. I was a red-haired nut case. Of course, I knew he wasn't going to actually kill me. He couldn't, it was against the rules, I think. Everybody knew how the system worked. Well, not everybody.

The speaker inside the helmet was always ON so everyone could hear what happened in the helmet at all times, but you couldn't hear topsides unless they called or you called them. On one of my qualifying dives, I was almost completely suited up; only the faceplate remained to be screwed in place. Just as my tender went to dog down the faceplate the Chief, the one who smacked/liked me, tossed a fat housefly into the helmet. I spent the next forty-five minutes trying to kill that fucking fly with my face, head, nose and tongue. I tried to suck it into one nostril so I could smash my face against the glass and kill it. I tried to catch it with my lips so I could eat it or trap it in my ear so I could smash my head into the side of the helmet. The fly continued to fake me out as I mashed my head into the helmet in hopes of a kill. You can't get your hands inside a helmet. The Chief keyed the microphone, "accidently" and I could hear him place his bet on the fly. I could hear my buddies laughing topside. The fly escaped me during the dive. I finished my project and went up the ladder bleeding from my crumpled nose. When they opened the faceplate I struck.

The fly buzzed out, experienced one nano-second of freedom and died suddenly from impact with a known combatant, my gloved hands. Someone stuck a burning Marsh Wheeling stogey (a cigar butt) in my mouth to kill the wafting stink from the suit. I picked the disfigured fly body out of the web of my glove and handed it to the frowning Chief who reached for his wallet. The divers split their winnings with me. You have to be present to win. I was.

My dive partner was named Capitano Claudio Jorge Raoule' Mendoza. He was from Colombia, South American, about thirty-years old with the well-tended flab of a wealthy family evident about him. The poor fellow had no idea what the school was about or, if he did, he hid it well. It was part of his family tradition to serve in the military. At thirty he was already a Captain in the Colombian Navy. His family must have thought the offer of attendance at this school was a friendly international gesture and a way to build contacts with the Gringos. No one thought to ask what was required to graduate.

I spoke *"poquito"* Spanish, so they made him my partner. The only thing he had been taught to say in English before he got to the school was, "Yes, I understand."

No matter what you said to him he replied, "Yes, I understand."

The poor *caballero*. He was very polite, very courteous and almost very dead.

One day, in the middle of the course, I was again Mendoza's tender. I dressed him as he sat hunched and damply depressed on his wooden stool; he had begun to "understand." When he was suited up we put him down on the bottom of the Potomac with a high-pressure water hose to dredge in the mud of ages and politicians gone by. They are of similar viscosity and mix well. Mendoza was okay at this point in his training but was always getting his dump valve (air out) and his inflation valve (air in) mixed up. The way it worked, you hit a button in the helmet with your chin to let air *out* while, with your left hand, you turned the valve *on* to put air into the helmet and equally important, the suit. You worked with your right hand and had to balance yourself carefully. You were inside a stinky canvas balloon. We ventilated the suits, a lot. If you get upside down in a deep-sea suit the air goes into the legs of the suit, the helmet goes down and you blow to the surface ass-first where the suit explodes. Then you sink back to the bottom, head first, quickly. That was not encouraged and considered "poor form" in Navy diver circles.

Poor Mendoza was always screwing it up. He'd turn the air off, hit the chin button and deflate the suit. The external water pressure collapsed the suit, but it couldn't collapse the spun copper helmet, so the pressure tried to push his military body up and into the helmet.

I heard that when this happened, in deep water operations, the Navy (with the family's permission) buried the helmet with honors. Water doesn't compress. People do, but shouldn't.

That day Mendoza, with great intent, finished the project and mounted the ladder on the side of the barge for his courageous return to the staging area. He had decided it was his last dive. We all rooted for Mendoza as he started up the ladder leaving the river depths for the last time.

"Mendoza made it, Chief," everyone yelled, money started to change hands. But part way up-Mendoza stopped.

Coming up the ladder you don't stop, you're carrying two-hundred pounds of gear. You get your momentum going, you "choogied" (choogie is the way Vietnamese women walk when carrying two buckets of water on a pole across their shoulders for five miles), you got up that ladder and didn't stop. Mendoza made it halfway up the ladder and stopped. He looked up, I looked down. Then he looked down and I looked up. Damn.

"Mendoza, don't stop," I yelled to penetrate the helmet *"No Halto, No Halto*!! Don't stop. Keep coming, keep coming, *rapido, rapido*. Mendoza, hold on! Mi amigo, keep coming! *Aqui, aqui*! Move your *zapatas*."

He hung on as long as he could, then let go and plummeted down into the fertile bottom of the Potomac River like a Spanish speaking plumb bob.

"Aiheee!" echoed through the COM box speaker.

We tried to stop him but he was too heavy. We ripped the skin off our hands trying to gain control the snaking hoses and wires. Mendoza got his buttons mixed up, as always. We were wrestling 350 pounds of wet Aristocrat and dive gear. His suit was deflating, making him even heavier and his body was slowly being crushed into his helmet. I was holding on to the air hose and COM line. We tried to get him stopped; I heard him breathing heavily over the radio.

I reached for the COM box, "Mendoza, Mendoza, put the air ON, put ON the air, *abierto gaso*!"

Mendoza farted. The crew dropped to their knees in spasms of laughter. I tied off his hose and returned to the COM box. All I heard was, "OOOOH, my friend, my friend, my friend......"

Somehow he hit the right button; near death has a way of sharpening your recall. So does a bad fart in a deep-sea suit. He got some air back in the suit, it was survival.

"Mendoza," I squawked, "hold on amigo, *esta llegando la ayuda*. Help, to you, is coming."

"Yes ... I ... understand."

We lowered the stage; a metal box-like platform supported by a cable, and got Mendoza on the stage with the help of a safety diver in SCUBA gear. There was zero visibility below the surface. The Chief was worried; he didn't want to come up short 1-each-Mendoza at the end of the day. It would look bad on his permanent record. We started to bring him up. The platform came out of the water and Mendoza, completely exhausted by now, teetered back and forth like a drunk ready to keel over. I could see through his foggy faceplate as he approached deck level. I saw that he was "Fritoed," fried. The stage was connected to a boom about three-feet out from the edge of the barge, with the river fifteen feet below. As the stage reached deck level Mendoza saw me and, mustering great effort and sincerity said, "OOH, my friend!" as he stepped forward, without looking, to embrace me in the traditional Latin manner. ZOT! POOF-SPLASH, there went Mendoza again, straight to the bottom of the Potomac for a second time.

We finally got him up and on the barge. I spun the face plate open and said, "Mendoza, mi amigo, you should go home-*vaya su casa*."

"Yes," Mendoza nodded, shaking his bloody head, "I understand."

In his final evaluation report the Chief wrote, "Mendoza does not do well under pressure."

There was a diminutive Vietnamese fellow who chose to attend Dive School, a nice guy, but he was only about five feet tall. He was an officer in the Republic of Vietnam Navy and would have been safer in Nam. His name was Captain Nyugen Bo. Nyu' (pronounced 'nhew') for short and, of course, we called him the "Nyu' guy."

Our training included running sprints and drills around the parking lot with two eighty cubic-inch metal dive tanks on our backs. They weighed about 40 pounds each. The purpose was to condition us to carry the weight of the deep-sea gear. The training was intense and we always helped the other guy, usually Nyu', when we could. I came back from these drills with my shoulders cut up and bleeding from the thin nylon straps, I was tired, my back and hips ached from the tanks pounding into them. I'm not sure why divers had to run with rifles and helmets but we did, and we took turns dragging the Nyu' guy. He always smiled politely during the entire ordeal. Never leave a man behind. We didn't have to be taught that.

When Nyu' stood upright alongside the pool with his tanks on, the tanks were on the ground. During one of the first sessions they put the little guy in the pool with two tanks on his back. Nyu' wasn't just off the paddy; he was an educated Vietnamese officer. But he refused, under any circumstance, to take a breath underwater. He simply thought it was a bad idea. So they put him in the pool and Nyu' laid on the bottom, chest down, pinned by his tanks and weight belt. He looked like a dead Asian Dung beetle. The instructors swam around and checked us out then swam over to Nyu' who was very well mannered for a person that wouldn't breathe. Ol' Nyu smiled, though it looked more like a grimace with the regulator in his mouth. Nyu' nodded and waved at the instructors. He had two days worth of air for his skinny ass in those bottles! Then, when he didn't think anyone was looking (of course, we knew what he was doing but we didn't want him to lose face), he crawled over to the edge of the pool, pulled himself up and took the mouthpiece out. After taking several big deep breaths he put the mouthpiece back in and sank back to the bottom of the pool. The instructors came by and, because there were no bubbles, they knew that Nyu' wasn't breathing. Apparently Nyu' hadn't thought that one out. Nyu' just could not bring himself to overcome that human instinct that told him breathing underwater was a bad habit to get into. He would neither take a breath nor be rude under water. He simply could not do it.

Navy Dive School was designed to break down your human instincts into two parts, fear and more fear. After reviewing my notes on Nyu', I decided that it might better, in some cases, to lose face…than ass.

Chapter 11

Return to the Army

After Dive School, I was again stationed at Fort Belvoir, Virginia where I met Flat Vanatta, we shared an apartment in Woodbridge, Virginia. One night I came back from work and Flat was having a party. I went into the bathroom, turned on the shower, real hot, to soothe my military body and, without turning the lights on, stepped into the tub. It was full of live Maryland blue crabs on ice, ready to be steamed. I re-entered the party abruptly to the amusement of almost everyone. Life was good.

We were both assigned as Combat Engineer Company Commanders and right off the bat we got into trouble with the Base Commander, Colonel Byrd. Flat took it in stride. The trouble, I believe, was directly related to the two French sisters we'd "cottoned on to" (an old corn husker's term) and secretly, this was the bad part, brought onto the base. They were contortionists from a circus in France, "performing" at a Washington DC club. Contortionists, French. One of them could put both feet behind her head, or yours. We thought of it as International Relations. Flat later said his contortionist had "helped extend his…imagination." The girls had no ID's with them and a security check at the Officer's Club proved to be our downfall.

We were ordered to report to the commanding officer for a verbal reprimand. We arrived at the colonel's office as ordered. His secretary informed us that the colonel was going to "masticate us a secondary anus." I looked at Flat, "Don't worry, it's a military term," he informed me.

In his office, the colonel had a set of ceiling to floor red velvet curtains. Yards and yards of red velvet just hanging there. He didn't decorate the office; he like others used it the way he found it.

We came to attention in front of Colonel Byrd and proceeded to get our butts chewed during which time Flat mumbled something in my direction. "What did he say?" asked the colonel, who was not used to being interrupted. "What the hell did he say?" he repeated.

"What did he say?" the colonel barked at me for the third time, though why he was asking me and not Flat, I didn't know. Flat could be a little scary.

"He said," I looked at Flat ... "He said, *'It looks like a whorehouse in here!'* Sir!"

The colonel stopped masticating our buttocks and looked around his office. You could tell he pictured himself sitting in the Madame's lounge in a New Orleans whorehouse and, he imagined that people who came through his office every day probably thought the same thing.

"What do you think I should do about that?" he finally said. "Is there anything you can do? Can you boys take care of that?" (in lieu of an ass chewing was implied).

"He's running scared," Flat whispered.

"Yes, Sir," I said. "We'll look after it right away, Sir."

We got the hell out of there, but came back that evening and gathered up all the curtains, all the red velvet we could get our hands on and left many feet of rusting curtain rods and mildewed strings behind. Flat graciously left a list on a cocktail napkin he found in his pants, describing the approximate size of each curtain needed to re-furnish the office. We took it all to our apartment where we made our own red velvet bar, red velvet bedspreads, red velvet towels, red velvet throw rugs and red velvet curtains. Every place you turned was red velvet. It was fabulous. We hoped the colonel took it in the right spirit. I'm sure he did, although our orders to "ship out" arrived sooner than expected.

Flat and I were bachelors and stationed at Fort Belvoir for a year. We each had a brand new Corvette Stingray and lived in Georgetown, across the street from the Nurse's School. It was reportedly a good school and convenient, since we each had numerous and continuing afflictions that needed attention.

I had a Studebaker before I got the 'Vette. A little four door, robin's egg blue Studebaker Lark sedan. After being home on leave, where I found I was treated with a new found respect, I bought the Lark. It was in new condition. I drove it back to Washington, D.C. However, upon arriving back at the fort I realized this nifty little sedan wasn't going to do me any favors with the ladies, and what else was there? So I traded the Lark in on a new Corvette Stingray, a Burnt Tangerine, four-hundred-fifty horsepower convertible Mistletoe. It was great but I missed the Lark. I was driving by the Corvette dealer a month or two later and there was my little Lark still sitting in the lot. Alone. Still robin's egg blue, still cute. I stopped in and the dealer told me they couldn't sell the damn thing! (Maybe they shouldn't have parked it between two new Corvettes).

I said, "Why not, it's such a good little car?"

"Well, if it's such a good little car, why don't you buy it back?" he counter-offered.

So I did. I paid him $200, picked up my buddy Flat and away we went. I had a car that I didn't know what to do with, but it was such a good little car. One night Flat and I got a bit tangled up in the old Studebaker. Alcohol was a factor, I believe.

We were invited to attend a birthday party for some older retired military folks. They asked us to play our guitars and sing folk songs. Upon arrival, we were surprised because it was supposed to be a "dry" event, but it was far from it. It was a geriatric Gong Show. They served a bowl of innocent-looking punch and a giant chocolate cake. Soon, "too soon," some would later remark, everybody started eating the cake with their hands, not a good sign at 7:00 PM. We were playing music and I decided that, for training purposes, it would be a good idea to spin around the pole in the basement. For an even less clear reason a number of the elderly people at the party decided it would be a good idea for them to do it, too. It was not a good idea, not for me, not for them. Flat strummed away at Johnny Cash's "Ring of Fire" as the old-timers started spinning around the pole.

Unfortunately they didn't have the strength to hang on and went spiraling out of control, aluminum frame walkers knocking over drool cups and a few other people. Girdles snapped and dentures flew through the air. One guy could barely walk. Of course, he'd been like that when we got there; everybody was drunk as hell. Being good sports and patriots, Flat and I got hammered with the rest of them. We had the 'right stuff." At some point we felt it had come time to, and were actually *asked to*, depart the scene. Perhaps it was because we got caught eating handfuls of cake and pissing in the sink. It wasn't premeditated. We were too drunk to find the bowl and to dizzy to lean forward. We dropped our members over the edge of the sink, turned the cold water on and continued to party down. Unfortunately, an older lady at the party chose this moment to walk by the bathroom. She saw two idiots with cake smooshed over their faces, a cup of punch in one hand and a dick in the other. For some reason, old people can be sensitive, she screamed.

That was the end of that part of the night. Almost. These were civilized older adults, almost nursing home age. Finally, the hostess came up and said that she thought we "boys" should leave. We obliged her and made ready to leave. We packed up our guitars, but Flat could not depart without an encore. "Lets give em' an encore!" Flat bellowed. He was a true showman. Up until that point *things had been going well* I thought. Five old timers helped push Flat up the staircase. Flat was a big boy. They just about got to the top of the stairs when Flat let go of the hand rail and fell backwards, taking the whole band of "Q Tips" down with him. A heap of twisted, wrinkled, bodies laid moaning at the bottom of the stairs. Flat was on top of the pile still humming Johnny Cash's "Ring of Fire."

Finally, after untangling numerous bodies and garments and grabbing at last cup of punch, we left in the Studebaker, trying to find our way home. We should never have gone anywhere.

While heading back, we spotted a Krispy Kreme donut shop on the other side of the street. Being an officer and blessed with the ability and training to make quick decisions, I made a sharp left but failed to notice the curb, or the hedge, separating the two sides of the street. Immediately we were stuck on top of a two-foot high row of bushes, four little Lark wheels spun wildly in the air. It was then we noticed a bunch of cops across the street, their backs to us, sitting in The Donut shop having coffee. We rocked the Lark back and forth like mad men,

"Rock, God damn it!" Flat screamed.

"You rock!" I replied.

We rocked, got sick from the effort and puked out the windows. Finally, we got some wheels on the ground and powered off the hedge. Just like in the Army. We made it to the drive-through window of The Donut shop. Not a single cop noticed us. It was a good donut. The last one for awhile.

Before being deployed I went home and looked up my ex-girlfriend, Holly. We were high school childhood sweethearts. She wanted to get out of Milford and had large breasts. I was lonely and liked large breasts.

So, of course, we got married. We were married for one year before I went to Vietnam. She was tired of rural Michigan life and saw me as her ticket out. Another perfect example of the little head leading the big head.

Chapter 12

In Country

In August 1969, after a twenty-four hour flight from San Francisco, I arrived in Vietnam where I spent the next twelve months and nineteen days. I would come home a hero, or in a box. I had been to Vietnam once before, serving as a Top Secret Courier for the Army in charge of a crypto trailer full of electronic equipment. The "unit" was loaded onto a US Air Force C-130 military transport aircraft with a flight crew of five Air Force guys and me, the elite Army grunt. We departed Wright Patterson Air Force Base in Ohio and jumped across the country and then the Pacific, from Hawaii to Wake, Guam and Subic Bay in the Philippines before landing at Saigon. I almost didn't make it, but not because of any enemy action. We played "nose wheel roulette" at every landing.

Prior to landing each crew member picked one of the twelve numbers painted on the nose wheel. If your number was at the top of the wheel when the plane stopped you won the pot of $24.00. I won every stop except one. The Air Force guys were pissed, until I used the money to buy them drinks.

When I arrived in Vietnam for my one-year tour it smelled the same as it had the first time. The hot, dusty military base, the fetid scent of fear and diesel fuel and the exhilaration of war are forever in my memory.

I had a letter with me that I hadn't opened, and wasn't allowed to open, until I reported for duty. Arriving at the Saigon Airbase I reported to Colonel Beakwright at the 523rd Port Engineer Company, and handed him my orders.

"Well," said the Beak, none too happily after perusing the paperwork, "I am short of officers and had hoped you would remain here, but General Honker wants you to take command of a black ship and go do some projects." It actually was a "black ship" - it was painted black and carried no identifying numbers.

"What kind of projects?" I cleverly asked.

"Read the letter for yourself," he said, handing it to me.

The colonel was upset because he wanted me in his company, and the Commanding General of IV Corps jerked me out the day I got there. I read the letter. "That doesn't sound too bad," I said. He rolled his eyes at me. The letter read something like:

Commanding Officer
523 Engineer Co.
Subject: Orders
RE: 1st Lt. M. Perkins
Offer and provide Lt. Perkins any and all assistance required in furtherance of my directives.

Honker
IV Corps, Commanding

I was detached for TDY, temporary duty. I had been accused of being detached before, but now it was real. I didn't have to report to anyone except the general. The reason for that was not in the manual. I thought I was going to an Engineer Company as a diving officer, to build bridges, docks and facilities using barges, floating cranes and dive support. I was wrong. I finished reading the letter and said,

"If I'm not a dive officer for a port construction company what am I, exactly?"

"Special warfare," he said.

"What does that mean?" I asked the Colonel, noting that... I was special!

"Nobody knows," he said. "It's a nebulous term for 'what it is,' and nobody knows 'what it, is.' That's what makes it special. That's their way around specifics...is that clear Perkins?"

"Yes, Sir."

I was issued a nice army jungle outfit: olive drab shorts, olive drab shirts, olive drab socks, olive drab undies, two pairs of jungle boots and an antique .45 calibre pistol with a shoulder holster, no Bible this time. After changing out of my Class A uniform I hopped an outbound Huey helicopter and headed to Vung Tau to meet my ship and crew.

At the end of a peninsula that juts out into the South China Sea and formerly known as Cap Saint Jacques, Vung Tau was the Key West of Vietnam, the Paris of Southeast Asia. Vung Tau had been and still was a resort city. Even during the Vietnam War many opposing interests met in peace on the tree-lined streets with exotic scents and French café atmosphere. I felt the terrible excitement of war. It intensified my senses.

The women, beautiful, floated past me in their silken Ao-dais. The food was an exceptional combination of French and Vietnamese cuisines. Before dinner we went into town to get a "steam blow and a bath job." Small rooms, the walls did not extend to the ceiling, like a field emergency room. The girls were very petite and did not have enough body weight to give a good massage with their tiny hands. Instead, they walked on your back, stepping, or doing other things, on the points that needed attention, and all while eating chicken on a bamboo skewer and talking loudly to each over the top of their rooms. Their combined voices were sweet. I lay on my face and watched the shadow of fan blades. My head looked like a helicopter on the floor.

Prior to taking command of the ship I reported to General Honker via radio.

"Perkins, you are working for me now and I don't have time to read reports, you savvy?"

"Yes, Sir."

"And keep your goddamned radio on."

"Roger, WILCO, Sir." Finally, something I was good at...not writing reports.

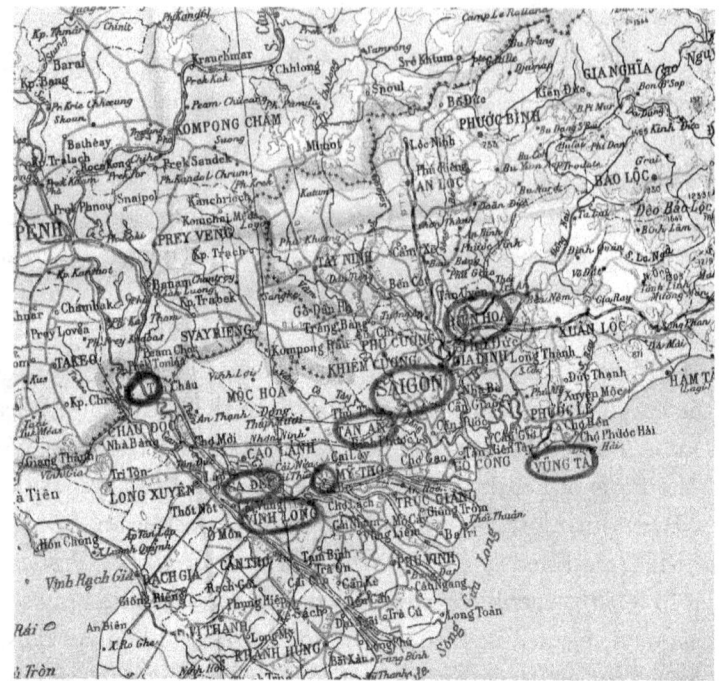

Map of Vietnam

"Honker Out."

It pissed off my fellow officers, because that's what a junior officer does, writes reports. On my occasional return to our base at Vung Tau, I reported in to Colonel Beakwright.

"Excuse me, Sir, are you busy?" I said, locating him by his voice behind the piles of paper on his desk.

"What have you been doing?" he barked back.

"Just some things."

"Things ... Like what?"

"I don't remember exactly ... I ... ah ... I forgot, Sir" His face appeared above the stacked papers.

"Don't you keep a log Perkins?"

"The monkey ate it, Sir."

"Monkey? Unh huh ... I'm worried about you, Perkins."

"Thank you, Sir."

He shrugged and went back to his paper bunker.

I shrugged. I didn't have to tell him anything, he knew that. One less report to read.

It was just me and the crew. A war born family and I had 'the letter,' to protect me from putting up with the usual bullshit. I just had to put up with the unusual bullshit.

After a five-hour ride, my Jeep driver screeched to a halt near the ship. I dug some flies out of my teeth, stepped on a dog turd and inhaled the sweet smell of napalm burning up wind. Home sweet home.

I was in Tan An and in command of "the black-boat down at the end of the pier," as the colonel described it. A black, steel, 150-foot, 300 Dead Weight Tonnage dive support vessel with a crew of twelve. I was number 13. The ship had no name or number on the hull. It was an old French river freighter converted to a Special Warfare/Dive Support ship. The ship carried two .50 caliber machine guns, numerous small arms and fighting devices, a double-lock recompression chamber and a ton of high explosives.

First Sergeant Jones, the Senior NCO (non-commissioned officer) and a Master Diver, met me on the pier. Together we formally inspected the ship and the crew. I introduced myself to the men and asked, "What is the ship's name?"

It was quiet. Everyone looked at each other. Maybe I hadn't been briefed. "Our ship has no name, or number, Sir!" Sgt. Jones said and winked at me.

I knew it had no number but I remembered my uncle telling me that a ship had to have a name.

"We won't paint it on the hull, but let's call her the *Irish Pennant*. Irish Pennant is from the Royal Navy during the time of sailing ships. It was a loose or untidy end of a line. In Navy and Marine Corps parlance today, an Irish Pennant is a loose thread on a uniform."

"Huh?" the crew responded as Sgt. Jones looked at the sky.

Sgt. M. J. Bassett was my eyes and ears on the boat. When Bassett first called me "Red", I called him "White." That's how his nickname started, as did the modest beginning of his unrepentant disrespect.

Before I arrived in country, White had been on the rivers for six months running a PBR (Patrol Boat River) for a Military Police unit that guarded the perimeter of Ton San Nhut air force base. He was transferred to the Port Engineering Company shortly before I arrived. White was a trained First Class Army Diver and we were short of divers, plus he had been "in country" for awhile. His experience would come in handy.

On the river or in the jungle, whoever was "in command" could be as much at risk from his own men as from the Viet Cong. Out in the middle of the Mekong River I told a dozen men (mostly draftees) who didn't know me, things they didn't want to hear about things they didn't want to do. I wasn't all that clear myself. They could vote to mutiny, dump me over the side and head back to base after a few days to report a casualty. I didn't get a vote.

"Gee, Sir, he musta fallen over at night taking a pee, Sir, "would be the story.

I needed someone I could trust on the boat; White was that someone. He was a stout hairy lad with a movie star face. White appeared to have little respect or regard for my obvious talents but, I was the best and the brightest. I was an Officer and a gentleman and, I needed to know what these guys were up to.

White was bat-shit crazy, but unusual alliances can be forged in the fog of war

Hearts Minds and Bullets – White on the right

Looking back from where Toby got sniped

The night before I arrived, the *Irish Pennant* was been moored near the riverbank in the city of Tan An. That night a sniper had nailed a crewman named Toby while he was standing on the foredeck, taking a leak. The poor bastard went over with his shorts down. I thought we should wait a day or two for him to "blow" to the surface because after two days in a hot jungle river a body starts to puff up and, full of gas, pops to the surface, unless the alligators find it first. But the crew didn't want to wait. I never met Toby. Still it was my responsibility to find him. The crew was naturally upset. I took the job, got dressed in a deep-sea suit and went down the ladder. I groped around in the black fetid mud under the ship, trying to find a body by feel. Welcome to Nam.

There was no light one-foot below the surface. It was my first dive in the real thing. I didn't want to do it but I knew my crew were watching. I looked for Toby, no luck. We were all disappointed. We found him the next day when he bobbed up near the ship. The medics bagged him. I stared at the hot black bag; suddenly things weren't as much fun. A few days later a messenger delivered a letter from the colonel expressing his sympathies to the crew. It was my job to inform his parents. It was a hard letter to write since I could offer no reasonable explanation for their loss.

River Mission

When I had showed up as "Captain of the Boat." I heard that I replaced a less than loved Lieutenant, so the bar wasn't set very high. My inherited crew was a bunch of highly trained, glue-sniffing, untrustworthy, madly motivated, wild-eyed, chronic drunks, women lovers and masturbators with guns, good eyes and training. Misfits, a gang of fearless losers, I thought at first.

White and a couple crewmembers showed me the current sapper-boom project and filled me in on necessary procedures for my survival.

The *Irish Pennant* was tied alongside a pier near the Tan An bridge. We crabbed along the bridge's walkways inspecting the structure. "Sappers are enemy divers," White said "who try to float explosives down river at night, just under the surface of the water and hopefully blow up bridges, with us on them, if possible. They get extra points; they're nasty fellows, sir!" White refused to capitalize Sir when he spoke. He made it sound like slur.

Our mission was to build sapper booms to stop the sappers. The big wooden floating booms were forty feet long with chain link fencing and razor wire hanging eight feet into the water. They were secured in front of the bridge, on the up-current side, theoretically to keep enemy divers away and ensure the bombs would not make it under the bridge, its weakest point. Occasionally the booms collapsed from all the debris they trapped, including a few bodies. The Viet Cong fired the explosives with time fuses (not an exact science) and they didn't always get the length just right. Sometimes the VC blew themselves up, sometimes curious fisherman or, not infrequently, one hundred pounds of unfired explosive would get caught in the boom. We had to go and get it. White told me that we even blew up our own bridges occasionally, simply to prevent the enemy from having the pleasure.

Walking across the old French bridge with White and several of the crew I passed a little twig bird nest and, on the way back, White spotted the nest as well. The nest had two little speckled blue eggs in it guarded by mama bird. Cute, I thought. White stuck the barrel of his M-16 into the nest. Mama bird attacked the barrel and got her beak stuck in the flame suppressor. White pushed mom aside, getting pecked heartily in the process and picked up one of the innocent little eggs. Holding the egg between his bird beaked thumb and well-pecked forefinger he looked at it, rolling the egg around slowly as though he was a scientist or bird person. Interesting, I thought.

Then White popped the egg into his mouth with a flourish and swallowed. Slam, swallow, burp. It was revolting. I looked at White. White looked at me. With a slight nod and a wink toward the remaining baby bird egg he waited, patiently. Drawing on an unknown reserve of foolishness, I reached in and grabbed the egg, like I was going to eat it, though I sure as shit wasn't. I didn't have to; I was an officer. I was the Captain. I held it out toward White.

"Here you go, Sergeant Bassett, you seem to enjoy these."

White stared at me.

"You're a sick bastard," I said.

"Hey, don't be a pussy, sir," he piped as the crew eagerly looked on.

Now, whenever someone calls you a pussy you must respond immediately. It can be painful in some cases. My bluff had been called. I looked at the egg, while being heavily eyeballed by White and the crew. I was distracted, but I could swear I heard money-changing hands. I tucked my chin in, put my chest out, screamed "LAY HOLD-HEAVE!" and with proper military bearing I popped the egg through my dry lips and crunched down. Instantly, shell, bone, feathers and beak of bird, exploded in my military mouth. A skinny bird leg, with a tiny bird foot attached, popped out and flapped wildly between my lips. It was fighting for survival. I tried to push the leg back in and gagged.

"Don't puke, sir."

Where was the respect? I was the Captain.

I chewed and swallowed the still kicking bird, it was tough. I didn't want to kill it, but I had wounded it. White nodded in approval. I donned a nonchalant air and prayed that the egg, which I now realized White had swallowed whole, would hatch before he took his morning dump.

In the macho world of war you can't let anyone think they have the upper hand. It didn't matter what the setting - you had to be crazier than the other guy, and convincingly so. The more fucked up the better, otherwise your men would take your sanity as a sign of weakness and start working it. The crew knew they would eventually win if they were crazier than me. I wasn't crazier than them, but I knew I had to look that way. Plus, I was a natural and it was my duty.

Many relationships were brief in-country. The crew had a puppy onboard for a few days. Before we had a chance to name him he disappeared. One morning, when the dog tried to take a drink of water out of the toilet he may have encountered an unforeseen problem; our toilet hung off the back of the ship. Air sip, gone!

(No real dogs fell through the toilet bowl. Only a fictional dog)

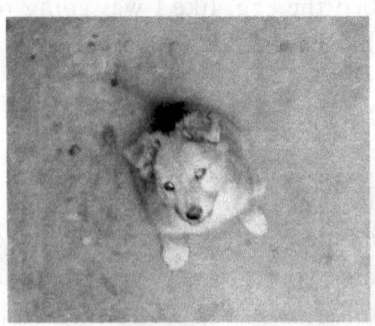 

Our dog named GoneOops Bye Bye

After two months in-country I wasn't sure about anything. Did I have the guts to do this? Did my crew respect me, even like me? Did I know as much as I thought I knew just a few months earlier? There is no adequate preparation for war.

New Message:

Extract LRP team. 50 K upriver from present position / side of bank west/ coconut on stick/ four SF (Special Forces) Coordinates to follow. Nothing further/out."

Whatever you say, Sir!

I still believed. In what, I wasn't sure. Things were becoming fuzzy.

A few days later, in the middle of the night, four of us headed toward a river bank near the Cambodian border. We pulled the black raft into the weeds and set up a perimeter. I found the coconut on a stick and crawled into a wet hole in the stinking mud. There were three guys in the hole. Without thinking I said, "I'm here to pick up four guys." No one spoke. The team couldn't recover their buddy's body. It was quiet as we headed to the raft. I should have counted before I opened my mouth.

We worked around bridges, but sometimes we got orders to head out and wait for further instructions. The old "Stand BY to Stand BY ... Stand BY!" We went upriver, sat around swatting bugs and then received another order via radio:

"Situation developing/anchor off shore near Can Tho/ Nothing further/out." Sometimes it got boring. My favorite message was, *"Initiate termination of previous initiative, Out."*

We had a double lock recompression chamber down in the main hold of the ship. It was our "home entertainment center." We liked to go "down" fast in the chamber, using air pressure instead of water pressure to induce nitrogen narcosis. The chamber was operated from outside by a reportedly sober individual. At ninety feet you get a build-up of nitrogen in your blood. It causes nitrogen narcosis, the "Rapture of the Deep." It was stoning and euphoric, like nitrous oxide, and air pressure wasn't illegal. When we "came up" the air decompressed and a miniature cumulus cloud formed in the chamber as the air grew cooler. It was one of a few times we would get cool in-country. The rapid decompression also blew a squad of boogers out your nose that looked like an Apalachicola oyster in free flight. It was nasty, but if you wanted to get rid of a sinus cold and be stoned at the same time, that was the way to do it. Jungle air conditioning and no hangover.

It seemed like we were always on the way to the small hamlet known as ...*U Binh Phucht.*

The Enterprising Vietnamese

Above, the little people are busy gathering bits and pieces of wood, metal, wire and cement to make more booby traps.

Almost everywhere the American GI's went, little markets popped up in minutes. The variety of goods was impressive, anything from a python skin, to Tampax, from dried dog meat on a string with flies, to fish eyes in a glass, or tattered "Playboy" magazines, could be had for a few dong. Dong was the name of their currency. After the war, in 1975, the North Vietnamese changed the name to the "Liberation Dong". One of the Liberation Dongs was worth 500 of the South Vietnamese losers' dongs. A lot of dongs changed hands in Nam.

There was a lot of unorganized activity that I was not a party to, and didn't want to be party to, although I did want to party, too. My training had been "Take what you know and apply as needed" which meant I shouldn't be too busy. That made things simple and left time for fun.

The General's letter gave me access to anything. When we needed to re-supply we'd hunt down U.S. Navy ships at anchor in the rivers. The Navy Commanders puckered up when they heard me on the radio. Many of them knew I had "The Letter" and they knew what happened when we got onboard their ships.

Unfortunately, in the Navy you can't drink beer on the ship, but you can drink beer on a barge tied off to the ship. It was a tradition.

One night we tracked down a black ship, No Visible Exterior Lights, a Navy vessel anchored in the dark middle of the Mekong River. They wouldn't answer us on the radio when we hailed them. Radio silence. It was so dark we couldn't see the bow of our own ship. There were no lights on our vessel, either. However, our Vietnamese cabin boy, Boway, knew where the Navy ship was and told us which way to head... mmm? Head on in we did. Then, Boom! We hit the down current side of the Navy's one-hundred-foot steel "beer barge" so hard we got stuck in it.

"Might as well put out a line," said first mate White.

"You can do it for safety," I said. "But we're not going anywhere."

We were wedged into the beer barge, which was okay considering what was on it.

My crew dispersed into the bowels of the Navy ship to "trade." We carried booze, the occasional 'evening companion,' captured AK 47's, Montagnard spears, animals and whatever else the crew gathered. I went onboard the ship and up to the officers' ward room with my letter. I was not always welcome, but the food was good.

The Cho Gow canal

One day we got orders to travel to the village of Phuct Tup Luc. If we took the Cho Gow canal it would save us seventy miles of jungle river passage. The Cho Gow canal was manmade, very narrow, very shallow, and very dangerous. I decided to take the "Choke," as my crew called it.

Watching for the enemy

We were heading through the Cho Gow canal; three Republic of Vietnam (RVN) gunboats ran alongside. The enemy was out there and a 30-mile run through the jungle lay ahead. We got five or six miles up the "Choke" when our RVN allies, our Brothers in Arms, our friends, our buddies, our guards, turned their gunboats around and left us. Rude. They wouldn't answer the radio, nothing. Even when we shot at them they wouldn't come back.

"ASS HOLES!" we screamed to no avail. Now in the "Choke" we were on our own. The word 'asshole' echoed between the mud banks.

Once the ship was in "The Choke" we could not stop or turn around. If we stopped, the ship would displace the water in the shallow manmade canal and get stuck to the muddy bottom. We had no choice but to go ahead. Or did we?

Some hours later we heard and felt gunfire erupt from the banks on each side of the river. I didn't know what to do, so I stood there with my mouth open and hoped that something intelligent would come out. I hit the throttles full ahead and screamed, "INCOMING." Small arms bullets bounced off the hull, sounding like a drunken drummer beating on a church bell.

Meanwhile, the crew scattered below deck leaving only Sergeant Locati and me in the wheelhouse. My men swung into action. Great! Suddenly most of the crew came back up on deck with…cameras. They ducked down behind the 3000 psi high-pressure air tanks located over the '"High Explosives Locker" and started shooting… pictures. No one was hit, the crew scooped up a few flattened enemy bullets for souvenirs and soon we were out of range.

I immediately gathered the crew, "What the fuck was that? What about things like guns and grenades and fighting back, air strikes, napalm, Army shit. You know …War!"

"Well, look, sir," said White, "it's not a good day for killin'. We get shot at a lot. It's kind of pointless to waste our ammo shooting into the jungle. If we got lucky and hit one of them gooks they would really get pissed and try to follow us. Better to lose face than ass, sir. Best to just let them blow off some steam, and besides they don't have a lot of ammo either. Best not to make them break camp and chase our military asses through the bush."

"Hmm?" I intoned. "Well, don't let it happen again!"

Sometimes we did shoot back, just for fun.

Finally, an hour after the ambush and still in the 'Choke' I said, "Men, you know what? This is not a good idea." Many nodded; the pucker factor was palpable. I stood tall and issued my orders to the crew, "We have only two choices men… Get fucked up …or…Get more fucked up… Let's go back." More nods. So we turned back by ramming the bow of the ship into the bank and pushing the stern around with our 500-horse power bridge boat. We came back down the Choke at night and either the gooks didn't see us go past or, more likely, they moved from a known position, in case we called in an airstrike. Clever fellows.

White, molesting a mollusk in the South China Sea

We were tied up in Nha Bang to fix an engine. Fifty yards away from our mess tent, across the river on the mud bank, was the Wood Pile, a stinking heap of North Vietnamese and Viet Cong bodies stacked up from kills in the area. Our snipers were good. The bodies were sprayed with lye to keep the flies and other creatures away. The bodies lay there until the Republic of Vietnam soldiers, who weren't known for speed, could come and get them. They stacked the gooks like firewood, out in the open. I called them gooks too; it made it less personal should I have to "counsel" one. We smoked and joked as we looked out the window at the grim collection of expired souls. It was hard not to look. We weren't particularly gracious to our enemies. No one was gracious to anyone; still, there was a certain appeal to the madness.

I rarely used a rifle, except when we went on patrol, they were too awkward. I carried a .45 in a shoulder holster for close-in counselling, but my main weapon was a M.79 grenade launcher. It held one grenade the size of a frozen orange juice can and made almost no sound when fired, just a *"tuunnkk"*, harder for the enemy to discover where it came from. The shell detonated on impact and was much louder on the other end, I was told.

I got a carpenter's holster with a metal jaw designed to hold a hammer. I bent the jaw open to hold grenade launcher. With that rig all I had to do was swivel from the hip and fire. I didn't have to pull it out or aim very carefully. It was quite efficient and the barrel looked awfully big from the wrong end. That grenade launcher may have saved us one night.

The *Irish Pennant* was disabled at a gravel loading dock upriver near Chou Duc. An Army recon aircraft radioed us, warning of an impending attack by about sixty Viet Cong. Shortly thereafter, we were advised that a nearby Combat Infantry Company wouldn't be able to get any reinforcements to us for four hours and no gunships were available. The war business must be good, I thought.

We couldn't move the ship. White and I went up to the top of a gravel rock pile as High Observers/Ground (HOG's). We were well armed, enough to cause the gooks some serious indigestion should we cross paths. The rest of the crew manned the vessel and readied the .50 cal. machine guns, the M60 machine guns and their M16's. They set up a perimeter of Claymore mines and detonator cord. We could clear an area half the size of a football field in two seconds. White and I sat on top of the gravel pile for an hour or so waiting for some sign of impending doom; we dug a hole and cooked a few C-Rations over some C-4 plastic explosive (C-4 burns like Sterno when you light it and it doesn't smoke). I brought my guitar and extra ammo; White brought his harmonica, a box of grenades and a six-pack of Tiger Beer. We started singing songs, quietly, but they reminded us too much of home and so we made up some new ones while waiting to die.

"Sitting on a rock pile singing our song
Out in the bushes are Viet Cong ...
Oh ... what a groove we're in.
We up here and they're out there
they don't know and we don't care
Oh ... what a groove we're in."

I was just dicking around and for some reason, perhaps to test range and trajectory; I decided to try to blow the top off a coconut palm tree fifty-yards from us. It was near an old brick kiln. We were getting bored and there's nothing like the smell of burnt cordite to get the juices flowing. I didn't aim very carefully, just fired ... *tuuunk*. I hit the tree by sheer luck but, unfortunately, there was a gook in it. When the grenade exploded near the top it blew him out of the tree. With a faint *iiiiiiieeeeeeeeee!* he plummeted to earth, his white shirt and baggy shorts flapping in the wind. It looked like he was trying to fly on the way down. Thump. He got up and ran into the bush with a bunch of coconuts! Oops. Turned out it was a local farmer.

The next day, after I apologized, he confirmed that no one, including himself, heard the *tuuunk* from the M-79 and that the Viet Cong had been in the area as reported.

"VC go *didi mau*," he said through toothless gums, "see you makee blow me out tree."

The gooks thought we had them spotted. Sixty of them, twelve of us...we were lucky. It was a good night to be alive.

Me with the "Flying farmer," all is forgiven

Son Ri was our cabin girl. She was on the boat for everyone, along with her girlfriend whom the crew called "Mumbles." Mumbles always tried to eat chicken, talk, and learn English, while giving a blowjob. White taught her to say "restaurant."

One night, after I'd finished, *Son Ri* looked at me and said, "You do me now, *Dai'wi,* You do *me* now." She'd never had an orgasm and apparently wanted to know what the big deal was. Who doesn't?

Another time we nearly got blown to hell, but were saved by our young cabin boy. We had inherited this skinny little Vietnamese kid as part of a package deal. When *Son Ri* came onboard so did her little brother. We called him *Boy san'*.

Cabin Boy san'

One night, we were tied up near Dong So. Everything was quiet; it was almost dark. We were getting ready to eat dinner when out of the bush *Boy san'* showed up. He ran quickly up the gangplank and onto the boat, "You go! GI' You go!" *Boy san'* insisted.

I didn't know much Vietnamese and proved it. "What you meanee *Boy san'*? We no go, we makee tie up here. You dinki dow! We makee chop chop," I replied pointing at my mouth.

"No, no. You go, Captain! You go! You go now fast! He was panicking. There was something about his voice I thought, panic perhaps. I ordered the crew to cut the lines with an axe, "Bang!" steel blade on steel bitt. I turned the wheel to starboard, punched the bow into the bank, swung the stern out, then backed down full, the engines screaming for mercy. With no lights, black smoke blowing out the exhaust pipes and shit sliding everywhere, I spun the boat stern first away from the dock and into the river. I looked back at the dock where we'd been tied minutes before and thought, "What the fuck?"

Not five minutes after that insightful question, two rockets came screaming in and hit the dock.

The "wee folk" had sighted in on us in during the day. *Boy san'* had been ashore and saw them doing it. The rockets were lashed in a tree and were aimed at the ship during daylight, while they could see it. All they had to do was wait for dark, when most of the crew would be onboard, trip the rockets and Boom! *Boy san'* had seen them getting ready to launch just before dark. He knew where they were aimed and also knew his sister was onboard.

Later on, *Son Ri* moved over to an eighty-foot long tugboat to make a trip down river at night. The tug was pulling a large gravel barge behind it. Vietnamese fishermen lived on platforms out in the river. They strung nets between poles stuck in the mud. Lots of nets, but no lights. On the way down river the tug Captain spotted the nets with his searchlight and turned across current to avoid them. He didn't make it. Then regrettably, he decided to turn around and save the people he'd spilled into the water after going through their living room. When the Captain turned up river, the two-hundred-ton gravel barge behind passed him going down river. Before the Captain could get the tug around into the current, the barge's towline pulled high and off center on the tug's towing post and flipped it over. Within ten seconds the tug was gone, dragged along the bottom of the Mekong River by the still floating barge. The fishermen went for an unexpected late night dip. We never did find the tug, or *Son Ri*. *Boy san'* was alone now and we took care of him after his sister was gone. I hope he made it after we were gone. Most Vietnamese were gentle people and even though their world had collapsed they tried to make the best of it. In the end I liked them and felt bad about what was happening.

Chapter 13

Bugs and Bullets

Flat Vanyatta, my buddy from the "Red Velvet" days in DC, and I were in Vietnam at the same time. Flat had a crazy job, which suited him.

Everybody talks about marines or infantry or other elite troops being the "first ones in." Well, they were not always the "first ones in." Sometimes you couldn't get "in." South Vietnam and the Mekong delta was jungle, you savvy? It was Flat and his bulldozers, the Mechanized Corps who were the "first in." They were called "The Stingers," and most of his men were volunteers. Flat had been issued his own helicopter and he reconnoitered the designated areas. The military wanted to go into these places because they were "hot." Hot equals dangerous. There were no allies, just Victor Charlies, as we called the Viet Cong, snakes, spiders, leeches, tigers, bugs and bullets. Flat's mission was to cut a swath through the jungle with bulldozers, large earth moving machines and explosives for the armored cavalry troops to follow. His unit typically encountered some "resistance" as Flat put it. The company had a high casualty rate, as they drove into remote areas with small arms, explosives, tractors, bulldozers and beer. Bulldozers, the size of a small apartment, had gigantic piercing blades called "stingers." While living in tents for weeks at a time, Flat and his men would slice through the virgin jungle cutting down all the vegetation in their path. Snakes, bugs and bullets fell from the jungle canopy. If something was too big to push over or tear apart with a stinger blade they'd blow it up with high explosives. God, it was good to be young, but a little rough on the vegetation where life had flourished without interruption for thousands of years. Now a new creature had arrived in the jungle, the "Bullet Bug," it flew fast and it had a bad bite.

Occasionally, Flat would chopper down to wherever I was in the Delta. We'd hang out for the night in a lovely jungle setting, tracer rounds lighting the evening sky, and a few times in the exotic bars of Vung Tau or Saigon. Things seem more exotic in wartime, at least to some participants.

Flat's visits were welcome, as I didn't get many chances to chill out in "The Nam."

One evening, without notice or "proper clearance" from the authorities, Flat's Huey came out of the jungle, hot and low. He landed his helicopter anywhere he wanted and with shit blowing everywhere and MP sirens screaming in the distance, Flat kicked open the chopper door and tossed out a case of Tiger beer. "Hey Pards...you thirsty?" I was. The MP's raced up and had to decide between fighting with Flat or drinking cold Tiger beer. They made the right choice.

I got the chance, how lucky can you get, to fly with an advance aerial scout in an airplane that looked like a dragonfly called the "Bumblebee." A two-seater aircraft with a glass bulb in front, a Bonzai altimeter, a ten-foot camera pod and a sixty-foot wingspan. Pilot and cameraman sat side by side in the "eyeballs." The skinny arachnid of a plane, with long wings, tubular fuselage, cameras and early infrared sensors mounted below were employed to give fifteen-minutes of fame to those pesky VC.

I met "Vertical Vern," the pilot, (he spelled it-Pile It) in a Saigon bar. Vern told me what he did and I thought it sounded like fun. I had been drinking. I asked him if I could come along sometime.

"You betcha, Red Rider, how about now?" Vertical Vern burped. "I got a flight up country in forty-five minutes outta Ton San Nhut, we'll fly 'the nap,'" he chuckled and cracked his knuckles, "hot and low over the tree tops, one hunner' and fiffy' knots...up towards Black Virgin Mountain, we'll try not to die ... Sheeeeet! ... sure you want to go? ... don't eat if you do." He kicked his chair back, got up, guzzled his beer, winked at me and wobbled away, trying to find the door made out of beads.

I kicked my chair back and guzzled my beer, "Sounds like fun Vern, let's turn and burn," I barked with beer foam in my nose hairs.

We took off from Ton San Nhut airbase and flew along at one-hundred-fifty knots. Vern had an instrument called a "Bonsai" altimeter and we watched the red, two-inch digital altitude numbers flicker. We cruised just above the treetops, the Nap as Vern called it.

"By the time the Viet Cong hear the plane, we're past them. They can't shoot at us, the forest canopy is too dense," Vern said over the headset, grinning optimistically.

"Roger that," I said marveling at American technology and thinking about how much fun I was having.

Our "Bumblebee" crossed the jungle canopy, contour flying above "the nap", using the infrared cameras. When we got to the end of the run Vertical Vern yelled over the roar of the engines, "Okay Red, I've got to go VERTICAL, hee ... hee ... hee ... and hey man, don't puke on me, I won't be able to see!" He pulled straight up in 2-G climb, spun her around, and dropped back down on the nap inducing a few more "G's."

He didn't want to be a target. I felt like I was going to drop out my own asshole. We could hear pop, pop, pop and saw tracers behind us. Maybe the VC saw us or heard us when we pulled up to turn around. But the jungle canopy saved us and we made it back to the airfield. I was a little disoriented and forgot to thank Vern. He was gone before I finished puking.

Zoo in the Jungle

Monk

It is easy to get detached from everyday courtesies when you are trying to kill someone or, when someone is trying to kill you and pets, the crew had come to find, were a natural and necessary way of keeping some humanity.

We had a monkey on the boat; no one admitted knowing how it got there. The monkey didn't like anybody, nobody, except White. No one knew why, but that's how it was. That monkey was a terror, mean and dirty; you could smell him if you were down wind. Monkey see, monkey do do ... but in the beginning, the crew wouldn't let me throw Darwin's Nightmare overboard. I couldn't get near enough to catch him anyway. A Vietnamese man told me a person should never go near a monkey that didn't like people, and most of them don't. And, he said, never put your face near a monkey or try to kiss a monkey, it would bite your lips off and eat them, because they're easy to chew. That made an impression. I never went near that crazy monkey. To this day I don't try to kiss monkeys. See, I have learned something.

One evening, I came back to the boat and there, on this one hundred and fifty foot ship was the monkey controlling about twenty feet of deck, his own section. The Monk patrolled daily as though he, too, was in the Army. Did I mention this was a big monkey, all muscle, teeth and attitude? White managed to keep it on a chain sometimes, but it was a long chain and no matter where you were or what you were doing the monkey came over and checked you out and, if you were eating, the monkey got some. The monkey always got fed. No one likes a hungry monkey.

We came back from a land trip to Chow Duc late one afternoon. The ship was moored alongside a concrete loading dock near Soi Rap. On this hot jungle river day, I spotted White, sitting in a modified lotus position, possibly asleep and lying back in the shade, against the .50 calibre machine gun mount. He was guarding the ship. And there, sitting behind him in exactly the same position, like he was White's shadow, was The Monk. The Monk was also doing guard duty and there is no better guard than a monkey, they don't miss a thing. However, from a distance it appeared they were both asleep. The Monk quickly stood up as my jeep approached (at least one of them was awake!) then walked over and stood in front of White. The Monk stood upright and inflated himself to his full height in front of White, teeth bared. I didn't know what the monkey was going to do and White did not move a muscle He was either asleep or paralyzed with fear...sleep most likely. The monkey may have felt that his "Monkness" was not being properly respected and assumed an aggressive, dominant position. I got out of the jeep, drew my .45 and stabilized on the hood for a shot. White snored. I ignored the incessant sound of mosquitoes drowning in the sweat on my face. It was a long shot for a .45. I focused and thought of the earlier bird egg incident. It would be a tough shot, and a tough choice.

The monkey wasn't as big and scary as he thought he was and finally sat down on White's feet. This woke White up; they looked each other in the eye, though White was not focusing. The monkey stared at White, maybe thinking, *Damn! This is one cool dude.* Finally, the monkey reached over and picked something off White's hairy chest. A bug, a leaf, a tick, a marijuana seed, I couldn't see. Sweat was running into my eyes, I was hoping I wouldn't have to shoot. The Monk sat back on his haunches, looked at the picked object, bit it to kill it and spit it out on White. White fully opened his eyes. He recognized the nature of The Monk's gesture. What did White do? He dug the dead bug out of his chest hair and flicked into air then reached over and picked something off the monkey, looked at it, bit it and spit it back on The Monk. Monkeys need love too. Now they sat grooming and spitting dead bugs on each other, White and The Monk, face to face, family. In the jungle you make friends when you can.

By now the rest of the crew hated the nonhuman primate, they had to clean up all the monkey loafs baked on deck. The Monk knew it and took a shit in a different place each time. It was like an Easter egg hunt gone bad. One day the crew went into the village and bought a dozen cheap lounge chairs the, "Made in China Numba" One G. I. ... you buy ... cheap! cheap!" patio furniture set. The crew set them up, looking forward to some relief from the hot steel decks. Then we got called out on a land-based mission and were gone most of the day. As I looked back out at the ship anchored just offshore (we anchored out when we could to keep the animals, snakes and bugs off) there was something comforting about the cheap patio furniture and Tiki torches set up near our .50 calibre machine-gun. Homey. The boat looked good and we left *Boway*, our fifty-year-old cabin boy, onboard. *Boway* would not go near The Monk. The monkey had free reign on the ship (no one messes with a bad monkey) and whenever we were at anchor in a secure area we let the monkey roam around, he couldn't get off the boat and would attack any strangers. Monkeys can swim but don't like to. Unfortunately, we never knew where The Monk was going to be when we returned. That was the fun part. Anyway, we came back from our job and were driving up to the dock when we saw the damned monkey in the midst of the patio set. He picked up every single piece of lawn furniture and tipped them over the side. Our lounge chairs, tables, our beloved Tiki torches, all of it went overboard into the Mekong to be sucked away by the fast moving brown water. (Two months later we went down river and thought we saw an old man sitting in one of our chairs.) We watched The Monk do his deed and express his feelings for cheap patio furniture. "Hey, screw you guys," he screeched in *monkese* as he hauled ass up the radar mast. Now everybody *really* hated the monkey. They were going to kill The Monk, but I couldn't let them do that, even though I had suggested it.

I had a buddy, a Special Forces Captain named Coleman. He stopped by the ship one afternoon. I said, "Coleman, I've got a problem. I've got this fuckin' mad-mean monkey and my guys are going to kill it unless I do something about it." I had come to admire the monk for his fierce independence and didn't want *Mama' san* to cook him.

Coleman had met The Monk before. An introduction that included having a monkey finger stuck up his nose. Coleman liked The Monk. He covered his nose and said, "Hey, 'Fuckin-A' Red, I'll take that monkey, no problemo." The Monk didn't like many people but he liked White and he appeared to like Coleman. So, that was it. Problem solved. Monkey gone. And we didn't have to kill it, although our housekeeper, *Mama'san,* had offered to cook it. "Yoo rike me cookie Monkey? Numbah One! Chop Chop GI," she said flapping her bright red betel-nut stained gums with relish.

A week later, Coleman's jeep came careening out of the jungle and skidded to a halt in a cloud of dead bugs and water buffalo dung. He was wearing a black VC pajama shirt, several sizes too small, with two bullet holes in it. He said he took it off someone who "didn't need it anymore." And there was The Monk, hanging on to the front of the jeep hood with a leash around his neck. The monkey loved it, like a dog with its head out the window. It was our monkey all right; The Monk, but now he sported a Regulation- Special Forces -Mohawk haircut. Coleman called it a "riding cut."

"Is that our monkey, The Monk?"

"You're righter than rain, Cappy, he's Special Forces now!" He made a little move with his hand and the monkey jumped up on my shoulder. I covered my lips and mumbled "Great." The Monk stuck his wet bony finger in my ear and looked for bugs in my beard as White came out of the bush.

"Hot Damn look at that monkey!" White said. "A real Special Forces M-Fing Mohawk monkey ... THE MONK... Damn...Look at him now!" We were proud. The Monk had found a home.

A few days later I was not surprised to find out that Coleman, who studied cats for strategy, had another monkey, a female. That day, after the rains stopped, Coleman showed up at the ship with the new monkey on one fender and The Monk, riding "Mohawk High" on the other. With a leash in each hand Coleman couldn't get out of the jeep easily. "Let's go for ride, Red!" he said. I jumped in back. The driver punched it and got the Jeep going as fast as it could down the rutted and probably mined dirt road. The driver had the front window folded down. Coleman turned around in his seat, got slapped in the back of the head by a palm frond at forty miles an hour and cried through bug filled teeth, "Watch this, Baboo!"

He called me Baboo ... or was it the monkey? He let the monkeys off the leash. The horny primates crawled onto the center of the hood as we careened through the jungle at forty-five miles an hour. The driver, foot flat on the floor, was going all out. He began to smile. Coleman turned and comforted me with his theory ... "If you hit a mine going fast enough it goes off behind you."

"Right," I said, from the back seat.

I thought Coleman was an optimist, if nothing else, as the female scrambled up front, partially obscuring the driver's view. She grabbed the hood and held on for dear life. Then The Monk scrambled up, grabbed the female from behind and started humping her for all he was worth. We tore through the jungle with two monkeys humping on the hood. The driver was grinning like a fool while Coleman held on to the dash, laughing so hard he cried. I sat back and let the tears of laughter land on me.

The Monk, the dog and the cat weren't the only animals on board. All personalities combined, we had a floating menagerie, a real zoo.

Up in the wheelhouse of the ship, I kept a bamboo birdcage with two wild jungle birds. They were lovebirds, very pretty and sweet little birds that chirped beautifully. I slept in a cabin in the wheelhouse and the birds lent a touch of civility as well as an early warning system to the cabin. One day I called White into the wheelhouse. "White, there's something happening with my birds." I said.

"What exactly do you mean, sir?" he asked.

"Look." I took him over to the cage. "I think they're trying to escape."

"That sounds pretty serious, sir," he said. "Maybe we should keep an eye on them." So we kept an eye on them. The next day White came up to me "sir, I think you're right." (He'd gone undercover). "If they don't think you're looking at them, they're pecking on a piece of the fucking bamboo over there" pointing to the back of the cage. "But if you walk into the wheelhouse, they scramble over to the other side of the cage and start singing and shitting. If you reach in to touch them near the side of the cage they're trying to break out of, they start pecking at you." White had studied this; he showed me his scarified finger. So we had a discussion about it that night. I asked White what he thought I should do.

"Do you think we should repair the bamboo bars?" questioned White.

"No, I don't think so, I think we should wait and see what happens. Monitor the situation."

"Yes, sir, I love that choice."

It took two more days. On the third day I went into the wheelhouse and the birds were gone. They ate their way out of that bamboo cage. They were tree smart. We observed and let it happen anyway, like a lot of other things in war. I threw the cage overboard. I didn't have the songbirds anymore, but I had my guns. They made chirping sounds too.

We were tied up to a Navy pier in Vung Tau. We had an older Vietnamese woman onboard, the one who had offered to cook The Monk. We called her *"Mama San."* She cooked, cleaned and helped establish the bare minimum of sanitary procedures.

One afternoon White was down in the galley with Mama San, sarcastically telling her how much he loved the light green colored pound cakes in our WWII vintage C-rations. *Mama San* looked into the OD colored can and poked at the damp lump with her boney finger. Her eyes lit up. *"Mama San'-Can Do, Mama San'-Can Do!!"* she cackled through her betel-nut stained lips.

So White, trapped by misunderstood sarcasm, gave her a few hundred *Dong*. She came back the next day with bags of ingredients, a big pot and some wood. Before anyone knew what was happening *Mama San* came out of the galley, covered in flour. She cackled incoherently and proceeded to build a campfire on the deck of the ship, the steel ship, our ship with the painted deck, the ship with the ton of High Explosives underneath the deck. She set up camp between the eight High Pressure air bottles to keep the wind off the fire. *Mama San* stoked the fire, scuffled back and forth and finally spread the embers over the top of the pot to make an oven. The deck blistered and smoked as the paint burned off... *Mama San* would not be denied. Voila!

"Mama San makee chop chop, you rike chop chop GI?" she asked the crew as she removed the baked item from the coals somehow wearing two pairs of sandals to save her feet.

I poked at the unidentifiable, paint scented, brown lump with my gun barrel, "Yes, Mama San... we rike."

Sgt. Mooney and *Boway* the 50-year-old cabin boy

Being the only Officer on the boat with a twelve-man crew was not necessarily a good thing. I didn't trust a single one of these malcontent dingleberries, except White, maybe.

The wheelhouse and my cabin were on the stern, the crew lived at the bow. During the night my faithful cabin boy, *Boway*, lived in the middle. I trusted that gook, it was easier that way. He could have set us all up to die any time he chose. Sometimes we got off the ship and left him there alone, this Vietnamese man of unknown tendencies. On the other hand, we did protect him. He was probably as safe with us as he was anywhere.

Boway was my advance guard, my early warning system, protecting me from my own crew. Every night, before I went to sleep, I tied a monofilament fishing line to my big toe with a slipknot. This small, almost invisible line ran from my cabin to amidships where faithful *Boway* sat with his back toward me, staring ahead. *Boway* stayed up all night, every night. I know, I checked.

If anyone came more than halfway down the ship *Boway* would tug on the line. None of the crew seemed to know about my setup, the fishing line was hidden and hard to see. The late night tug came more than once, probably caused by guys who couldn't sleep or had to take a dump at 0300 hours …right. I also had two sets of beaded curtains, one at the entrance to the wheelhouse and one on the entrance to my cabin. Beaded curtains are difficult to get through without making noise.

Nothing personal. I didn't dwell on it. In the infantry knocking off your commanding officer was called "fragging," as in fragmentation grenade. My cabin was too small, you didn't need a "Frag"…comforting and, it would save the government money. We were doing hazardous stuff and some of the crew didn't think that the work was worth the results. I'm not sure I disagreed with them then and I certainly don't now.

One night a guy did try to get to me. I felt the fishing line jerk and snapped out of a half-sleep, seconds later the first set of beads began to talk. I racked back my .45, a sound that is unmistakable to the trained or even the untrained ear, untied the line and slipped out of my bunk. I lay on the floor and pointed the gun up at the door. The sound of a .45 racking back may have led the late night visitor to reconsider his dedication to the cause. It was quiet for a minute, there was some thinking going on. The beads talked again, "Bye Bye," they swished on his way out.

One morning, inspired by my level of success, as in STILL ALIVE, I decided to hold swim call. A command decision, "We'll take a swim, men, to stay in shape and get some exercise."

I heard some grumbling but, fearlessly leading the way, I jumped overboard shouting "GO ARMY!" and plunged into the sticky green-brown water. I came up, spit some unknown object out of my mouth and cheered the men on. I was followed slowly by the rest of the silent crew who looked like they were walking the plank. Splash! Wow! We could really swim. We were Army Divers, calmly stroking away as the jungle shore swept by. But when I ordered," Back to the ship, men!" we turned and met a two-knot current against us. Swimming like mad men, we gained only a few yards. Soon we would be carried away, up and into the jungle and perhaps get a chance to enjoy the local nightlife.

Local Nightlife

Boway stood silently at the stern, staring at us. Finally, I screamed out, "*Boway* throw rope…Throw rope…*Didi Mau!* (hurry up)." I tried to do a charade of a rope while swimming for my life. *Boway* walked away up the deck.

"We're fucked," someone behind commented. "Nice call, Captain," another chimed in.

One crewmember made a wet fart sound with his armpit to accompany the speaker. I was swimming too hard and couldn't turn to see who the insubordinate was. He was a rude fellow, but a good swimmer I had to admit. Minutes later *Boway* appeared with a bunch of mooring lines knotted together. He tied a float to the end and started letting it drift down current toward us. With the fear of death as an inspiration we held our position, then grabbed the line and hauled our asses back to the ship. Wet and exhausted I nodded at *Boway* and gave him a handful of dongs.

Occasionally, things did get unpleasant. Snipers, lobbing rounds in and hoping to get lucky, can get on your nerves even on the best days. The Mekong is a giant river, the Mississippi of Southeast Asia. However, some tributaries are not so large, not large enough to turn the ship around. One time, we got caught in a cross fire on one of the smaller tributaries. We heard gunfire from both sides of the bank. The shooters were on the high ground. We couldn't shoot because we didn't know who was who. We didn't want stop or turn around to investigate. Fortunately, they had to shoot over our heads in order to kill each other. We sailed under a bridge of bullets. We were getting used to weird stuff and this incident only rated a 5 on the adrenalin boost scale.

We'd been on the rivers for two weeks without any amenities and decided to pull into a small hamlet for some R&R. We hadn't shaved because we only had river water to bathe in. Most of the crew had beards. Bad infections can develop from river water. White and I left our guns onboard and walked into the town where we noticed a barber shop. We went in, sat down and pointed at our beards. We were tired. Suddenly my barber turned my head to the right and pulled it back. White's barber pulled White's head to the left and tilted his head back. Two jungle veterans staring at each other's white soapy faces and, in a moment of lucidity, realized we could be about to get our throats cut. We bolted, still lathered up, barber capes flying behind. We did some damage to the bead door on the way out. Tangled in the beads we ran into the nearest bar. The barbers laughed softly behind us.

During the rainy season, floating weed islands the size of football fields came downriver from the north. They were big enough to stop a 150-foot ship and carry it backwards. If one of the islands surrounded the ship it was serious, so we sat on the bow and blew our way through with .50 calibre machine guns, grenades, M79's and weighted balls of DET (detonation) cord.

Typical Weed Island

A message came over our PRC 10 (Prick Ten) radio.

"We have Intel that a VC sapper team is planning to blow up a bridge near Tan An. Do you have enough time to build a few sapper booms and get them in place? Over"

"Negative, Over"

"Roger that, then take a team and blow it up first, in case we're right."

"Roger."

We had to go north to an old French bridge. We couldn't get there by boat nearly as fast as going through the jungle by truck. We had to take out this bridge.

Sophisticated Mission Equipment

The dive team arrived at the bridge and started inspecting the pilings. Rusty concertina and razor wire coils were wrapped around the pilings. The wire was full of river trash. A diver would have to go down to set the charges while holding on to the piling. The current was so strong that a diver couldn't go out and around the wire; he had to go through it.

That was a problem. We snagged the wire with a grappling hook and rope and had our one-ton truck pull the wire back. That was helpful, but there was still a lot of wire around the first piling and we needed to get under it to set the charge. Finally, after cutting more of the rusted steel wire away it looked like there was enough room inside the H-beam piling. I sent a diver named Locati down to put thirty pounds of pyramid-shaped C4 at the base of the piling.

Before he finished, Locati came up, "I can't finish it Sir, I'm out of air."

"You fucking pussy, give me that thing." I grabbed Locati's tank and made ready to finish the job. We didn't have any more dive tanks; we'd used the others while diving to cut the wire. If we didn't finish the job we would have to stay in the jungle overnight or come back the next day. I would be a hero to my men! I pulled the reserve valve and eased myself down the piling. The current tried to pull the regulator out of my mouth. I gutted it out and in less than a minute I set the charge, just in time to hear the truck line snap after it rubbed on the razor wire too long. I felt the impact of the steel grapnel hook as it crashed into the rusty razor wire above my head. I was trapped on the bottom of the Soi Rap River with no air left, no way up through the wire and thirty pounds of C-4 set to fire. It's a good thing the water was brown.

The concertina wire closed over my head, I couldn't get out, I couldn't swim against the current and if I let go I'd get cut up and be swept away downriver, bleeding, and perhaps get a chance to feed the local alligators, up close.

I could feel the razor wire cutting into my scalp as my air ran out. The sound of trying to breathe, when there is nothing to breathe, is memorable and unpleasant. You can get a similar sensation by putting your wet lips on a refrigerator door and sucking hard. Death would not be much fun. I would probably never be found, assuming anyone looked. I was in black water, I couldn't see anything but I was close enough to the surface to reach through the wire and touch Locati's foot, The Foot of Locati, the guy I'd just called a pussy. He knew instantly by my touch and the severed line that I was out of air and/or luck. He'd been "out of air" when he came up, as he so eloquently pointed out several times later.

Like a good soldier, Locati acted quickly. He got his body into the "H" groove of the piling and without anything but an olive drab T-shirt, he took the wire onto his back and legs. The wire closed over him like a steel octopus. He crouched down and pushed back hard slicing himself up bad. I had taken off all my gear because I insisted that at least part of me was coming out. I made sucking sounds like a sword eater with asthma. I felt the wire open further, got in the channel and with a final chance to live, came up between Locati's legs. Another minute and I was dead. If Locati

Locati

hadn't stayed on site I was dead. If he'd been extra pissed off at me for calling him a pussy, I was dead.

The next day the mission was cancelled. Oddly, surviving a bad situation only served to make me want to try it again. I guess you don't know what losing is like until you do.

I should have been dead, but I wasn't. Another random miracle?

We had to Medi-Vac Locati out. He was badly sliced up like cracked conch. He was no pussy.

It happened one hot, fly festooned afternoon. Locati and I sat in our three-quarter-ton truck waiting for a river ferry to take us across to Vin Long. We were supposed to meet up with a special ops team and have some fun. The ferry was controlled by the Vietnamese Army. A group of natives unloaded the ferry. The loading gate guard watched me drive up and stop at the gateway. The RVN (Republic of Vietnam, pronounced R-VIN) guard walked over to the open window. "We go now!" I pointed at my Captains bars and at our guns and gear. The guard shook his head sideways and to demonstrate his importance, turned his back and left us parked in the dust. The workers finished loading the ferry and crossed the river. An hour later it came back and the guard still wouldn't put us onboard. Hours passed. Two ferries came and went. It meant we'd be driving through the jungle at night. It was 1600 hours and we were sitting in the dusty, fly-flecked heat. Finally, I told Locati to pull up in front of the guard station.

"Look, *Nuoc Mam*," I said to the guard, (*Nuoc Mam* is fish oil that is put into a container that looks like a paper wasps nest and left to ferment; you can smell it for miles. It is one of the most distinctive smells in Vietnam and tastes good, after you get past the stink).

"Look, Nuoc Mam, I waiteee four hour (holding up four fingers), I havee go ferryboat NOW! You savvy?"

The guard gave me a blank look, holding up one finger.

I did the math and told Locati to put her in gear and get on the damned ferry, which he started to do. But the RVN who was fucking with me fired a couple of warning rounds at us. The bullets went through the top of the truck, through the canvas above my head and into the nearby market blowing two holes in a tin sign. The sign advertised *Nuoc Mam* and was nailed to a wall at the entrance to a "House of Pleasure."

Locati wasn't impressed and kept on going but I said, "Ok, goddamn it... . Stop the truck."

I jumped out and pulled my .45 out of a smelly shoulder holster. Unfortunately for me, the pier was near a marketplace and there were too many people to start shooting. For the same reason the guard couldn't fire at me, not that he was trying. He sprinted away toward his shack.

Ferry Crossing

I went after him on foot and chased him toward his guard shack, both of us scuffling through the crowded marketplace knocking over live chickens, bags of rice, monkey skulls and baskets of snakes and bananas. I noticed some condoms, stuck to flypaper for display purposes. Clever marketing, I thought. Then it dawned on me that this was going to get "real." I caught up with the gook at his guard shack. He tried to hold the door closed but that didn't work, he was an underfed skinny 85-pound gook and I was a crazed GI. I got in, grabbed him by the front of the shirt with my left hand, picked him up and pinned him against the wall. I grabbed my well- honed dive knife and, finding a good target, I went to swing the blade, but I couldn't move my arm. It felt heavy. I looked down. Hanging off my sleeve, about a foot off the ground, was a little Vietnamese girl. She was dressed in a plain white smock and her sandals were dangling from her tiny toes. One small hand grasped my sleeve as she swung back and forth like a tiny trapeze artist, her other held a small brown paper bag.

She looked up and smiled. Her two front teeth were missing, "G.I.! G.I.! You want buy feenut … cheap cheap! Numbah one feenut … yoo rike feenut G.I.?"

I was getting ready to skewer a gook while a tiny Vietnamese girl swung back and forth from my shirtsleeve trying to sell me a dong bag of peanuts. I paused. Was this really happening? I shook it off; I shook her off, "No fucking feenuts!" I put my knife away and dropped the gook... with a quick right. Contemplating what had just occurred I said out loud to myself, "Perkins, I'm worried about you, you need a drink."

I slapped the guard back into semi-consciousness and frog marched him out of the shack. I found Locati outside the door with his M-16, locked and loaded, covering my back. I grabbed a couple of Tiger Beers on the way and got in the truck. The RVN guard put us on the next sailing quickly and stood watching just to make sure I didn't have any second thoughts.

I found out later that I am allergic to peanuts. The girl saved a guard; I saved a dong.

Coming downriver toward Nha Bang we took an RPG (rocket propelled grenade) hit in the starboard forward hull just above the waterline. The rocket didn't go off. That was a plus, but it was sticking through the hull about twenty feet forward of our High Explosive locker. We were in the bush. We turned and went back upriver to a small navy River Patrol Boat outpost. When we got within five-mile radio range, I called in on the Prick 10 radio and asked for dockage. The American MACV (Military Assistance Command Vietnam) advisor said "Sure, Come on in, Captain!"

As we approached the dock I saw eight guys standing by to help us tie up. MACV called back on the radio, "What's the problem, Cap?"

"We've got a rocket stuck in the side of our ship; it hasn't blown up … yet"

I heard a click and the sound of sixteen boots running away on the dock boards. We tied the ship up ourselves and pulled the rocket out with a truck. No big deal.

Out Back

For entertainment, I spent some time with the Australian Special Forces near the Cambodian border. One night, tied up near a multi-national Special Forces river camp, I met Ackerly, a sergeant in the Australian army. Ack brought me into camp where we "skulled some piss" (Australian for drinking beer) and after a few hours and more than a few Tiger beers we decided to go into town. But there was no town, only a nearby village. We were in a camp with foxholes and sand bags, encircled by razor wire and claymore mines. The surrounding jungle had been cleared for better fields of fire.

Ack told me he'd spent days memorizing the paths used by the villagers who came to work in the camp. Maid service in the jungle. About two in the morning Ack decided it was time to party. We crawled out through the concertina wire, dragging a duffel bag full of party favors and left empty beer cans to help us find our way back through the mines. Guards don't watch for people leaving.

In the deep jungle there is no concept of time. When you're in the bush you do what has to be done when it needs to be done. We needed to party.

We stumbled into the village and woke up the headman. We'd brought food, cigarettes and beer, but no weapons, Ack said they might "put a damper" on the party atmosphere. The headman was happy to see us with no weapons. The whole village got up and we ate and drank until just before daylight. Ack figured we should go back before we were missed. We straggled back to the perimeter but the beer cans were gone. The gooks collected the cans and made small houses out of them. Ack hollered out to his mates to let us in. The Special Forces lieutenant was not happy to see two drunks standing outside the perimeter at 0600 and made us wait until the villagers arrived for work a couple hours later before letting us back in. Ack hollered at his mates to throw some 'piss' over the wire.

Near the end of my tour the Aussies tried to recruit me to return, as a civilian, and teach night warfare to the Cambodians. Underwater combat. An Aussie civilian brought me down to Vung Tau to meet the boss. We boarded a small speedboat and went out into the dark. Speeding through stinky water we came alongside a barge anchored in the middle of the harbor. An authentic, full sized pagoda welcomed me. Scents of exotic incense, cooking fires, *nouc mam* and French perfume powerfully embraced the night air but could not overpower the stink of war. Teddy, the boss and the "liaison" as he described himself, had a security team stationed around the perimeter of the barge and in nearby boats. There were several beautiful, richly perfumed French Vietnamese women dressed in silk *Ao dai* with classic slits up the side and square collars, flowing from cabin to cabin. Teddy's chef was cooking over a charcoal pit in the big open room that overlooked Vung Tau harbor and up toward Big Mountain. Cigars, women, perfume, smoke, food, fish and booze. War is swell!

"Cheers mate!" Teddy was immaculately dressed in a classic British Colonial gentleman's jungle outfit and was smoking a Cohiba Esplandida. I commented that he sure had a nice setup for being in a war zone.

"War ... Crikey, its bloody damn good sport, Mate!" he bellowed, handing me a glass of effervescent Dom Perignon.

There were quite a few Aussies "in-country." The soldiers were good fighters and the civilians even better merchants. They set up all types of nefarious deals and many made a fortune. They were the middlemen and couldn't be held accountable for anything, as far as I could tell. My mate Teddy made me some good offers but I wasn't interested. Call it a weakness. The job involved teaching an unsavoury skill-set to a questionable student body. He wanted me to train a team and take them out on one mission each, I assume to prove the quality of my instruction. He was going to pay me $2,500 a week, American, cash in a bag. That was a lot of money back then. I still wasn't interested.

Everyone gets a little nuts when you have a gun and no law. I only knew a couple of guys that were clinically insane, but there was no clinic. I met Rat Tail during one river trip. He was from Oklahoma, stood about six-foot-six inches tall and was called Rat Tail because he was long, skinny, ugly and didn't have any hair on his head. He didn't like to kill people, something to do with his religion. But Rat Tail did have a nasty thing for ears. He was an RVN advisor, an American who worked with the Vietnamese Special Forces, the Tiger Teams. One of his buddies told me that when Rat Tail was in a firefight, he didn't use a gun; he just sat and watched for a VC to break cover and run. The VC usually did just that when they were out of ammo. And, if conditions were right (paddies can be a tough patch), he would literally "run them down," catch one and cut off an ear. He was a skinny trooper with long Texas-range legs, twice as long as the VC's so he could easily outrun them. He cut an ear off and let them go. I guess he figured that was as effective as killing them. His theory was that the gook whose ear he'd nipped would go back and tell his friends about the crazy son of a bitch down in the paddy. Plus anyone seeing a gook missing one ear would know he was VC. Rat Tail had a combat bootlace that had three or four ears on it, it stank something awful. He hung it outside his hooch. A strange sort of wind chime, or maybe a charm. I've never forgotten that smell. It made me puke. Rat Tail thought it was funny.

Just north of Binh Wa, "in-country"
and upriver near Can Tho,
lay the small hamlet of Yu Bhin Phuct.
Not a good place to go.
The Nouc' mam stinks but so do we
eager young men with good intentions, guns
and beer, we were no match for ourselves.

Then there was my long-suffering colonel who commanded the Engineer Company, Colonel Beakwright, "The "Beak," no doubt thought I was telling the General how I was being treated (the general never asked and I never told). The problem was that whenever The Beak got new guys in the unit he always sent the best ones to me. The best ones on paper that is. I had to take them, interview them and then send most of them back because some of the "best" guys were educated and even worse, *normal*. I'd ship these guys back to the colonel and he'd say, "Are you crazy Perkins, these are the best guys I've got. What is wrong with you? I pick the best troops they send me and you keep shipping them back."

"Did any of them cry when they got back here, Sir?"

"Huh?"

That was a problem

"Look Colonel." I said, "You don't know what it's like out there ...Sir. All my guys are crazy and it's better that way. I've got a Q-tip addict (he used half a box a day, no one knew why or for what,) I've got a glue sniffer, a guy into Buddha, a guy who blows on everything before he touches it and a chronic masturbator. I got all these nut cases, Sir. I've got a Navajo Indian who won't speak a single word to anybody and lives in the engine room with a box labelled Webb's Shit, because he doesn't like the pale face. I've got a guy on sick leave, he got burned trying to light farts...for the second time.

"What?" the colonel asked and shifted uncomfortably in his chair.

"Sir, when one of those new guys gets onboard and starts showing pictures of his kids and wife and mom, why it's enough to make you puke, Sir. The new guy says, '*See my dog, that's a golden retriever and when I was a* kid we used to put up sheets and watch movies and blah blah blah'. This is the kind of guy who will screw up everything… Leave us to be crazy; it's much easier…Sir."

"Perkins," he said, "I'm worried about you."

***

First Sergeant and Master Diver Sergeant Jones kept me alive long enough to figure things out. Thanks, Sarge.

The crew were all nuts in their own way and it was fun…sort of. Like a big armed family with no parents and plenty of ammo. Jones taught me how to grab sea snakes by the tail and pull them underwater when they came at you in the river.

"They won't bite underwater," he said with a wink. In some cases it was easier to "just believe."

Sgt. Jones on the South China Sea

I knew most of my crew were whacked-out on something, but I didn't know what and I didn't care. Most of them were seriously twisted but I had yet to learn just how twisted one could get. I had never done anything except drink and choke the chicken.

Docked in Vung Tau, I went into town one night and got so drunk that I ended up passed out on a cool tile floor in someone's home, last night's bar journey lost in the pickled baffles of an unwinding mind. Early the next morning, I heard a guy puking, gagging and choking. He woke me up. Man, what an asshole! I pulled out of my own stupor and yelled at the guy, "Hey, shut the fuck up Asshole, I'm trying to sleep!" I yelled it several times, or perhaps it was an echo. I nodded out again.

Later, as I regained consciousness I looked around and there was nobody else in the room. It was me talking and me being sick. I was so drunk I was two different people. One of them was sick and puking, and the other, the compassionate one, was telling myself to shut the fuck up. I stood up and the room was empty. So was I. I had seen the other side of sunrise.

"The Room"

In August, two months before my departure, General Haines rode his Huey helicopter into the jungle with a 1ST AIR CAV escort. We were tied up near Cho Lai. News of our close call with the VC at the rock pile had made it to headquarters.

The Official Fool

The thumping, hard hitting rotor winds of the lead Huey cleared the LZ (landing zone) as the Commanding General of IV Corp circled in his chopper. Once the site was secured he landed and set out a Special Forces perimeter.

With the chopper's rotor still spinning, shit blowing everywhere and his entourage consisting of another general and two colonels, General Haines boarded the *Irish Pennant*. I came forward and stood at attention. It was only one of a dozen times I put a full uniform on in-country. "Lieutenant Perkins reporting as ordered, Sir."

The Adjutant approached and Haines reached for a case containing a new set of Captain's bars. He formally took them out and started to pin them on my shirt.

"Lieutenant Perkins, you are hereby issued a battlefield promotion to Captain, FUCK! ... Ahem ... ah ... I stuck the damn pin in my thumb," he laughed jerking his hand back. His entourage nodded in sympathy while trying to keep straight faces. "Ah ... Perkins, you are now the highest ranked diver in the United States Army, **and** you are hereby awarded the Bronze Star for your courageous leadership ... Good Luck."

Was it a medal or a "blood stripe"? Was the attrition rate higher than published? What did he say? I reached out to shake his hand and ask him, "why me?" But he was gone, his blood on my collar. Simple endurance can sometimes be mistaken for courage.

I was the highest ranked working diver in the Army and a distinguished fool.

Chapter 14

Almost Normal

Since none of my crew killed me, I felt I owed them. In September 1970, at the end of my tour, I showed a small token of appreciation.

We entered Vung Tau harbor at night and passed near two large Navy power ships anchored offshore that provided electricity to the military compound. As we approached the ships I went to the wheelhouse, "Okay, Locati, I'll take her from here." He gave me a look, but said, "Aye Sir, I'll go get the lines ready for docking."

"Don't bother Sergeant; I don't think we're going to need any lines."

Locati grinned when he saw my crazed and determined expression. He yelled to the crew, "Rig for collision! Fuckin' A!" and gripped the helm station. I rammed the throttles full speed ahead. Our ship, the *Irish Pennant*, God bless her flat bottomed, one-hundred-ton soul, drove straight toward the shore between the power ships and the pier. The white bow wave foamed and grew larger, observers would later say she had a "Bone in her teeth." We ploughed toward the oily beach and, with full power on; I drove her straight up onto the stinking war mud.

Unfortunately, it was high tide when we hit the slick, foul smelling black sludge. The *Irish Pennant* steamed doggedly ahead, her propellers corkscrewed into the silt throwing muck, garbage, old condoms and beer bottles fifty-feet in the air.

At the end of our "last run," as the crew later referred to the incident, we rammed, bow first, into Mama San's "Butterfly Girl" whorehouse and knocked it over. The lashed bamboo walls folded down like dominoes in slow motion and our dying diesels screamed in sympathy. The "girls" scrambled out of the squeaking, slowly collapsing building and the GI's ran for safety with their dicks in one hand and a Tiger beer in the other. They had to drop one of the two to get to their guns. For some it was a tough choice.

I let the engines run at full throttle. The ship convulsed and the "Butterfly Girl" collapsed into the mud. Shortly, one of the engines exploded, throwing hot shrapnel around the engine room, the other finally died out with a relieved death rattle. It was an entertaining spectacle, but it smelled bad in the area and Webb, our engineer, his Navajo hairdo in disarray, was pissed as he stood on the sloping deck with a box of oil- soaked belongings labelled "Webb's Shit" cradled in his arms. The MP's and the base photographer arrived shortly thereafter.

"Concerned parties" complained and I was standing at attention before the base commander early the next morning.

"What happened, Captain?" his voice was tight with anger, his face ready to burst.

"I guess I'm not a very good navigator, Sir."

"Cut the crap Perkins, this isn't the goddamned NAVY…you deliberately decided to destroy that ship, that's Government Property, didn't you, Perkins? … huh? huh … didn't ya … didn't ya … huh huh?"

"No, sir," I replied, modifying the account. "I was putting her up on the beach to clean the bottom."

"You put a 150-foot ship up on the beach; going full speed ahead, at high tide, in the dark and let the engines explode … TO CLEAN THE GODDAMED BOTTOM! What are you up to Perkins?"

"I …"

"… you didn't want your guys to go back out, isn't that right?" he said through tight white military teeth.

"I …" It was but I couldn't admit it.

"Speak up Captain!"

"I … I don't want them to die for no reason, Sir. Does that count? We completed **almost** every mission." I mitigated.

"Almost" only counts in horse shoes!" he snapped.

"And dying." I countered.

"… do not confuse the issue with facts Perkins," coughed the Colonel. "We're going to have to arrest you."

"That's fine," I said. "I could use a break, Sir."

"Perkins, I'm worried about you."

"Too late … Sir."

My light hearted romp through hell was over.

I wasn't arrested but the threats went on for days during which I hoped most folks "in-country" would be too busy trying to save their own asses and wouldn't have time to worry about mine.

I didn't panic. I should have. A day before I left Vietnam I had to report to a different colonel concerning the "boat incident." He gave me his colonel look, "Well, Captain Perkins, as I see it, you have two career choices facing you."

"What are those, Sir?" (Two didn't sound like a lot).

"Well, you can undergo a court-martial for destroying government property, endangering the lives of fellow soldiers, endangering the lives of civilians, conduct unbecoming, and **I could go on** ... Or ... Or you can be sent to the War College at Carlisle Barracks, where we'll fast track you. You have certain qualifications, you know. You'll probably be a general by the time you're fifty."

"That's kind of a big spread isn't it, Colonel?" I said. "A convict or General."

"Well, not really Perkins, that's the way it works," he said leaning forward. His calloused and wrinkled elbows provided good traction on the desk top, his blue military eyes locked on mine, his hair was high and tight. *I could be him,* I thought.

"So ... what'zit gonna to be, soldier?"

"I'll take the court martial, Sir, I don't mind testifying. You know how we officers love the truth, Sir, and I've seen a lot of fucking truth over here, Sir."

"Perkins, I'm worried about you."

I didn't respond.

"Get the fuck out of here, you wiseass son of a bitch!" he screamed, a fleck of foam flew from his lips. A parting shot? I forgot to salute on the way out.

What happened to the "Officer and a Gentleman" routine?

I was out, I didn't feel loved, but I was out!

There was little time for reflection and forty-eight hours later I was in San Francisco getting my physical exam for discharge. The doctor asked me how I was doing. Only my words stood between me and the door.

"Fine, doc," I said. I didn't say, *I'm back in the States, I'm out of the Army, I'm alive, THIS is my discharge physical. How do I feel? Pretty damn good, is how I feel.*

The doctor didn't mention Agent Orange. He stamped my wrinkled forms with authority and seemed relieved as he handed me my papers,

"Welcome back, Soldier," he said, pointing at the exit. So much for the physical. I opened the door and stepped onto streets of San Francisco as a civilian with an honorable discharge. All the others had been cured by penicillin.

I didn't realize that I had lived through an adventure of a lifetime.

Chapter 15

Civilian Daze

Captain Perkins rapidly adjusts to society

I return to civilization and tried to adapt to the American culture. Holly was living with her parents. Things weren't good between us. There was not much money in the bank. She'd spent most of it.

I had my severance pay and made a trip to Miami to meet up with White. I couldn't go back to Michigan. I was on my way to open a bank account. I wanted to find a job and maybe rent a place. Try once more with Holly. We were driving along US 1 in White's Thunderbird. White looked over, "Hey, you want to smoke a joint ... sir?"

"I guess so," I said. "What's that?"

"Uh, it's marijuana, Chief."

We fired off that bone. It was an ember to remember.

"Man," I said, "that smells just like Vietnam." White gagged.

It may be hard to believe, but I never smoked pot in Vietnam and had never seen or heard about it growing up. If an enlisted man got caught smoking herb he got a reprimand, if an officer got caught he was dismissed from the Army. In the bush everybody cooked on fires and burned incense, I thought that's what the in-country smell had been. White looked over at me and tried to smile but his face muscles did not respond to his brain waves, "I'm worried about you, Red."

I thought back to the bird egg incident, I think he did too, we both laughed like idiots.

I had never been stoned before and spent the next hour trying to open a checking account. I failed my first civilian mission.

Each time I spoke to the teller, words came out of my mouth and turned into little white clouds. They floated over the counter, it was funny. I laughed too loud and my bungled attempts cracked me up even more. Finally, the seventy-year old security guard, apparently not a 'smoker', firmly asked me to leave. I had, after all, filled two waste baskets with applications. Maybe I should go home.

I was out of the Army. I didn't know what to do in Miami, and returned to Michigan to resume a normal life. I started to think that maybe I'd taken enough chances. I needed to grow up. A regretful decision that, fortunately, didn't last long.

In October 1970 I was back on the street, not that I knew anything about the "street." I didn't know what drugs were or even what sleeping through an entire night was like. I had no idea what was going on in the American culture. Everything had changed.

During my four years in the military I rarely mixed with civilians and if I did it was always on base where they were "normal" people. I didn't realize there were hippies. We didn't have much music in Vietnam, at least not on my boat. The gooks had good ears, noses, eyes and guns so we didn't listen to loud music, cook outside, or wear tie-dyed T-shirts. You don't make any unnecessary sounds in the jungle. A fart could get you killed.

What was I going to do? I wasn't trained for anything that would be useful in society. I was trained to dive, drink, fight, fuck... and, oh yes, eat raw bird eggs. That was going to come in handy out there. Still, I would simply... return to normal. I tried for weeks to get a job, any job. During what turned out to be my last attempt I almost got a sales job at Robert Hall's selling men's polyester pants. I needed the money, my hope lasted three heartbeats. After the rather brief interview the manager said, "I am sorry, Perkins, but we can't hire you."

"Why?"

"Look Man, you're too much for this place. You're going to take my job, you're probably gonna take my girlfriend. I mean like- sorry man, but you're a real threat to the rest of us here."

"Got it, Lima Charley (loud and clear), thanks."

Dopamine Diving Daze

Hearing about the Experimental Diving Unit at the Atlantic Undersea Test and Evaluation Center (AUTEC) on Andros Island in the Bahamas, I flew to West Palm Beach and underwent an interview that consisted of insuring that my adrenalin gland was equal to or larger in size than my brain. I passed with room to spare and was advised I could move to Andros Island and live on a boat with free dockage. Holly, flew down to meet me, we bought a twenty-six foot sailboat and headed for Andros where we lived aboard the LIZBETH in a mosquito- infested backwater bog called Fresh Creek, a haven for old time pirates who came for the fresh water. After one month we kept the boat at the dock but moved into an air-conditioned trailer with a bathroom.

AUTEC was a military facility run mostly by civilians, where they did things that had not been done before, like recovering nuclear test torpedoes in a "High Sea State."

The test torpedoes cost a significant number of frog-skins (dollar bills). The government decided it would be a good idea to recover the torpedoes instead of allowing them to sink and turn the Tongue of the Ocean into a colossal body piercing. Our assignment was to develop a method of recovering the torpedoes when it was too rough for the seventy-two-foot Torpedo Retriever Vessels (RTV) to go out. The torpedoes were about thirty feet long and three feet in diameter. If the sea was rough, a torpedo could come off a wave and hit or sink the RTV boat. Under those conditions ship-board recovery was too dangerous. The Experimental Diving Unit (EDU) was set up to handle that inconvenience.

AUTEC was a top secret installation. Nobody knew what we were up to, not even us. All projects were segmented. No one knew the whole plan, if there was one.

One day our honcho (boss), a retired Navy Master Diver, got us together. I invited White to share in the fun He was standing next to me when honcho said, "Okay, boys, you're going to be called experimental divers an' ...you'll go out... an' figure out how to recover these torpedoes by jumping out of helicopters. Any questions?"

"Where's the bar?" someone mumbled.

There were no other questions. Odd, but after what most of the divers had been through recently, jumping out of helicopters in a high sea state seemed a reasonable idea, and fun, too. The water was clean and blue and no one was shooting at you. I was a civilian now, working for the government, no longer the one in command. I was just another worker bee.

It was impossible to get life insurance but I was married and had to think of my wife even though I was getting some strange vibes from her. We didn't know what we were doing. Some things never change. However, looking on the bright side, if I died I got $2,500, my month's pay, even if I died on the first day of the month; well actually my widow got $2,500. I didn't care and it was around this time that my marriage was breaking up anyway. When Holly and I got to AUTEC, I knew we weren't going to make it with me being "down range" for days at a time or up in a Bell Jet ranger helicopter and her, back at the base, fucking the snack bar manager behind the hot dog cooker. Being gone does not lend itself to a stable relationship and I'd been gone most of our marriage. However, I was amazed at how emotional I could get and still not really give a shit.

At first, I thought Holly was a bad girl. I liked it. Looking back I don't know if she was a bad good girl, or a good bad girl. I bear her no ill will. I signed everything away. I had nothing; it was easy. Holly moved in with Mr. Hot Dog. She's a Jehovah's Witness now.

There weren't a lot of people or, things to do, on AUTEC.

After work, the jumpers, a squad of ex-Explosive Ordinance Disposal, Special Forces, Army Rangers, Navy Seals and Special Warfare guys, all civilians, all expendable, all with top secret clearances, went to the Officers Club. A seedy bar in a seedy, but air-conditioned, trailer. Everything was in trailers. The base looked like a pile of tin cans from the air.

Yet, because we were willing to risk our lives for $2,500 a month (tax free), we got the privilege of going to the O-Club.

Most evenings, off in the corner, sat four guys with dead eyes. They lived on Thorazine and booze. They called each other Al.

I sat next to an Al one evening and noticed that his fingertips were white. From personal experience I thought it was from holding a beer bottle for an extended period of time but, when I looked closer, the tips of his fingers had a Teflon-like coating grafted on them. No fingerprints. These guys were "specialists" left over from Vietnam. No one knew what to do with them. They were kept on the island pretty well calmed-down until it was time for the next war. The Al's weren't very outgoing or pleasant, but no one teased them about it. They had the classic "thousand yard stare." The look of someone who seen too much, or gone too far. Someone who wanted to unfocus and forget. I was glad not to be an Al.

The bar was a creature of circumstance, like "Star Wars" with lifelike characters, most of whom didn't give a fuck about anything or anyone. Some nights it got a little rough. It was an oversized, air-conditioned Petri dish with chairs, dark memories, cheap pretzels and booze.

We were on Andros Island. To the east was the test area known as the Tongue of the Ocean, an abyss between Andros and Nassau, six-thousand feet deep. There is only one entrance to the Tongue, at the north end of Andros near Morgan's Bluff. The US military liked the Tongue because no "potential enemy" could spy without us (US) knowing.

Which Way is Up?

On days off we sometimes went up island to a dive resort called Archie's Hole in the Wall. The dive began at the edge of the wall, about 1/2 mile offshore. Descending to 60 feet the "Hole" leads you through a large passage that turns and exits on the side of the Tongue. When a diver came out of the hole in the wall a safety diver waited with a sign that read "WHERE ARE YOUR BUBBLES?" At this depth most novice divers were "narced" from an accumulation of nitrogen, nitrogen narcosis, the "Rapture of the Deep." Fish always swim with their bellies toward the bottom therefore the divers thought that "up" meant swimming away from the bottom. The bottom was actually the side of the wall and if you didn't look to see where your bubbles were going you would swim straight out at a hundred-plus feet and probably die. A bad habit to get into and you didn't get your badge. It was considered poor form in most sport diving circles.

Back at base we tested underwater lasers. We set and checked deep sea buoys and sonar arrays, sometimes diving two-hundred feet on compressed air. The arrays could monitor every sound in the ocean. They could hear a whale fart (I have a recording available on CD). To build this audio file, the navy ran test vessels of all kinds over the sound arrays to collect their hydro-sonic signatures.

When it came to jumping, none of the retired navy chiefs would. They said they were "Too Old" or, they were too smart. However, even knowledge of the truth didn't keep me from doing it.

One day, during the developmental stage, our boss said, "Okay, boys, today we're going to go out in the chopper and jump until somebody gets hurt. You know, see how far we (meaning you) can *really* fall before somebody gets killed."

"All Right, Chief!" we said. "Sounds like fun! Hoo-Rah!" Fools rejoice. Perfect.

There wasn't much to do on the island, so on jump day some folks came out and watched to see if anyone got killed. Some sat eating picnic lunches in their cars while others walked or rode bicycles. If I died at least somebody would find it entertaining, but I still wouldn't get my full fifteen minutes of fame.

We loaded into the helicopter and lifted off. After several preliminary jumps the chopper was moving at ten knots forward, sixty-five feet above the water. I was carrying twin tanks, a full wet suit, weights and a mask. The wind was twenty knots on the surface and the seas were running about six feet high. The safety/recovery boats were steaming in circles below. This jump was "just for fun" as the chief put it. Even during our "fun" jump we had to be completely sealed, I was "vapor-proof" as I waited to jump, the wet suit dry and tight. I squeezed my butt in fear. When it was our turn; we got the nod and jumped. My partner, Bobby "The Leaper" Leeman, looked like an Appalachian "whammy doodle," his form was as unpredictable as a broken high pressure air hose. He looked like a scarecrow in a wet suit.

It only takes a few seconds to fall sixty-five feet but as I fell I heard a curious whistling sound ... t was me ... falling toward terminal velocity, (182 feet per second) or at least faster than anyone would want to fall.

If the divers don't jump at exactly the same time the helicopter loses cyclic (stability) and the jumper on the low side can get sliced and diced. I had US Navy "Duck Feet" flippers, made of two-inch thick vulcanized rubber on my feet. I jumped at sixty-five feet moving ten knots forward. When I hit the water the flippers were driven up my legs and over my knees. They squeezed tight, cutting off the blood to my calf muscles. I couldn't feel my feet and when I looked down I hit myself in the face with the flipper. My leg started to spasm and I was beating the shit out of myself with my own flipper. The backpack and tank broke off and hit me in the back of the head. I was dizzy, bleeding from the back of my head, my mask had been ripped off and I couldn't see. Additionally, when I hit the water, my wet suit exploded, the air in the suit compressed and blew my hood off. It was like jumping inside a big whoopee cushion. A human fart and getting paid, could life get any better? A few nano-seconds before hitting the water, I remember thinking, "Perkins, I'm worried about you."

After the jump we were debriefed and voted unanimously not do it again. There were ten jumpers but only nine votes cast. Number 10 was in the hospital.

I'd signed a one-year contract, and White was down there with me. We had to complete the mission. I couldn't let him beat me at being a fool. I made my year, but it was one of those situations where you knew you'd die if you kept doing it. I began to resent that, knowing it would probably be sooner than later. Nobody could do it for long, even the guys who truly didn't give a fuck. "Not giving a fuck" provided no protection in this instance

We lost two guys from nitrogen narcosis, "The Rapture of the Deep." Nitrogen narcosis is the result of too much nitrogen in the blood. Its effects are similar to those of nitrous oxide and, like Vietnam, it was a cheap party, unless somebody died.

One day, we were taking underwater pictures of a US Navy battleship running speed trials through a set of buoys. The buoys were attached to a U shaped underwater boom with markers on both ends for the ship to steer through. We grabbed the boom with our knees as the ship passed seventy feet over our heads. The test was designed to collect sound signatures, and the Navy also wanted hydrodynamic/laminar flow photos. A team of six divers manned the boom. Unfortunately, it was the first time we had attempted this procedure.

We crotch-locked our legs around the booms and readied our cameras as the battleship passed overhead. The first pass was slow. The next pass faster. When they went through on the fourth pass the ship was cranked up to flank speed. The ship displaced a thousand tons of water and the suction pulled almost everybody off the booms. Then, belly up, we were sucked toward the bottom of the ship. No way to stop. We clicked away like idiots, mission oriented. We got our pictures. By the time we reached the surface, the ship was gone and we were left floating and swirling in its wake.

Unfortunately, one diver had fallen off the boom. He had too much weight on his belt and he was "narced out." He went the other way, down. His depth gauge only read to one-hundred-fifty-feet so every time he looked at the gauge it read one-hundred-fifty-feet. He thought he was okay. The water was so clear we could see him falling backwards, into the abyss, still clicking away. Click, click, click. Six thousand feet deep, all we could do was watch. There was no way to catch him. He went deeper every second, so stoned he didn't realize it was his last dive. He just disappeared, still checking his depth gauge and shooting … click, click, click …

When several days of torpedo recovery work were scheduled we stayed down range. After a twenty minute ride by helicopter we landed on a rock, a small rock south of Fresh Creek called Goulding Cay. The rock had a trailer, a generator, a fresh water tank and a helipad. That's it. Like Robinson Crusoe cast adrift in an air-conditioned trailer, the Site Manager, Olli, lived alone for weeks at a time. He worked out, ate and worked out. Alone. The guy was in great physical condition but his mental condition was of some concern. He took to diving and exploring along the coast of Andros to kill time. At least then he wasn't alone; there were always friendly sharks.

One day he decided to dive down into a blue hole he had discovered. At slack tide he descended into the hole and came upon an underwater cave. To get into the cave he had to take off his dive tank and push it through a hole in the coral wall. He followed the tank in and when he got inside he found a cavern with stalagmites and stalactites. That meant at one time this cave had been above water. He told us about it and we decided to explore and film the phenomenon. Ollie had discovered it so he was chosen to lead the expedition.

Down we went, Ollie leading the way into the cavern. He went through the hole first and helped pass the gear in and then showed the divers around the cavern. After ten minutes Ollie helped guide us back out through the small hole. At one hundred twenty feet we didn't have much bottom time and had to get out before the tide changed. Commercial divers are trained to work under the influence of nitrogen. Olli was not. Being the first one in and the last one out Ollie was seriously narced by the time it was his turn to come out. He swam up and looked through the hole at us but would not come out. We signalled, yelled through our mouthpieces, waved and pointed. We yelled through our mouth pieces. We could see Ollie, but he wouldn't come out and no one would go in to get him. Ollie was too strong and worse, crazy on nitrogen. The hole was small, only big enough for one diver at a time. We had spare tanks outside the entrance. We switched tanks and watched him until he ran out of air. Then we got him.

As if our job wasn't stressful enough, we had to jump with all kinds of spear guns and power heads because the sharks in the area could get a little excited and aggressive. These were the deep water, open-ocean, pelagic sharks. White tips, black tips, tigers, makos and the occasional hammerhead.

Nuclear or otherwise, the torpedoes we recovered were propelled by a set of nine unguarded, razor-sharp propellers. If you bumped a blade you got cut, if you got cut the sharks came, if the sharks came you got eaten, if you got eaten you died, if you died someone got $2500, and another fool got a job. The torpedoes also dumped jet fuel (JP4) when they surfaced and if you got it on your skin it burned like acid.

We flew out in helicopters and stared at the seemingly vacant ocean, but down below a nuclear submarine was waiting. While we hovered above, a test torpedo was fired and ran exercises underwater. The submarine sonar pinged away, choppers chopped above. And when the torpedo surfaced two divers plummeted, ass first, into the roiling sea. There was so much noise and vibration the sharks always knew where the party was. Sharks like to have fun too.

At first, we jumped with twelve gauge "bang sticks," as well as .57 magnums and .45 power heads on a pole. But the best weapon looked like an ice pick. Inside the handle of the "Faralon Shark Dart" was a CO2 cartridge that fired on impact and blew a bubble of CO2 into the unlucky shark. You could hit it anywhere...no blood, no meat, no concussion. The shark lost control of its buoyancy and started to spiral away, hopefully. The other sharks would turn to each other, "Lunch!" Off they'd go to eat their buddy-and they hadn't even been to law school.

One day when we jumped it was a little nasty on the surface. They only sent us out when it was too rough for the seventy-two-foot torpedo retriever vessels, that is to say in eight-foot seas or higher. We developed a method of recovering the torpedoes. We threw a set of nylon slings with a float attached out the chopper's door. Then we jumped, attached the lifting bands to the torpedo and signalled for a pick up. Occasionally, if conditions were really bad or the sharks were too numerous (one is considered "numerous" in my book) we threw out a packed US Air Force surplus fourteen-man life raft that we always carried. The raft had a CO2-actuated nose cone attached. The plan was to put the cone on the nose of the torpedo, fire the actuator that set off a pneumatic clamp that locked onto the nose of the torpedo. After we rigged the torpedo, we inflated the raft and climbed in. The torpedo couldn't sink, theoretically, because it had the raft to keep it afloat and we, the divers, became less appealing as *haute cuisine*.

We had a Bell Jet Ranger jump chopper, a Huey heavy lift chopper, and another Bell Jet Ranger with a diver/spotter above it all, watching the show. White and I jumped out of the Bell Jet Ranger and got the torpedo secured to the raft. Then the Huey helicopter lowered a set of slings to lift the torpedo. We connected the lifting cables and disconnected the raft. Sometimes it was hard for the spotter in the third helicopter to find the divers in the breaking seas, the orange life raft helped and we always stayed with the raft. The helicopter could only pick up one man at a time and the remaining diver was known as the Last Man. The pilot always picked up the lighter guy first, so everyone tried to get a fat partner. Sometimes I was the Last Man. A foolish honor, I suppose.

On this day, after we secured the torpedo, the chopper picked White up in the sling and hoisted him onboard. If you grabbed the sling before it touched the water you would get a 25,000 volt static discharge. It wouldn't kill you, but breathing water while waiting for your heart to re-start might. Today I was "The Last Man," waiting in the water, in the life raft. Suddenly the helicopter, which was not very far above the water, turned as fast as it could and came straight at me, with the rotors tipping over at an angle, as if the pilot was trying to brush the water away. I didn't know what was going on. I thought the pilot was trying to kill me. Most of the pilots were ex-Vietnam guys who were fearless and very good at their jobs. White was hanging out the door, making peculiar hand signals, signals I'd never seen before.

Underneath the raft a fourteen-foot Tiger shark was circling, getting closer and bolder. The helicopter pilot saw it but I didn't. The pilot tried to distract it. He used the rotor blades to frighten it, but pelagic sharks don't scare easily. A guy alone in a raft in the middle of the ocean does. The shark turned its attention to the chopper. The Jet Ranger was low enough that the shark, seeing the chance for a new food group, leapt out four-feet out of the water and tried to eat the chopper. I remember seeing the wrinkles in the back of his neck. His head was as wide as a line backer's butt. I could see its neck. They say sharks don't have necks, but this shark had one as it tried to bite the skids off the helicopter. He could have brought it down on top of me.

I took off all of my gear. A shark can hear or feel almost any sound and I have an old ankle injury from my ski jumping days that clicks when I move, so I couldn't use my right leg. Hoping the shark didn't hear me or see the bubbles of fear escaping from my wet suit, I slipped into the sea. I kept my hands under the surface and did some slow one leg kicking, drifting away from the raft. I drifted away; it seemed forever, far enough away that the crew in the chopper could see I was not in the raft. They spun back around and lowered the sling. At first they were going too fast and the sling couldn't touch the water where it would discharge its 25,000 volts of AC current. If I grabbed the sling when it was live I was dead. Fuck it, I was getting out. They say if you grab hold of an electric cord you can't let go. Well, that was my plan. I'd rather be fried than sushi. Overhead the chopper, with the sling skipping across the water, came straight at me. There was no time to put the pickup harness on; the shark had turned toward the chopper again. I locked my arms around the harness, closed my mouth so I wouldn't drown if I was hauled through the water, then...Swoosh-Zot-Boom, I was snatched out of the water, swinging wildly underneath the helicopter, while the pilot tried to stabilize from the high speed retrieval. He had snatched me out of the water at ten miles an hour and managed to ground the sling before I grabbed it. Hoo Rah!

I couldn't see anything as I swung back and forth underneath the helicopter. White told me later he'd seen it all. Shortly after my recovery the shark realized I was gone and got pissed off that he had been faked out. Sharks do not have a sense of humor when it comes to food. The shark went back to the raft and angrily bit into it. In a canvas pocket on the inside was an emergency steel CO2 cylinder about the size of a fire extinguisher. It was used to inflate the raft if the primary cylinder failed. The shark ate the cylinder. He ate a twelve-pound piece of steel by ripping it out of the raft. Unfortunately, for the shark, it inadvertently tripped the trigger on the CO2 cylinder while swallowing it. The cylinder expelled its gas and the shark exploded in a ball of meat and blood flying fifty feet into the air, the colors lending a certain texture to the setting sun. As we flew back over the Tongue of the Ocean I contemplated my situation, stared at the blood mist on the floats and examined my career choice.

On another torpedo recovery, one of the divers was pulled out of the water wearing his two-inch thick US Navy Duck Feet flippers. We hoisted him up and pulled him into the cabin. He reached down to take his flippers off. Most of the flipper on his right foot was gone, a perfectly curved bite mark in front of his toes. The shark's teeth were so sharp they cut through two inches of rubber and the guy didn't feel it. He counted his toes just to be sure.

On one of my days off I swam offshore and shot a couple hog snappers for dinner. I cleaned the fish on the beach ramp. There were fish guts all over the ramp so I hosed them into the water. A bonnet shark, about four feet long, swam in and commenced eating the fish entrails. After gutting the fish, I washed my gear with Dawn dish-washing soap, streaming the water, fish entrails and soapy bubbles off the ramp and into the sea. The gut gourmet swam in again. Suddenly it stopped, as if it had hit a plate glass window, shook its head, went back around, came back up, stopped, shook its head, and went away.

It dawned on me, it was the soap! So I took note and decided to test my theory. The next time I jumped from the chopper I took a condom full of Dawn soap with me. I carried it down the inside of my left leg just for effect. When I hit the water I unzipped my wetsuit, pulled it out and popped it. The soap dispersed around me. I was completely sealed in the wet suit, protected from the fuel the torpedoes jettisoned, so the soap didn't bother me. Sharks came up in a spiral from the depths, in a cone that got smaller and smaller as they neared the surface. They slowly came close and finally, if you looked interesting, they'd bump into you. They rarely came straight up and bit a diver. They had to taste you first, not that they are picky eaters. Sharks can taste through their skin, a little bump, to get a taste or maybe a small bite to see if you have blood. Then the big bites followed, but sharks didn't like the taste of neoprene rubber, so they usually left us alone after tasting our stinky wet suits. The JP4 fuel didn't bother them either, it was on the surface, but the soap did. We drifted in the soap shield. Sharks, divers and torpedo moved together in the ocean current. The big eaters came up and started to close in but suddenly stopped, as if they had hit a glass wall. They got soap in their gills and couldn't breathe and the soap kept dispersing. The sharks circled, but they would not come inside our invisible fence. Still, we continued to carry other means of protection, just in case.

We had the power heads (shot gun shells in a cylinder on the end of a stick) as a secondary weapon. The problem was that you only got one shot. One is not a lot when facing an ornery shark. The strike had to be dead on and a diver had to be accurate under pressure to hit the shark on the top of the head while he was coming at you. If you didn't kill it right away, well, you were pooched, (pooched comes from the Latin *poochus screwum*, meaning you screwed the pooch). You were screwed because all you've done is blow three pounds of meat off his ass, pissed him off and remained in the vicinity of the blood and meat. Not good. Then the wounded shark would turn around and try to eat you. That gets old. When my contract was up it was time for me to leave. I had had enough of this adventure.

Chapter 16

Key West Daze

I left my money with my wife, my wife with "Wiener Man," my job with AUTEC, and the Bahamas with the Bahamians. Looking for greener or at least dryer pastures, I sailed my mortgaged sailboat toward Key West with Bobby, The Leaper, Leeman. Like me, The Leaper was tired of jumping out of helicopters and plummeting ass first into an unforgiving sea. He was getting soft. When I told him I was getting divorced he said, "Let's go to Key West, I know people there."

On our way to Key West I sailed the *Lizbeth* onto the remote coral reefs near Morgan's Bluff, on the north end of Andros Island. The Leaper and I spent a long, sad night listening to the *Lizbeth* crunching through the coral on our way across the reef.

Four days later we sailed into Key West Harbor, anchored out, swam ashore and went into the Chartroom Bar at the Pier House Resort. We were wet. We had no choice; my dinghy had been lost on the reef during our voyage. However, we did have a little money, the greatest survival tool of all and unlike today, where most people work two jobs to survive in Key West, in the early 1970s most people didn't have even one. It was easy and cheap.

Just before we sobered up, days later, The Leaper and I decided to start a charter business. Leaper arranged for us to meet Miss Floy Thompson one afternoon at her home, where she served us sweet tea in the southern way. Miss Floy had lost her son and, years before, had sort of adopted The Leaper. He introduced me as Captain Reef, a backhanded slap referring to the grounding incident during our trip from AUTEC several weeks earlier. The name stuck.

After a few hours of congenial conversation she said, "What do you boys need to start your business?"

"A dock."

Key West Charter Business

The next day we had a dock, courtesy of Mr. David Wolkowsky, the owner of the Pier House and a friend of Miss Floy. It was a great spot right next to Tony's Fish Market where, several times a week an ambulance screeched up in a cloud of coral dust and medics raced into the restaurant to start pumping some unlucky diner's stomach. We thought of naming the business Ptomain Tours.

Our business was called Ocean Charters. We had two boats: my Westerly twenty-six-foot sailboat and an eighteen-foot Boston Whaler outboard that the Leaper borrowed from a friend who was in jail for smuggling. Along with The Leaper, Gorgeous George and Marcus the Biker served as shills and crew.

George was a handsome fellow, with a bad attitude and a colorful vocabulary. He was a charismatic fellow who worked at the Pier House pool between shrimping jobs. He booked charters for us. Everyone assumed they would be going out with George to see the sights.

However, when the guests showed up in the morning they found Captain Marcus, an ex-Hells Angel, passed out in the bottom of the Boston Whaler, an inch or two of water sloshing the empty beer cans, dead bait and Marcus, back and forth in rhythm to the swell. Marcus was a rough looking character, to say the least. He'd seen his share of hard times and it showed. His front teeth were missing, he was always sporting a bandage on some part of his body, and tufts of his hair were missing, the result of bar fights. He'd been asked to the leave the Angels brotherhood after he got caught sucking air out of his Harley's hot tires trying to get high. It was too weird even for the Angels, he said. He still wore his leathers from the biker days, which were a little ripe in the tropic heat. To my knowledge Marcus was the first person to wear a fish hook in his ear. His got there by accident. Once, while Marcus was trying to bait a hook, he reached up to slap a "no see'um" (a tiny biting bug found in the tropics). The hook snagged his ear, but Marcus figured it would be less painful to leave it in and let it rust away than to try to get it out since he didn't have anything to cut the metal hook with. The hook finally rusted away and left a nasty, festering hole in his ear. But Marcus had come to like the look, and the attention he got. So he put another one in. Finally Neil, from Sun Lion Jewellers, made him one out of gold to help reduce the inflammation.

When the guests showed up and saw Marcus they tried to leave quietly, but I was there to guide and counsel them. I already had their money.

To wake Marcus, I grabbed the nearby garden hose and sprayed him. Once he found his teeth and started talking the guests saw that he was actually a nice guy and his stories were so intriguing that almost all of them decided to take the trip with him. They were happy just to come back alive. The small joys.

The Chartroom Bar was the center of Key West's political commerce in the 1970s. Around three in the afternoon, the cream of the Bubbas began to float to the top: the sheriff, the mayor, the fire chief - Bum Farto, the crooked and the good cops, the state's attorney and other nefarious characters. There were always enough locals in the bar to ensure that no "tourists" could find a place to sit. Some of the city's business may have been conducted in the Chartroom. The Bubba system. It works.

I was dating a girl from Canada named Martha. She was very pretty, had unusually large "casabas" and was not too bright. No, I didn't marry her. She was the perfect woman, or so the State's Attorney thought. He was a regular in the Chartroom and he loved Martha and her Afghan hound. One afternoon, after some tacit encouragement from the State's Attorney (he did want Martha to be happy), Martha and I went to the Federal Building and falsified forms to get her a social security number so she could get a job and stay in Key West. After we finished filling out the forms, we took them downstairs to the clerk and a few minutes later we were met by a US Marshall who informed us we were under arrest for making "false declarations." I asked if I could make a phone call.

"*YOU* have an attorney?"

I was a little scruffy and had an "outdoorsy" look about me. I was poor, un-employed and unsuccessful, who wasn't? Could he have mistaken me for an honest man?

"No, I need to call the Pier House." He handed me the secretary's phone; I pulled the cord tight and called the "Fartroom."

"Hey, Tom, is Ed there?"

"Hold on."

"This is Ed."

"Ed, its Reef"

"Where's Martha? I want to buy her a drink."

"Well, Ed, Martha won't be in today."

"Why not?"

"Well, Ed, we just got arrested for falsifying Federal Documents that, as you suggested, might behove Martha ... oh and Martha says *Hi!*"

"Oh shit, Reef...put the Marshall on the phone."

I gave the Marshall the phone; he listened for a minute and hung up. "Don't do this again," he said sternly. He shook his head and sighed, as he walked out the door, tearing the arrest papers into small pieces, pieces about the right size to roll a bone I noted.

The first to feel the pinch of the 1970's bad economy were the dancers in the titty bars like the one next to Cecil's Sub Shop on Duval. The performers got fewer and uglier as the depression wore on; it was one of the worst things about the depression and very depressing.

On Duval Street, where Rick's Bar now stands, was the Old Anchor Inn, a bar that was home to many wayward souls. It was owned by Bud Man and his wife Dorothy and operated by anyone, occasionally me, who happened to show up that day. The Anchor Inn was a small building that opened at ten in the morning, but a select cliental, who slept in their cars out back, came through the rear door between eight and nine. When the door and windows opened, it was already full. Bud Man said it was "good for bidness." Some of the patrons, who had left only hours before, could be grumpy but we always agreed to listen to Maggie May play over and over for the first hour. It was our glorious new day anthem, our call to arms or at least elbows.

"Wake up Maggie I think I've got something to say to you
It's late September and I really should be back at school
I know I keep you amused, but I feel I'm being used..."

There were two doors into the Anchor, each only half as wide as a normal door. The side walls of the Anchor were open windows, cut out and down to within eighteen inches of the ground outside. Patrons who sat in these three-foot wide cut outs occasionally fell out backwards, the result of drunkenness or other forms of alteration. Only their feet remained in the building. Sometimes there would be four feet sticking in, other times four feet with toes pointed in opposite directions, sometimes a dog was mashed in between the patrons. It was hell sorting out the flip-flops, but the arrangement added significantly to the capacity of the bar. When other patrons arrived, they gently pushed the fallen ones legs apart and sat down between them.

Inevitably, some passersby felt compelled to call the cops. The local authorities arrived, eventually, and determined that, since the patron's feet were still in the bar, they could technically be considered customers. The Bubba System. It works.

At night, in front of the Anchor Inn, on a folding chair completely obscured by her massive buttocks, sat a woman named Tiny. It was rumored that Tiny had recently been released from prison in Texas where she served hard time for manslaughter. It was alleged she *accidently* sat on a guy's face with whom she had been arguing and smothered him.

"That's tough," my dad would have said.

She claimed it was self-defence and no one disagreed with her, except the judge. Who would want to die like that? A number of socially unacceptable events took place in the Anchor and if you talked about them out on the street you never got back in. Period. Tiny had a world-class intelligence network. If you tried to enter the Anchor she turned her little eyes, the size and color of pink marbles, on you. If that didn't stop you, she held her twelve-inch thick arms across the doors. No one ever tried to get past Tiny. You were out and you would stay out.

However, one guy did get back in. His name was Stoney.

Stoney was having a "go at it" with a willing female on top of the jukebox one evening when he experienced an "uncontrollable thrust" as he explained later. To the great distress of the first light patrons Stoney managed to scratch our only copy of "Maggie May." When he admitted it the next morning, Stoney got 86ed.

Stoney's exile resulted in his moving around the corner to Capt. Tony's Saloon. However, for a few weeks after the incident, he returned every morning to stand in front of the Anchor and stare at his old friends. We stared back and every time Maggie May's scratch played we would snarl at Stoney. But, he took it like a man. Stoney stood about six-foot-two and was a big, dark haired, rough fellow. The fact that he was sorry enough to stand on the sidewalk day after day suffering the scorn of his peers eventually qualified him for re-entry. Still, Stoney never came back early in the day.

Back then, in hard times, manners were the only social fences.

Hard times can be hard even in the best of hard times. We never locked our bikes or houses; we couldn't afford a lock or a bike and didn't own a house. We had nothing worth stealing anyway. Everyone knew each other, or was so stoned they thought they did.

While walking around town it wasn't unusual to see the front door open at a friend's house, stop, say hello, and be invited for dinner. We shared what we had, which usually doesn't work for long.

***

Ocean Charters didn't make much money and the business ground to a halt. I took on odd jobs. I worked as a carpenter with a guy named Billy. He had cancer some years before and said he had part of a goat's stomach implanted. It appeared to work pretty well. Billy could talk; I mean really talk, about anything, all day. We built a closet for an older lady one time. It took three weeks (eight hours of actual labor) and cost $3000. But she was happy; she liked Billy because he listened to her stories and laughed a lot. He had a way about him, especially after lunch when he pointed to his grumbling stomach and said he had to "go outside fer a spell." It's a good thing he did.

Johnny "The Wing" Wingfield was a charismatic ne'er do well I met in Key West during the 1970s. The Wing was good looking, stood a little over six feet tall and had a mop of long straight hair that he was always pushing back out of his face. He was so tall that he often leaned over to be polite when talking. He looked like a sheep dog when he did. The Wing and I had no jobs and very little money so we decided to fly to Jamaica with cash that we borrowed from a couple of Wing's girlfriends. We would smuggle some herb back and repay them, The Wing said.

As we waited to board our Air Jamaica flight I noticed that I no longer cared about being a hero, I just wanted fun and money. I also noticed a number of arriving tourists, about my age, carrying hand carved turtles. The turtles looked good; they were quite big and must make great souvenirs, I thought.

We were seated and, after a couple of in-flight beverages, The Wing thought he remembered the name of a guy who, he had convinced himself, owned or was a friend of the owner of the Cheela Bay Resort Hotel. Cheela Bay was next door to the Playboy Club in Ocho Rios.

We landed at Montego Bay airport and taxied to the hotel about 2:00 am. Wing woke the security guard, who was armed with a half-eaten banana, and told him we wanted to check in. We had no baggage. The security guard was not fully awake. Wing said we needed to check in right away because we were tired. "One hundred dollars a night, Mon."

"You may not have been properly notified, Mon," The Wing said, "but we are good friends of Mr. Grandis (a name he made up), THE OWNER! We won't need to check in but there is one fine thing you can do, Mon. We're hungry and need to eat."

The guard was beginning to come to, but it was too late as The Wing carried on in his gentle South Carolina drawl. The guard was hypnotized and happy. Wing winked at me as we headed for the kitchen where the guard cooked up some chicken, peas and rice and, for dessert, a fried banana on vanilla ice cream. The groggy guard found us an empty room, opened the door and walked back to his guard table where he fell asleep instantly. We settled down to eat our dinner.

The next morning The Wing went to the front desk and found out the owner's name, it wasn't Grandis. He went over to the owner's table and introduced himself, dropping names, like quarters in a slot machine. The Wing thanked the owner for his generosity and proceeded to try and convince him that they were old friends via a mutual acquaintance back in the States.

It took the owner two days to find out if The Wing was bullshitting. We only stayed two days.

We had two choices, we could move over the fence to the Playboy Club at one hundred fifty dollars a night or move across the other fence and stay at Aunt Clover's Guest House for five dollars a night.

Aunt Clover was a robust Jamaican woman about sixty-five years old and a force to be reckoned with. She had an extended family living with her. She saw herself as a queen and dressed in colourful, flowing XXX sized muumuus. Aunt Clover liked The Wing and me. She called me her "little earthling" and let us sleep in hammocks over a concrete slab above the dog food dishes and next to the septic tank. We had dogs to scratch, spliffs to burn and papayas to eat. We were in Paradise.

Not long after we moved to Aunt Clover's, we decided that some income was needed. I went to look at a sailboat that had gone aground near Ocho Rios. Maybe I could salvage it and make some money! However, while I was up the mast during my inspection, a wave hit the sailboat. I lost my grip and fell, my right leg tangled in the rigging on the way down. My right foot was messed up badly. Wing wrapped my wound in a banana leaf and got me to a Christian Mission where, if I would sing and swear to God, I would be treated. I told them I had been swearing to God since the fall but they didn't buy it, so I had to swear to God again, right on the spot. They let me put off the singing until later.

After about half the day, I got to see the doctor, Dr. Palmer-Malcolm, but not before I had spent several hours in the waiting room with another fellow, an elderly native Jamaican. He was also at the clinic for an injury to his right foot. X-rays had been taken of my foot earlier and when I met with Palmer-Malcolm, he explained that I had a broken foot that needed to be put in a cast. Okay. While I was waiting in the lobby for my cast to dry and crutches to arrive, the old Jamaican came out his foot wrapped in an Ace bandage. "Mon, how do you feel?" I asked.

"Rightly, Mon, de foot don't feel better than he did, dee Doctor say "Mon, be cool, don't hackle de' foot."

"Sorry."

A few weeks later, back in the States, when I took the cast off early because I couldn't stand it anymore, another doctor (American) looked at my foot. It wasn't broken. I told him about the Jamaican and his foot.

"They must have gotten the X-rays mixed up, they put you in a cast with a sprain and wrapped the "Mon's" broken foot in a bandage," he said shaking his head.

Oh Mon!

During my convalescence at Aunt Clover's, The Wing, Aunt Clover's twenty-five year old boyfriend Roy, Aunt Clover and I, the little earthling, again decided we needed money. We would open a bar in Aunt Clover's thatched hut down on the beach.

We pooled our money, about $85, and set about fixing up the bar and getting supplies. I wasn't much use, but I could talk. I still wasn't much use. "Mon, we gone need to smoke it out, to kill de' bugs," Roy said through a pungent but pleasant haze. We opened "Roy's Ting" two days later. Unfortunately, our advertising budget was limited to about $5 so we couldn't promote the Grand Opening as much as we would have liked. Only the locals came and since they were all friends, broke and mostly related to Aunt Clover or Roy, Wing and I found we couldn't charge for drinks without being considered "Colonialists" (at best). So we opened one night, drank till the liquor and our money was gone and closed the next morning at sunrise. Aunt Clover loved it. She clapped her hands and laughed so hard she couldn't stand up. Roy caught her.

Before we left Jamaica we borrowed $ 85.00 from Roy. We decided to take advantage of a little cottage industry that had developed on the island. A few talented wood workers carved good-sized wooden turtles out of the native hardwoods, like the ones I had seen at the airport. They ingeniously hollowed out the inside (there were no seams visible on the outside), and packed two pounds of herb in through a very life like hole in the turtle's butt. They plugged the faux anus with a bung and finished coating the outside with paint.

We arrived in Fort Lauderdale airport on the late night flight. Because of my injury I was put in a wheelchair and pushed down the hall by a uniformed attendant. I had smoked a spliff before we left Jamaica and now, as the effects wore off, I suddenly realized that I was wearing a dreadlock hat, a Rasta Mon T-shirt, carried a big wooden turtle and had no other baggage. I did not look like the average tourist and began to get nervous as I approached the immigration desk. Wing had gone ahead and was already through both immigrations and customs. I got through immigration then suddenly, before I got to the Customs area and for reasons unknown, (random miracle?) my attendant hit a red button on one of the sliding doors and pushed me out into the lobby. Huh?

I coasted to a stop, got up, grabbed my turtle and limped out the door. A friend picked us up and we headed south. We were able to repay the girls and Roy the next day. Dat's cool Mon!

After returning to Key West from Jamaica, I found there wasn't much to do. Especially if you didn't want to do anything. As I had successfully managed in the past, I sat on my butt and waited. Then another door opened-a revolving door.

I was taking a whiz behind a dying palm tree at the Pier House the day Jerry Jeff Walker, his girlfriend, Murphy, and Jimmy Buffett came to town. Jerry Jeff was riding his motorcycle with Murphy on the back and Jimmy was driving an old pickup truck with supplies. We met in the Chartroom Bar and soon discovered, as new acquaintances did back then after a few drinks, that no one had any money. We promised the bartender, Tom Corcoran, that we would return to pay our tab. Jerry Jeff and Jimmy gathered up their guitars, I got my washtub bass and an artist named Vaughn got his washboard. We headed up Duval Street in search of work. We walked halfway up Duval to Moe's barbershop. Next door a building had been renovated. It was Ed Swift's first restoration project.

Crazy Ophelia's was a hippie joint. They had a limited budget so there were no tables or chairs, but the floor was slanted down toward the back of the building so everyone could see the stage. By the end of the night everybody gradually slid down the incline to lie "en masse" at the bottom of the stage. They looked like a smoking campfire someone had pissed on. We did a few tunes and made $7.00 then moved on, back down Duval Street to Howie's and the Old Anchor Inn. We did well, as far as I can remember.

***

Frank Bing was a large black fellow from Key West who had gone off to make his fortune wrestling alligators. After an apparently successful career, as in alive, he returned to town and started selling Conch Salad up and down Duval Street. He began in Black Town (that's what it has always been called) and rode his fat-tired bike over to Duval Street and then up and down Duval Street. His strong melodious voice could be heard for blocks, "Come on now ... Get YO CONCH SALAD!!! COOOOOOOOONNNNCH SALAAAAAAD!" ... toot toot on a rubber horn. Frank was a kind man and if he saw that someone was drunk or just looked hungry he would call them over.

"Here man, get yersef some of this here conch in ya', it'll make ya' right." Or if you were drunk he'd say something like, "Come o' heah, it's Big Frank talking to ya' son! ... Now you take this down (conch salad) and then get yersef home ... ya hear me, son?" He'd squeeze your shoulder till it hurt and you said, "Yes, Mr. Frank."

The Leaper, his friends "Pene" and "Brother," and I decided to market Frank's talents. We cut the side out of an old school bus that Pene found. We put in a counter and all the sophisticated equipment: a cooler and Dixie cups. Up and down Duval Street we went. Frank took money in on one side of the bus, we took the money out the other and got drunk. It was fun but it got old. Still, years later, I told the Leaper I missed the bus. He laughed and said, "You sure did."

I spent a few evenings at Frank's house in black town. One night we were in the living room. Everyone was slightly twisted, everyone except Frank. I looked out the nearby window into the hallucinatory darkness when a car turned the corner and flashed a powerful set of headlights through the window. Outside were a dozen little flower faces looking in. They peered into the house, like little children. It made me wonder what they did at night when we couldn't see them. Did they look in and watch us, just like we do to them during the day?

Thirty-five years later the vision reappeared when I attempted to attain "Arthood" in my garage. I developed an innovative technique that I call *Peque Tambon*.

Peque Tambon is French for "the art of drinking wine and dropping paint-soaked toilet paper off a ladder and onto a piece of glass salvaged from a dumpster." I developed it into both a fine art form and an interpretive dance routine. Sip, dip, climb, drop...splat...sip, dip, climb, drop. Finally, I tired of my exceptional creativity and realized I couldn't see the other side of the glass anyway, so I went to bed and slept an artist's sleep. The next morning when I got up I flipped the glass over and there was the same scene I had witnessed at Frank's house all those years ago. Later that year I entered the piece entitled "Flower Faces" in the Bahama Village Art Show.

"Are you an artist by profession?" the lovely Ms. Nowak, the organizer and an artist herself, asked me.

"No," I said. "But I'm trying to define art in my own way."

"Oh," she said. "And what's that?"

"To me, art is an object, an expression or anything that attracts the most amount of attention with the least amount of effort. Like the sky, like the ocean, like the wind, like me. That's my definition of art."

She didn't say anything for a few seconds, and then she murmured, "I'm worried about you, Perkins."

During the 1970s, I took on temporary jobs including tending bar at the Anchor Inn, posing for Carolyn Gorton Fuller and renting sailfish at the Sands Beach Club. Things got boring and I decided to go to St. Thomas to "find myself." While there I met my first and only Hippie Zen palm weaver, Don Wells. Don had been, among many things, the model/actor in the famous "Salem Man" cigarette commercials of the 1960s. I ran into him on a street corner in St. Croix. I was fascinated by his palm weaving, which he eventually taught me and which I eventually forgot. As usual, he (he referred to himself as "his hisness") was surrounded by a bevy of young hippie chicks seeking the source of "ultimate knowledge" and some good reefer. Donald could supply both. He sat in the shade of a palm tree assuming the full or semi full Lotus position and intoned words that sounded cosmic. Sometimes he played the flute. I think he sat as much as possible because he got so much pussy every night he couldn't walk. I learned palm weaving but it didn't work the same for me. Don was always very positive, and some people like that sort of thing.

Don taught me how to weave palms, or technically, the heart of the palm. The new fresh shoots would never know the joy of flailing in a hurricane-driven wind or dying of thirst in an un-tended snowbird's yard. But rather, the frond might end up as a basket full of single socks on a dusty shelf in Sandusky, Ohio. Palm weaving is, however, very soothing for the weaver, especially if the weavings sell. The gathering of the palm leaf is not always so soothing.

Once, during another trip into the bush to find myself I ended up on the coast of Guatemala. I was trying to impress a local well-formed bather with my weaving talents. I climbed a forty-foot coconut tree and was just about to harvest the heart when a three-foot iguana climbed out of the crotch of the tree. There were no introductions. He crawled on top of my head, got a fierce grip with all four feet/twenty-four claws, took a shit and jumped, driving my face into a bunch of green coconuts. I lived, but when I looked down the buxom bather was gone.

The Beginning of an Unexpected Career

I met Flash for the first time one inspired night in the early 1970s. I was in The Midget Bar, located across Simonton Street from Strunk Lumber and built around a tree. The tree trunk held the bar's roof up. I was feeling good and started performing hog hollers and the more sophisticated hog calls, none of which I knew how to do, but I thought I did. Finally, the bartender got tired of it and threw me out, right through the screen door. He told me to wait outside, " I'll be out to beat your ass when I get a break!" I was standing on the corner of Simonton and Greene wondering what to do next when a yellow Volkswagen convertible pulled up with a guy and three girls in it. The driver said, "Hey man, do you know where the Port O' Call is at?"

"I sure do," I lied. It was almost break time. The bartender wiped his hands and looked out through the mangled screen door. I jumped in the Beetle and pointed ahead.

"It's out that way. Just head that way as fast as you can, just go!"

"Hot 'Lanta, let's doer!" Flash (the driver) smelled the hunt and floored the Beetle.

It was dark. I was drunk. It was fun. It didn't last long. Rather quickly we got to the end of the road at the Simonton Street boat ramp. Screech, Zoom. Splash. Laugh. Scream. Fuck! Off we went, into the Gulf of Mexico. It didn't look very deep. The Volkswagen was floating along and everybody thought it would be a good idea if we took our clothes off so we wouldn't drown. We started doing that, safety first, when the cops showed up. Later, at the jail, I learned the problem was not that we'd driven a VW into the ocean, which could have been an accident, but that we were naked in public. Actually, I wasn't naked because I was too drunk to get my clothes off and I was a good swimmer. Anyway, the cops showed up and arrested everybody else for Driving While Nude, a DWN offense. I was the only one who was clothed. The Volkswagen started to sink. While the four wet nudes were put in the police cars, I decided to be the hero and find the girl's clothes. But I didn't try too hard. It was dark. Safety first.

The cops called a towing company and I stayed to help Arnold's Towing get a wire on the Floating Bug that looked like a giant fly-fishing lure envisioned by Hunter Thompson in his dreams. After pulling the Beetle up on the beach I went to bail my new friends out of jail. Flash had his pants back on and pulled the bail money from a wet wallet. Flash passed a wad of bills through the bars to a guard who passed *most* of them on to me.

A few days later I met Flash again. We sat off in a corner at the Midget Bar (different bartender). He cast a look around and tilted his blood-shot eyes down mysteriously. His sunglasses slid down his reddish, sun-screened nose and his eyes came up on me like a helicopter spotlight in a cop show.

His first words were, "I've…got something going down? You want in?"

I should have asked an intelligent question, or even a regular question, like "What?" but I didn't want to spoil the mood.

"Sure," I said. "Flaps up, gear up!" Later I would wish I hadn't used that term.

I went home to tell my girlfriend that I was embarking on an unknown but probably highly dangerous and very lucrative adventure! She paused and said she had something to tell me too, which was, "Like OK, cuz I'm seeing another guy anyway. He's like a tofu maker." She said, "He's the best in Key West."

"Oh well, that sucks," I said with limited emotion.

She was a true child of the flower and got pissed off at me because I was upset that she was porking a tofu maker, and not just any tofu maker, the "Only," she said convincingly, "tofu maker in town at this time." But I *was* bothered; I never did like tofu.

According to Flash, my job was to be the Captain. "Bale boys, bale!" I would find the boats, outfit them and Captain them. Trawlers, sailboats and "go fast" boats. We were going to sail to Colombia and Jamaica and transport "herbal products," and we did. We went by boat, by plane, by God! We'd complete a voyage spend all our money and start again. We lived paycheck to pay check, so to speak. Damn it was good.

One trip involved going to Europe to find a suitable vessel for a transatlantic excursion. We arrived in London and quickly noticed that our Key West attire, flip-flops, shorts and Eat It Raw T-shirts stood out. "Simply not done, old chap." We all went to the same men's store in the airport and for some reason got the same outfits and leather jackets. Smooth. Unfortunately, on our arrival back at Heathrow Airport after a short trip to Amsterdam (we needed to *re-fuel*) I was pulled over by a couple of airport "Bobbies." I had a large hash-ball duct taped under my nut sack.

"You look familiar," one said to me. "Are you a group?" The rest of my friends, those dingelberries, rapidly scooted past and left me to fend for myself.

"Ah, well actually we're a rock group," I choked and instinctively grabbed my crotch. The Booby looked closer. "I've really got to pee." I said quickly, looking suitable distressed. He nodded.

"Rock group aye! Blimey!... Yanks?"

"Yeah we're Yanks all right, (yanking on my crotch) ah, the Flying ...ah...The Flying Dingelberries," I said to the Bobby (and silently screamed at my friends.)

"Dingelberries...Don't think I know that bunch."

"Yeah, we, ah, like to come to England to hang...ah...to boogie and spend lots of money!"

"Yes, righto...well then ...Jolly Good, welcome back... Dingelberries?"

He pointed toward the loo and waved me through. Back at the hotel I spent several hours scrapping duct tape residue off my privates, and a few days later I was back in Key West. We never found the right boat for the transatlantic excursion.

Chapter 17

Business in the Isthmus

After a year or two sailing the waters between Key West and Jamaica, I decided to sail down to Colon on the east side of the Panama Canal. It sounded like a good place to pursue my new green matter transport career. I arrived in Colon and found some things were more complicated than I thought. I spent four months trying to make arrangements to sail east toward Colombia. Each time I tried to sail up the coast toward Cartagena I was stopped by weather and seas. I spent four days in a red circle on the pilot chart that denoted an area where wave heights exceed twelve feet all the time. I never made it to Colombia, but ended up having some fun in Colon.

I was up to no good and Colon was a good place for no good. It was the most dangerous place I'd ever been. Dangerous, but not for any obvious reason, like Vietnam or dive school, but because of the sort of people and business that took place in the Isthmus. The Canal Zone was a tropical Wild West, relentlessly and randomly hazardous. Most Panamanians were not allowed to carry guns, so during the day businessmen, dressed in *guyaberas* or mildewed white linen suits, walked to and from work conspicuously carrying the daily newspaper. Rolled up in the newspapers were ice picks. It was a legal weapon. The price sticker was left on to look like a recent purchase in case the police had questions, but they never did. With articles about murders and robberies wrapped around a sharp ice pick the businessmen warily walked the streets.

There was another kind of pick in Colon as well, the pickpocket. Unfortunately, the pickpockets didn't just pick your pocket, they took the whole pocket. Here's how it worked.

While you were walking down the sidewalk, two or three guys came at you from behind. The first guy hit you in the kidneys with his shoulder or fist, sometimes hard enough to bust a rib or an internal organ. The second guy quickly felt you up, then reached down and ripped out the entire pocket that appeared to contain a wallet and left the stunned tourist standing there, bleeding internally. The third guy was the lookout. He also took the wallet from the robber and ran his escape route. The pickpockets knew tourists had been told to carry their wallets in their front pockets to be safe. I did too, until I heard of a guy getting his nut-sack crushed as he held the thief by the neck. The Panamanian pickpocket had the tourist's balls and the tourist had the pickpocket's neck. A Panamanian standoff.

I adapted to the mood by carrying fishhooks wrapped in wax paper in my front pants pockets, and stopped carrying a wallet altogether. Panamanians are small people, but they're feisty little buggers.

I got one once. It happened in broad daylight, on a busy downtown street. I wasn't in a bad part of town and always looked behind as I walked. I noticed three youths looking at my shoes from across the street. Something was about to happen. In many Latin countries the bad guys look at your shoes to check you out and determine your value without alerting you.

I knew what was happening, I heard them coming and turned with the hit, but still got bumped hard by the first guy. The one who hit me kept on going. The other one, following behind, reached in and grabbed my pocket. He clamped down and got a fistful of fishhooks. His fist was balled up on the hooks, he couldn't let go and he couldn't get his hand out of my pocket. His two buddies immediately disappeared and left him with me for treatment. I had this little Panamanian with a handful of fishhooks right underneath my elbow. I had no choice, I had landed my first Panamanian. The guy had tried to rob me and my street rep would be enhanced greatly if I pounded the shit out of him. I hurt my elbow. Across the street the *policia* looked at me briefly, smiled and walked away. It wasn't pretty and I still lost my pocket, I had to cut it away to get rid of the blood, and furthermore had to remind myself not to reach too deeply or search too intently for change when I wore those pants again.

Shortly after this encounter, I went back to the Colon Yacht Club bar and ran into Eduardo the Ecuadorian, an underwater logger. Underwater logging requires diving into the vast swamps surrounding the Panama Canal and harvesting trees that were covered with water when they filled the canal and now harboured some nasty jungle creatures. It was very dangerous business and a 9 on the adrenalin scale. Eduardo looked like tree bark, ten times as rough. He was scarred all over, had a few gnarly teeth, though most of them were missing, and huge mangled hands.

I met him in the bar at the yacht club around lunchtime, just after I'd pummelled my Panamanian. As I sat down and rubbed my sore my elbow, Eduardo shook his head and mumbled, "Fuck, Fuckers, Fuck!" in Spanish, which sounded like English in this case.

"*Que paso?*" I said. "Eduardo, what happened?"

"I just be robbed."

"Me too!" I said. "At least they tried," showing him my pocket. "What happened to you?"

"I just be robbed too, my friend, in daylight, in front of dees club!"

I knew he carried a gun inside his shirt in an armpit holster. "Why didn't you shoot them?" I asked.

"They stole my gun, too," he said, shaking his head. "Fuck, Fuckers, FUCK!"

"Stole your gun?"

Rude. Being constantly in danger was a strange way to live but it was exciting.

Since I couldn't carry a gun, and carrying a wad of fishhooks tucked next to my nut sack had its drawbacks, I carried a rusty shark hook, a galvanized steel hook ten inches long. If I was going into an area I didn't feel good about, and that was most places, I slid the hook out of my sleeve and walked along with it at my side. I probably looked like a red-haired ballyhoo rigged for trolling. But I didn't care as long as it worked. People don't like hooks. They're not illegal and scarier than a knife, which wouldn't have fazed anybody in those parts of town. I told Eduardo about my weapon.

"I am making to have worryings for you, Senor Riff," he replied.

Also in the Canal Zone were Denmark Bob and his wife, Kazu, other people living on the fringe of society. To save money they tied up alongside an abandoned barge in Lake Gatun just outside the freighter lanes to the locks. My sloop was also tied alongside.

Bob was a Danish boat builder and after building a steel sailboat, sailing across the Atlantic Ocean and, on this afternoon, sucking down a Schnapps or two, he told me that he met his Japanese wife, Kazu, three years earlier. He loved her immediately. In the beginning "She would do *anything*" to please him, he said. But now she completely controlled his life and he couldn't take it anymore, he was desperate, but knew he was too ugly to find anyone else.

"Riff, what can I do, I am being made crazy?"

"Bob, don't be a pussy... why don't you shoot her?" I counselled.

"She won't let me," he said, "I asked."

El Moro was a fecund and friendly bar about six blocks from the Colon Yacht Club. It was convenient, and a whorehouse too. Tango and I went in to get a beer almost every day and almost every day, at first, the girls swayed and clustered around, offering various favors and constantly pulled at the hairs on our legs. After two visits I decided to wear long pants. I was friendly but I didn't get involved with them, very much. I only drank beer. I had my reasons: I was broke.

After awhile, in El Moro, the bar girls wouldn't even get up, they kept their knees together, giggled, made obscene gestures. They called out in the sarcastically nasal tone only Latinas can attain ... "Ah! ... Senor Cerveza Solamente esta aqui ... oooooh!" A romantic sounding name indeed but "Senor Cerveza Solamente" means "Mr. Beer Only." And besides, the girls fell in love quicker than me and theirs lasted longer than mine. In the civilized whorehouse you don't go in and have a different girl every time. Once you pick a girl, she's "your girl." Choose wisely.

One afternoon in El Moro the owner, Madame Olivia, came and sat next to me. Apparently, she had noticed my extended abstinence from the "pleasures of the flesh" and asked, in a voice normally reserved for good clients, if I would play Jesus Christ in their Christmas Parade. I don't know what her inspiration was. I had a mass of red hair and red beard or, perhaps it was my *holiness* in not seeking the pleasures of the flesh. Maybe she thought I owed it to her for being so cheap, maybe she thought I was a rump-ranger. So, I said, *"Si, Gracias!"* but it never happened. It may have been my only chance to at least appear holy. *Vaya con Dios.* Christmas in the Isthmus-I loved this life.

Although Panama was the most dangerous place I have ever been doesn't mean that it wasn't fun. Every police agency in the world had a presence in Panama, or so it seemed, and Panama was justly recognized for its pride in maintaining a "high level of international criminality."

There were "interests" from all over the world. The kind of place where you never asked anybody their last name and the first names were all false. The truth was rarely spoken in public.

An adventurer called Tango Limon flew back down to meet me in Panama. Limon had been in and out of the country numerous times both by plane and sea. So had I. It got complicated when we went through the slow bureaucratic passport procedure, maneuvering like cuds through a cow, to renew our travel documents. I had come in by boat, then flown back to the States, then turned around and flown back to Panama, to leave by boat, then return by boat, to leave by plane, to return by boat, etc. Too bad they didn't have airline miles back then. Completing the required paperwork was my occasional attempt to be "legal' or as legal as things needed to be in "Paneemar."

One afternoon we went into the Panamanian immigration office, *Oficina de Imigracion*. Tango and I walked into the immigration office and went up to the desk. Tango looked like a seedy Ricky Nelson and was pretty smooth with the ladies.

Tango and I had gathered the required paperwork to extend our stay. We claimed to be tourists and, even though we were Americans in the military zone, we had to go through the paperwork. The military was trying to keep track of everybody. They didn't seem to care what you were doing, but they wanted to know who was doing it.

Taking the lead, to show strength, Tango approached the two ladies manning the rusted grey metal desks in the mildew green colored un-air conditioned office and said, pointing at his chest, "Me Tango Limon." Then he pointed at me and winked, "Esta mi amigo, Reeeeeeef. We come Pa-nee-ma, (his lips puffed out), we come by boat, leave by plane, come back by plane, leave by boat..." He flapped his arms to demonstrate flying, and flopped his hands to demonstrate a boat going over waves. He spoke very loud Pidgin English with a distinct South Carolina twang, drawing out every word.

Finally, one of the matronly ladies looked up, wiped a bead of sweat off her warted nose and said, "Mister Limon, I believe that we, that is to say, my associate and I, understand fully what you are trying, most sincerely, to articulate to us. However, Mister Limon, perhaps a little less gesturing and a few more facts, such as the dates of your travel, and accommodation arrangements would be helpful."

Limon was rethinking his approach as the women shook their heads and stamped our damp, wrinkled papers. We didn't linger for much of a chat afterward.

During this time I met John Whiskey, he'd come down to Panama to become a crewmember. We called him *"Doctor Juan Moro, O.D."* because he spent all his time at the El Moro, where he almost OD'd on beer. He'd come down to Panama to help with the "project" I was working on. Moro, according to Moro, had been Chuck Norris's martial arts trainer until Chuck took to beating his ass on a regular basis. But he (Moro) was still quick, sort of. He was a tough guy.

One afternoon, after picking up our laundry, Limon, Dr. Moro and I walked out into the street and looked for a cab to take us back to the yacht club. Crossing the street, we unknowingly attracted the attention of a fellow intent on robbing us. The thief did not know our bag contained only laundry. I got in the back of a rusty cab with Tango Limon. Dr. Moro got in the front seat with the laundry bag. Faster than I can tell the story, the thief approached the passenger side of the cab and reached in to grab the bag. In the same instant Limon and I heard a *"tuunk"* sound from the front seat. The cab driver had seen the guy coming and when the thief reached into the cab, the cab driver pulled out his machete, and with astounding accuracy, stopped the would-be thief with the tip of the blade as it smartly embedded itself in the bone between his eyes. A drop of blood ran down the thief's nose, landed on Dr. Moro's lap and the would-be thief was gone. Immediately, Moro raised his hands in the classic martial arts position and said "Aiyeee!"

I looked at Tango. Tango looked at me. The cabbie wiped his blade. Moro looked at himself in the rear view mirror.

In the Bush

The San Blas Islands are an archipelago of islands to the northeast of Panama and are owned and populated by the Cuna Indians.

The Cunas did not have much use for the Panamanian government, then controlled by Mr. "Pineapple Face" himself, Senor Manuel Noriega.

The Cunas are very small and very self-sufficient people. They do not tolerate weakness, of any sort, even within their own tribe. The women carry most of the family wealth on their bodies in the form of gold jewellery and the men all carry machetes stuck down the side of their shrimp boots. They wear the thick white rubber boots with no socks to protect from snakebites.

In the process of sobering up one afternoon I was introduced to a chief from one of the Cuna tribes. He had missed the boat scheduled to take him to an important tribal gathering in the San Blas Islands. The Indians were said to be planning *resistance* to the development of the islands (Club Cuna?) by the Panamanian government. A Customs Official, who had done me some favors, asked if I would take the chief, on my boat, to the meeting of the tribes somewhere east of the Devil's Backbone in the San Blas islands. The chief had an armed guard with him. The Indians are very serious people. I was serious too, seriously hung over.

"What the hey!" I garbled, "*No problemo.*" I was serious, not smart, but serious.

After we got underway I realized that the charts I was using to get through part of the chain of islands called the Devil's Backbone were about a hundred years old with numerous areas marked "unexplored."

I saw only two other white folk on the way to the meeting of the tribes.

An elderly German couple were aground and marooned, their sailboat had been driven hard up on an uninhabited island during a storm, two years before. They had very little money and couldn't get their boat back in the water by themselves. I couldn't help them and gave them food. The Indians gave them water, but that was it. Every coconut tree is owned; you don't pick coconuts, the Indians sell them to you. The natives did take the old cruisers into town once a month and patiently waited for the tough old Germans to abandon their boat. They were still on the beach when I returned to Colon.

The Guardia (The National Policeman) assigned to get the chief to the meeting was a rough-looking hombre named Raoul Punjab. I called him "*El gran ojo,*" the Big Eye. He liked that moniker although his pleasure was somewhat diminished by the fact that he had a bad case of the clap. It was driving him nuts. He kept saying "If only I had known, if only I had just gone home, if my wife ..." If, if, if. We had no medicine so I tried cheering him up with jokes and booze. I tried to translate this joke into

Spanish: "If a frog had wings, it wouldn't bump its ass when it hops." Making frog sounds and hopping around on deck I tried to help, but I'm not sure it worked.

But somehow, with the old charts, passing Cunas and the help of *"El gran ojo,"* I managed, after five days, to find my way to the spot where I was to drop the Chief. We anchored out and went ashore in dugout canoes.

Who, me?

Everything was fine until I returned to move the boat and found that my anchor was fouled on their plastic water line, their only water line, that ran from shore, about a half-mile away, all the way out to the island. No one got mad at me; they just sat at the edge of the lagoon and watched. They let me solve it, alone. If I broke their water line, of course, I was responsible for their water. Not a good situation to be in. I dove down about twelve feet in the muddy backwater shit-hole swamp and tried to dig the anchor out. I found the PVC water pipe, among other unknown things, in the mud with my feet and eventually jerked the anchor out and re-set it. Then I spent ten-minutes drinking a beer and burning leeches off my body, during which time not one Indian said a word as the smell of burnt leech ass wafted over them. Love them Cunas!

I went ashore to the village where a little girl ran toward me with a mola. A mola is an intricate cloth design made of leftover fabric. The women take pieces of old clothing and stitch them together from the back, leaving a hand-sewn tapestry on the front. Some are very beautiful. The mola this girl was selling was not what I expected to find in the jungle but it was a nice one. It's the art form of Cuna Indian tribe and they are highly prized.

"Mici mola?" she said holding up a mola of Mickey Mouse.

"No, gracias." I replied looking closer at a Cuna version of Mickey Mouse and ventured farther into the village to talk to the local chief. I had to find out how to get through the island chain and back to Colon. The Chief and *"El Gran Ojo"* were gone, off to the meeting in the jungle. I had no guide, I had no chart and I had no clue. Scuffling down the dirt path, amazed at my own stupidity, I spied an old Cuna sitting in the shade. He looked like a wise man but he was asleep and wasn't any help. After almost destroying their water supply, I needed a favor. I knew that the Indians wanted my boat. Not that they'd attack, or steal it; they weren't like that. They'd only kill you if they thought you were going to die anyway. But if something went wrong, they'd sure as shit have been happy to make the boat their own. I was working my way back into the village when a new little girl popped out of nowhere trying to sell me a mola, the previous mola.

"Mici mola!! ...Mici mola!" she said. The mouse.

I kept saying, *"No, gracias, no, yo no quiero!"* Farther down the dirt path, a third little girl ran out,- same mola, different price. Four times crisscrossing the village, four different girls, and each time the price went down. In the end I bought it.

Finally, I reached the end of the path at the center of the village. There was a cleared circle in the dirt with a clay pot, a campfire. Nearby two girls crushed sugarcane using a bamboo frame crusher. The girls wore native dresses and had long bamboo balancing poles. They walked up a twenty foot long bamboo pole, about six feet off the ground, using long bamboo poles held vertically for balance as they slowly shifted their weight back and forth on the bamboo lever. The lever was fixed to the ground on one end and went slowly up and down across a shaped crossbar, the third member of the crushing team fed raw sugar cane stalks into the jaws as they opened and closed. The lever came down, crushed the sugarcane then slowly sprang back up. Girls bounced, crush, crush, crush, the juice fell into a bucket below. A combination of youth, balance and practicality in one useful act. A prehistoric juicer and a beautiful dance.

It appeared that no one in the village spoke English, but they seemed to be wealthy. Stubby brown necks sported heavy gold chains. Then there was me, "*El Blanco.*" I squatted on a log like a barnacle and waited. After some minutes the Chief came out of his hut. He looked at me, eyed me up and down and squatted on the ceremonial five-gallon pail. I kept his eye and explained, in pidgin Spanish with hand gestures, that I needed to go back to Colon, that the Chief I brought from Colon, was gone along with "El Ojo Grande" and I needed some help getting out. In Spanish the chief said, "You have done a favor for my people." I nodded enthusiastically.

As I was talking with the Chief a girl in Indian garb scuffled over, reverently holding a yellow gourd-like object. The Chief told me it was "*una vaso sacremento*" (a sacred vessel.) The words "Made in China" were stencilled in small letters on the side, I pretended not to notice. The Chief held it in his leathered hands for a moment, looked skyward and then handed it off to the girl who reverently took it to the cane crusher. She picked up the bucket below and poured some juice into the gourd, everything floating on top went into the gourd too. A natural, native blend of ants, bark, beetles, Cuna cuticles and leaves. Jungle juice.

Everybody was quiet, except for kids' muffled laughter behind the huts. I reached for the gourd, peered inside, and saw movement, numerous creatures struggling to stay alive. The gathered tribe stared at me; the Chief nodded solemnly, everyone nodded. I did not nod. No way was I going to nod, or drink it. Battlefield decision.

"*No es possible*-I can't drink this," I said to the Chief. "*Yo tengo* (I have) diabetes." Pointing toward my stomach and groin area. I didn't know the word for diabetes or where to point but I hoped the groin move would throw them off.

"Ahh..." The Chief nodded sagely, pointed toward his crotch and told the girl, "Diabetes."

The Chief nodded, the girl nodded, everybody nodded, including me, but I was still not sure which part of my body I should be pointing to, or if I had made a colossal mistake and said I had a small dick.

"Okay," said the Chief in English. "Get him a Coke."

"Thanks...no ice," I cracked. The Chief nodded again with a toothless grin and the whole village laughed heartily, none of them would have drunk that stuff either. They were just having one over on me, seeing if I was stupid enough to do it. It was a 50/50 bet.

Everybody laughed like fools. Indians like to have fun, their kind of fun. I laughed most sincerely.

San Blas Island Archipelago

The Chief drew me a map on an old paper bag. I grabbed my Mickey Mouse mola and headed back to the boat. I got underway and sailed from one island to the next, homeward bound. When I got to the next island I again went into the village. I didn't have a dingy, so the locals had to take me ashore.

A Cuna cab.

An Indian on the dock redrew the chart for me, making it a bit more accurate, he said, at least enough to get me to the next island. I made it to the next island, same thing again. In the end, I had half a dozen charts on the side of a paper bag, but only one mola.

Chapter 18

Plenty Blue, Plenty Green

Things didn't work out in Panama and I returned to Key West, a haven for the indecisive and geographically challenged.

It is said that the most important attribute a smuggler can possess is patience. Most days consisted of dreaming about the Big Bucks and sitting around, waiting. Waiting for orders and directions, while trying to guess who, or what, would get screwed up next. If a job that took months to plan went south, we'd start over from scratch. Dead ends were a common occurrence for the un-loaders. There were always rumors. People were watching us. Phobic fame. We had a plan that looked good on paper but we didn't use paper. There is some honor but little trust among smugglers. Trust got you caught. Quite often, we did nothing but maintain our blood alcohol levels. A certain amount of chaos provided a safety factor; it was necessary and to be expected. Then suddenly it would be "Shit-n'-Git."

The un-loaders weren't told the details until the last moment. Often they waited weeks in a cheap motel room only to learn there would be no "bidness" or the boat had been sent to a different unloading spot. Sometimes our leader, "Ice Cream," set up a job, planted someone in the reeds (it's cold in the reeds) and watched to see what happened when he sent an empty shrimp boat in. If the cops turned up there was a snitch. We never found one, but we were always watching.

Months later, I took a job as Captain of a seventy-two-foot shrimp trawler. With a crew of three I headed out of Palm Beach and down through the Windward Passage near the east coast of Cuba, looking for more "easy money."

I'd been off watch from 0200 to 0600 as we steamed through the Old Bahama Channel, north of the Cuban coast. I woke up and went out on the stern to take a whiz. I was abruptly joined by a second whiz: the whiz of an M-60 machine gun bullet fired by a Cuban gunboat less than half-mile behind us. A piece of wood suddenly flew off the transom. They were getting within range. The Cubans must have been trying to catch us all night, just barely gaining on us. I cursed the crew for not looking back, choked the chicken, ran forward and turned the shrimp boat into the sea and away from the coast. We put the outrigger stabilizers down; they gave us half-a-knot more speed in the rough sea.

I watched the gunboat through a pair of binoculars. I could see the Cuban machine-gunner was having a hard time staying on the gun deck as the smaller patrol boat pounded into the head seas. Swinging wildly back and forth, the gunner's fingers were locked on the trigger and grips to prevent him from falling overboard. He wouldn't fall overboard, but he couldn't stop shooting either! He finally swung around, out of control and hit the gun stops so hard they snapped off. Still fighting to stay onboard, he machine-gunned the bridge of his own patrol boat.

"*Hola Amigo! ... Hay un problema?*" we screamed back at them and delivered a formal one –finger salute.

Unfortunately, we did take a couple of rounds in the hull. I had to strip down and go over the side to plug the holes. Tied to a line, I slammed against the barnacle-encrusted hull at every roll while holding torn pieces of my jockey shorts and a flat-head screwdriver. I worked hard to stuff my sacrificial shorts into a bad leak in a plank and got the daylights beat out of me as the shrimp boat rolled, first down, pushing me away, then up, slamming me into her side.

After a long, hard, ten-day trip we arrived in Curacao where I went ashore with the guns and passports to clear Customs. While waiting at the bar for the Customs Officer to arrive, I ordered an Amstel beer and six others to take out to the crew. I had only been ashore a few minutes. Suddenly everything started to shift and sway. I grabbed my open beer, an ashtray, the bar stool with my knees, the six other beers and held on. Nothing had moved. An old sailor, who knew what was happening, sat next to me. He looked over, "Rough trip, son?"

On another voyage I sailed down south on a forty-five-foot sailboat and spent two weeks cruising back and forth off the deserted coastline of Colombia. We had run low on food and were eating split pea soup and Lipton tea mixed with seawater. We set the gruel on the hot deck in aluminum foil so it would warm. We couldn't communicate more than five miles with our radio and never knew if the transaction would take place on time. Some men began to weaken. I cheered them on day after day by intoning the sacred words, "Blessed are the meek ... We'll eat them first."

For two weeks after our arrival we sailed in toward shore at night, to get in radio range, I powered up the VHF radio and called, "Baby to Mama, Baby to Mama, COME BACK MAMA!" I kept trying. No answer. "Ready about, helms alee!" I moaned as we headed back offshore.

Conversation can be slow after two months on a forty-five foot boat when you have already said everything you know, twice. Toward the end I only used two words at a time. I pointed at the vast ocean "Plenty blue..." I intoned, to which one crewman would always respond, while rubbing his index finger against his thumb, "Plenty green..."

That section of the Colombian coast is a barren desert, nothing except sand and dust on shore for a hundred miles. Usually. We looked on the bright side; we could tell when we weren't alone. The loaders on shore showed up when they were ready. Period.

Fourteen times we sailed back offshore where we couldn't be seen. Twenty-four hours a day we sailed back and forth. There was nothing we could do but wait until our contacts showed up. Or die. We didn't have enough food or water to turn back to Jamaica. Finally, some Indian loaders came out in a canoe, carved out of a log, called a *cayuca*. They brought us food that, after crossing a hundred miles of desert packed in newspaper on a mule's ass, was not real tasty. There was fresh fruit of course, but we had to eat it right away. Unfortunately, that much fruit gave everybody the shits for the next week; we ate so many papayas we couldn't stand up. Mostly we ate gruel and looked for random bits of soft paper. Days could be long, "Plenty blue ... Plenty green."

Finally, the call came. We sailed in close to the beach. During the evening I barked out orders and drank hot rum. One of the Indians called me *El Picaro* during the loading procedure. I looked it up later. Picaro- "a rogue or a rake who makes his way through the world, adventure by adventure, never scrupling too much about common ideas of right or wrong or even about the law, except to keep it off his neck. Sometimes dishonest but easy to like, mind filled with imaginative ideas, very loosely tied to reality."

I didn't know what *Picaro* meant at the time, but it sounded good. Still does.

After fourteen days offshore, we were loaded up and headed back to a secluded spot on the eastern seaboard. During the passage our black spotter plane came out of Miami several times to confirm our position and airdrop instructions and food. We lived among the fragrant bales, slept on the fragrant bales and dined among the bales. We named them and talked to them instead of each other. We were wholly stoned. We did not have GPS or very good radios, so when we got close to the States we went for it, balls to the wall. Winner takes all, and we did.

One afternoon we were running into Key West harbor in an old lobster boat. The tide had turned against us. We ran out of fuel, up current of the Coast Guard dock at Mallory Square and had to turn hard right to get out of inbound traffic. We yelled out to the crew on the Coast Guard cutter tied to the pier. "Hep Me! Hep Me!"

Without power we lost most of our steering ability and crashed into the side of the cutter. Buzz got a line up to the crew. We were loaded down with pot, but it was hidden under cutout lobster traps. The Coast Guard refueled us by lowering five-gallon cans of diesel fuel.

"Love you guys," we shouted. They waved and we were underway to Brito's Boatyard.

One job was particularly disheartening.

White and I had invested everything we owned buying the *Whiskey Delta*, a sixty-five-foot sports fisherman, so we would get a bigger share of the job. Everything went well until we returned to the Keys with a cargo. We anchored near shore and waited for our guide. He arrived and tried to lead us through the channels to the unloading point. He got lost, but not before he managed to secrete away four bales of our best in his guide boat. We anchored again and took the dinghy ashore to figure out what to do. We secured the dingy, looked up and saw police cars with sirens on converging from east and west on the highway and bridges. Someone must have spotted us, or we had a snitch. White and I were walking down the road when our spotters saw flashing yellow lights coming our way. "ENEMY COMING! Hide in the ditch!" they called over a hand held CB radio that White carried.

We jumped into the dark vegetation, safe for the moment. Then, out of the infested darkness a yellow-lighted Monroe County Mosquito Control truck passed by, spraying us vigorously with insecticide-laden gas. Somewhat concerned and coughing, White and I stumbled back to the beach, got into the dinghy and re-boarded the *Whiskey Delta*. We headed south into the Atlantic and steered for the reef, hoping to escape to international waters.

There were cops on shore and we thought we saw a Coast Guard cutter in front of us. Was it adrenalin-induced paranoia? Time for a drink and a quick decision. We turned off all the lights and put her on autopilot, headed due south. I punched the throttles full ahead. White grabbed a bottle of rum. We took a mouthful, shook hands and jumped off, leaving the dinghy tied behind, we wanted the Coast Guard to think we were still on the boat. We were only a half mile offshore and, we would be harder to spot in the water.

We swam toward the mangrove-covered shore, climbed through the tangled roots and found an unoccupied house. I jimmied a window and we holed up inside the damp house with Palmetto bugs, scorpions, roaches, lizards and a nice dusting of spider webs. The cops came and checked the house next door but they didn't check the one we were in. They never did bring dogs, which surprised us. All night long helicopters buzzed around with their searchlights. We stayed holed up. The next morning we came out of the woodwork and smiled, nothing like being shot at and missed. We returned to Key West and tracked down our guide. White convinced him to tell us where the remaining bales were.

We got away, but lost everything, except our freedom.

Years later, I sailed down to Cuba with a mysterious fellow named Beryl Wongo. Somehow, during the height of the Cuban embargo, when the Russians were the most prominent, Wongo got permission from the US State Department to hold a "sailboat race" to Varadero, Cuba. The race had a field of four boats. I captained one of them. No boat went faster than six knots as we crawled across the Gulf Stream … some race. We got to Varadero, sailed into the harbor, looked around and there, sitting at a nearby dock was our goddamned boat, the *Whiskey Delta*. She made it all the way from Key West to Cuba on her own, where someone found her and claimed her. Our dream was now tied to a dock in Cuba.

While in Cuba, I managed to take a tour, an *"especial"* one. The Russians were everywhere, white, pasty-faced and none too happy to be in the hot tropical environment. A government-operated tour bus came to pick us up in front of the Varadero Yacht Club. The bus stopped in a spot that blocked the view of bus stop and that of our Russian "watchers." As everyone else boarded the bus, I stepped behind the bus stop. The bus departed, bound for a sanctioned tour of Havana.

The "watchers" had had enough and soon left, looking for shade. I stepped out from behind the bus stop and caught the next bus going the opposite way, toward Varadero Beach.

I walked around the city and noticed that all the clothes in the store windows were gray. I thought, "Man, it's bad enough being under Communist rule, but they have to wear gray clothes too? Bummer." I walked into a store and judged the clothing displays had been there for twenty-five years. The front of each garment had faded with the sun, time and hope. When I turned to leave I saw the backsides were still the vibrant colors and patterns of Cuba.

During my self-guided tour I visited the DuPont mansion, an impressive estate near the beach. The DuPonts called it Xanadu. The family still maintained the property even though it was under Cuban rule. It's now the clubhouse for the Las Americas Golf Club. When I arrived, there were only two French-Canadian tourists in the whole place. We lunched on DuPont china, DuPont silverware and DuPont linen. Later, after a good DuPont burp, I was thirsty and asked the waiter where the bar was. He pointed to the expansive backyard. I followed his finger and saw nothing but a couple of small hills. I must have looked puzzled.

"Si, senor, no hay problemo, esta' aqui!" (There is no problem, it is here.) He gestured rapidly with the back of his hand.

"Si, senor, gracias, no hay problemo," I said.

Dubiously, I went outside and started walking around the property. After a short stroll I noticed one of the "hills" had a door in its side. It looked like a bomb shelter, I peeked inside and there was the bar. It was a cave, it was cool inside. There were no customers and four stools. The bartender looked at me, nodded but said nothing. There was only one liquor bottle above the bar, a bottle of Havana Club Rum. The Old Devil Rhum. I sat down and looked up. He stood up and looked down.

"*Quiere?* What do you wish?" he asked wiping the bar in front of me. "Rum?"

He nodded, went outside and came back a few minutes later with fresh mint from the garden and something wrapped in a damp towel. He reached under the counter and pulled out a bag of unbleached raw cane sugar. He plopped the sugar and mint into a gourd and muddled it with a stick. Then he took a lime and squeezed the juice into the mix, all the while grinding with his muddle stick. He poured in a generous tot of dark rum and ground it again, then poured it all into a crystal glass etched with the DuPont crest. From the damp towel he took out one ice cube and plopped it into the drink. Abruptly, he stopped and looked around. We were in a cave. There was no one else. But look around he did and, sure that no one would see, covertly added another ice cube to the drink. Ice was more valuable than anything and he gave me a second cube. We were friends.

It might have been the best drink I've ever had, although my research is not yet complete.

The smuggling days were heady wine. I stayed in some of the world's nicest hotels, six-hundred-dollar a night rooms, back in the 70s. Unfortunately, the DEA had cameras in many of the hotels frequented by my type. I was on film for years but I wasn't ready for my close up. (For more on our group of "Gentleman Smugglers" see Jason Ryan's book *Jack Pot*.)

At one point, I lived in South Miami and occasionally met up with Flash and his girlfriend. He was a gangly nut case and fearless.

One afternoon, I borrowed his brand new Porsche Carrera and headed into Coconut Grove for lunch. I finished lunch and went out to start the Porsche but it wouldn't start, so I pumped the gas a couple times. Not only did it start, it exploded. I smelled burnt hair. Whoosh! Flames everywhere. It was fuel-injected and, now I know, you don't pump the gas pedal in a Porsche.

Nobody told me. It had a rear engine and thankfully the engine blew up behind me. The car caught fire and burned to a crisp before the fire truck could get there. I ran into the restaurant to get a fire extinguisher and a cannoli but to no avail. The Porsche melted on the pavement, right by the parking meter. Heavy styrene smoke, with a light scent of cannabis, swirled in the air.

I called from a phone booth, "Flash, I just toasted your Porsche, man."

"Shit. Really?"

"Yeah. Toasted."

"Really?"

"Yup."

"Okay, look, put some money in the meter so the car doesn't get a ticket, get a cab and meet me down at the Porsche dealer."

Flash walked in and bought another one. Cash. The dealer agreed to scrape up the one I'd melted. I didn't ask Flash for the money I had put into the meter. The Porsche was the most expensive car he could buy in South Miami. He would have bought a Maserati if there'd been one available.

Flash was a high roller and I wanted to be one too. Although we generally kept ourselves separate in case one of us got captured by the enemy, we did hang out occasionally.

Not long after the Porsche meltdown we decided to go to The Forge restaurant, a known hangout of old Miami "gentlemen." It was all old blood (probably somebody else's), a cozy criminal ambience with a very ornate interior. It was the tackiest and most expensive place I'd ever been. I liked it. Gargoyles and gold leaf everywhere. We were dressed in T-shirts, shorts and custom flip-flops as we pulled up to the valet standing in front of the red-carpeted entrance. We were rapidly surrounded by scooting valets in tuxedos. They eyeballed the new Porsche and beetled over to get our doors, but as soon as we stepped out they saw what we were wearing and changed their tune to "Dress Codes and Standards."

"Gentlemen, The Forge management requests that patrons dine in formal attire," burped one valet.

"Well, exactly how formal is it?" asked Flash

"Very formal, sir," said the alpha valet. "Extremely formal," he said again with a forcefulness normally displayed only by female bears.

Flash reached into his pocket and pulled out a wad of hundreds. He peeled off a couple and handed them to the valet. Bear food.

"Those look good on you," he said. "Is it getting any less formal?"

He kept peeling them off, until he'd given the guy five or six bills.

"It's getting considerably less formal, sir," said the valet. "In fact, in my opinion, you don't look bad at all. Welcome to the Forge."

The alpha valet took the money, jumped in the Porsche and careened away into the parking lot spraying the lesser valets with pea rock. It was not his problem anymore, but we still had to get past the maître d'. We flip-flopped our way to the podium and presented ourselves to the maître d'. He practically held his nose as he spoke. "I'm very sorry sir, but we have no tables available at this time."

"I see. Do you expect any tables to open up soon?" Flash asked handing the maître d' several hundred dollar bills. Finally, twelve hundred dollars richer, the maître d' grandly waved his arm, "Right this way Gentlemen, please..." From dirt bags to gentlemen in thirty seconds. It was good.

We were escorted to a table in a corner reserved for patrons who wanted to dine without being seen or bothered, which included most of the population of Miami at that time. It was a primo table without too many people around and our seating assignment served as an act of self-preservation on the maître d's part.

After we ceased to be of interest to the other diners, the sommelier brought us the seventy-five page wine list. Flash thumbed through it.

"Is this it?" Flash queried. "Is this your complete wine list?"

"Well, no sir, in fact it is not," sniffed the sommelier, a little peeved, his beaked nose twitching with displeasure. He was not sure we should be there but, well, we were.

"We do have a reserve list and also a collector's cellar in the basement."

Flash slapped the table, crystal glasses and fine silverware tinkled politely.

"Well ...Hot-Lanta, let's go have a look at her!" The sommelier didn't respond immediately.

"You look a little bottled-up," Flash peeled off another four or five frog skins.

Staring at the universal sedative in his hand the sommelier started to calm down, quickly, and managed, with unnecessary hip action, to lead us downstairs and into the "Collector's Cellar." We walked among the rows of fragrant old oak wine racks. Flash suddenly reached over and snatched a dusty bottle of 1960 Chateau Mouton Rothschild off the rack. The sommelier gasped.

"We'll take this one."

"That price, sir, two thousand five hundred dollars, is for those who wish to pack it up and take it HOME to be COLLECTED. To be served at dinner, it's four thousand dollars."

"Fuck it, crack it," Flash looked at me. I nodded, although I had hoped for something better.

Walk-around money, over-the-top days. No excuses. Stupid but fun. You can get lazy when there's that much money around.

Tired of the paranoia in Miami I flew back to the Key West International Airport. I had a little buzz on when I landed and floated out to get a cab. I carried a suitcase and a small leather bag full of some potentially embarrassing items, including a bundle of frog skins. I set the little bag down, loaded the suitcase into the trunk, closed the trunk, got in the cab and rode off. Straight to the Chartroom Bar. I didn't want to lose the elusive buzz. A few hours later, when it came time to pay the bill, it hit me.

"Oh Fuck, my bag!" It wasn't a question or a suggestion. Everyone looked up.

I rushed out, slipped on some fresh seagull guano and hailed a cab. I was distressed and beginning to sober up, which was even more distressing.

"Take me to the airport, I shouted, STEP ON IT!"

"I'd rather step on it than in it." The cabbie said with wrinkled nose and, at his request, I held my soiled flip flop out the window as he peeled out of the Pier House parking lot.

We screeched into the airport's crushed coral parking lot followed by a cloud of dust and wounded bugs. Sitting alone in the twilight was my little bag, untouched. God loves a fool.

White and Suzy in "The Day"

Chapter 19

California Here I Come

Around 1975, things started to get a little hot in my line of work: "Herbal Warming." The law can be annoying at times. I wasn't feeling that secure and I needed a break. I moved to California, to the Russian River Valley north of San Francisco in hippie country where they ate LSD for breakfast, peyote for lunch and stood around with their noses stuck in redwood tree bark trying to get high on ozone. It was not unusual to spot one or two people with their faces pressed into the side of a tree on the way up to my cabin.

I rented a shack toe-nailed to the side of a mountain. It was eighty-two steps up to the front door. I was still young; it didn't seem like much of a climb, the first time. The cabin was near Petaluma, California, "The Chicken Capitol of the World," where treasure hunter Mel Fisher's from. By 1950, Mel had moved to California, where he started a chicken ranch and soon opened the state's first dive shop in one of the farm's sheds.

It was a fine little house at the end of a canyon in a cul-de-sac, quiet, out of the way. I had to let things calm down back in Key West. As winter came the weather started to change; it got brisk and rainy. I met a few neighbors, "Hey man, like...ah... welcome to Ice Box Canyon!"

"What do you mean, Ice Box Canyon? This is California."

The guy's laughter echoed through the Redwoods. "Yeah, but this is also winter in California. We get sun from eleven to one and it can get nasty in the canyon when it rains," he said and pointed to the lovely trickling stream next to my house. "A wonderful water feature," the rental agent had told me.

"What," I said, "that little babbling brook?"

"That's the one," he said. "When it rains, that thing is a raging river."

"Yeah," I laughed, "Whatever."

"I'm worried about you, Perkins," he said. He stuck his nose in my redwood tree and inhaled.

Eventually the rains came and the babbling brook turned into a river. The water churned down the mountain, over the banks of the ravine, into the cul-de-sac that was Ice Box Canyon. My motorcycle was carried away with it. I never saw it again.

After the rainy season I decided to cut the top off a Bay Laurel tree in front of the cabin. I borrowed some telephone pole climbing gear and went to the top. I belted around the tree and got ready to cut. Down below a rusty Volkswagen bus painted with flowers pulled up and an old hippie leaned out the window, "Better take the belt off, man." He rolled up the window and drove away. Who was this clown, what does he mean telling me how to cut a tree. I hesitated just long enough to figure out that he must have had a reason. I took the belt off and hung on as I cut the trunk. Half way through the cut the tree spilt. If I had been belted to it the belt would have cut me in half. Random miracle time, again.

The "Beans Need Love, Too" organic grocery store and co-op was busy. I walked out the front door. My hands were full of groceries and I headed for my car when a hippie girl stopped me. Before I could speak, she stuck a piece of cheese, on a toothpick, in my mouth. My tongue instantly stuck to my upper palate, I couldn't free my tongue to speak. She thought the sounds I was making were a sign of approval. I was trying to breathe through my nose. She seemed happy that I enjoyed her product so much that I couldn't talk. She mistook my grimace for a grin. After awhile the saliva and a prodding tongue did their duty and I asked, "Wha' kind of freaking CHEESE it tha'? It tastes like Play Dough gone bad!"

"Oh! I just knew you'd like it ...it's new," she said happily, apparently having missed the Play Dough years. "My sister and I thought it up...it's made from cat milk ...we call it Kitty Curds." I didn't want to imagine what the "kitty ranch" was like.

After washing down the 'Kitty Curds" I came out of the Back Hoe bar, stared at the sun and walked into a parking meter. Clinging to the meter and gasping for breath, I noticed a red sign slipping past my eyes, *"Expired."* As I tried to compile information on my current situation, another young hippie chick walked up to me. Apparently she did not understand, or chose not to recognize, my circumstance.

"Hey, mister," she said. "Would you like a dog?"

"No thanks," I rasped. "I don't need a dog."

But I was under the influence and before I knew it she handed me a brown paper bag and walked away. I took it because she seemed like a nice young lady, I couldn't chase her and I didn't want to yell.

I carried the wiggling bag along with me, not making too much of it or looking inside. I went down the street to the next bar; I had been wounded for God's sake! I sat down and ordered a beer, the bag fell open. Inside was a puppy. She wasn't kidding. A male border collie right off the ranch and my dog, now. I called him Big U and wrote a song about him:

> "*A dirty old hound rolled into town*
> *It was late one afternoon.*
> *He looked mighty thirsty and he headed for the... local saloon*
> *He walked right in and sat right down*
> *Looked the barkeep in the eye and said in voice*
> *he thought to be rough and low,*
> "*Shut your mouth and grab your buns Fats, get me Black Dog rye.*"

I didn't spend a minute training Big U, but he was the smartest animal I have ever met. When I walked, Big U always checked ahead for problems like country snakes and city snakes. U could smell an enemy. If U saw somebody hanging around a corner, he innocently trotted over, took a whiff of the stranger, then came back and stood staring at me. He pointed back with his butt, signalling "Watch Out!" U could smell danger.

Every week or so I took Big U to the Mark Hotel in San Francisco and on up to the revolving restaurant at the Top of the Mark. I didn't take him in, exactly. I'd cut the collar off a white dress shirt and kept it in the glove box. When we went to The Mark I put the collar around U's neck with a little diamond stickpin to hold it in place. U was good-looking dog with "pumpkin seeds" over his eyes that make sheep think the dog is awake even if its eyes are closed. False eyes.

The valet parking attendant spotted U, "I'm sorry sir, but the dog is not allowed in the hotel."

"Roger that."

I shrugged, handed him the keys, a few bills, large ones, and asked him to leave the rear window down in my 1960 Mercedes 220D. I got out and went inside. U sat still and waited until he was of no interest to anyone, then jumped out the window. He watched the front door until everybody was busy then slipped into the lobby. I hovered nearby; I knew he'd get in. He scooted through the door, slinked up to me and lay down under a table by the elevator. He tried to look like a welcome mat. I entered the elevator and put my foot against the bottom of the door, U waited and watched, his eyes ever alert, then bolted into the elevator at the last minute. Up we went to the revolving bar on The Top of the Mark. Other patrons must have figured, "Hey, if you're already in the elevator of The Mark with your dog, then it must be okay."

We stopped at The Top. I left Big U by the elevator. The elevator was not visible from the maître d' stand. I shook hands with my friend Maurice, the maître d', and palmed him a bill. Once I was seated, Big U found me and slipped in under the table, where he couldn't be seen beneath the tablecloth. After I had absorbed a few beverages, eaten my meal and paid the bill with a generous gratuity, we strolled out together, past Maurice who, shaking his head with feigned surprise, every time, said, "Jesus Christ, where'd that dog come from?"

Once I had to depart California under urgent circumstances. I was gone six months. Big U befriended the neighbors and when I came back he was waiting at the cabin, same as ever.

Years later, back in Florida, my sailboat and I were hauled out in a boatyard in Clearwater for repairs. Big U was on the dock all day, every day. Little elementary school kids from other live-aboard boats in the marina went to school in the morning and came back in the afternoon. They passed our boat twice a day, each carrying their lunch pails and notebooks. As kids will, they teased the dog a bit, nothing mean, but Big U never responded. He lay on his stomach and day after day watched them go by, never moving a muscle.

One afternoon the kids got off the bus and as they passed they teased Big U. He'd had enough. He stood up, barked at them and suddenly fell prey to his natural instincts. He raced out and started herding them into a little flock. One of the kids, a brave little girl in her pink frilly dress with barrettes holding her hair back in pigtails, tried to make a break for it. She was a tiny little thing with cute straps on her shoes and she ran like hell, her little arms pumping, pigtails and papers flapping in the wind. She thought she was going to make her escape. She ran, smiling brightly, with the hope of the young, then came Big U. He caught her. U never bit anyone; instead he bumped into her with his hind end and herded her back into the flock.

Her schoolmates, who apparently had not read about Zebras in school, did not know that Zebras run only as fast as the slowest animal in the herd, even when under attack. Not these kids, the slowest one in their pack got left in the dust. The kids didn't tease Big U after that.

My west coast time was also my period of Arts & Philanthropy. In other words, I got screwed. I bought into a music school in Sausalito, California, the "Lightly Heavenish School of Divine Music." It came complete with a faculty of Haight hippies and New Agers. At this progressive music school students could learn how to make a bong of out a flute, a kazoo or almost any other musical instrument. I was the CEF (Chief Executive Fool). The school never made any money. Ever. All they did was sit around, get ripe, play music and call me "Sir." I was the only one who learned something. Do not invest when stoned.

Somewhere in the middle of those years, I went to see my dad back in Michigan. I arrived with some cash in a duffel bag. "What have you been doing for the last few years?" Bob asked when he picked me up at the airport's private jet lounge.

Not wanting to lie, I led him outside and whispered, "I'm involved in the vegetable transportation business... Pot, mainly."

"I knew it! I knew you were a goddamned criminal the day you were born. I knew you would never amount anything. Get out of my sight!" he screamed.

"Okay, Bob, shhh ... calm down." I said, "Will you just do me just one favor?"

"What's that? I suppose you want some money."

"Well, no, I don't, actually, what I want is for you to hold this bag of cash for me...just for a little while, in case I don't come back...Okay?"

Bob eyed the duffle for size and shape, "Hmm ... you know, son, I might have some property up north you'd be interested in," his tone warmed suddenly.

He wasn't kidding. "How much you want for it?" I asked him.

"No problem," I said. "Here you go." I gave him triple what he paid for it. Ten acres of land on an island in Lake Michigan. Only one problem, he never signed it over to me. BOB!

That was tough.

Chapter 20

The Last Run

"I guess being locked up occasionally is part of living free in this country."
—Pot-possession inmate,
Monroe County Detention Center

After years of banging around the Caribbean in slow moving sailboats getting the snot beat out of me on a regular basis, I decided to take an easier, quicker route. I signed on as crew to take a plane down to Colombia. The trip would take only a few days instead of a few months. It sounded easy.

Tony, the pilot on this mission, was "experienced" and it was said that he had worked quite successfully for Brother Louv and the Zion Coptic Church. Tony was straight and clean. He didn't drink; he didn't smoke; he didn't swear; he even shaved daily. His only quirk was he insisted that all his girlfriends have their upper lip waxed. Anyway.

We originally planned to obtain a large aircraft and bring in a cargo of the "Sacred Herb." However, after another fellow went to Colombia, drove out and looked over the "landing strip," we had to settle for a smaller plane. We bought an old turbo-prop workhorse known as a Lockheed Lodestar. Tony and I went to Oklahoma to pick up the plane. "Her name is Rita," the broker advised us.

A Lockheed Lodestar

Tony climbed into the cockpit and pulled out a tattered checklist that smelled like beer. We got ready to leave for Ohio. I was in the jump seat. I have logged a few hours in the air and felt compelled to ask, "Ah, Tony, ah ... don't we need a pre-flight inspection?"

"Oh yeah, damn, you're right, right as Rita!" Grinning sheepishly and shaking his head he climbed back down and walked around to the port wing. He jumped up and grabbed onto the wing tip. He bounced up and down a few times and tried to do a chin-up, but couldn't. He let go, patted Rita on the ass, hiked his pants up and climbed back into the cockpit.

"Looks okay to me, Reef, let's turn and burn." Tony was an optimist of the first order.

We took off in a snowstorm and flew east toward Ohio. Landed and taxied to a little hangar where a ground crew, experienced in these matters, gutted the old bird (sorry Rita) and made her ready for cargo. Days later we flew into Fort Lauderdale, met with the rest of the crew. We undertook the sophisticated planning and procedures necessary to ensure our success. In other words, we got drunk, and stoned and talked about spending money we had yet to make. A few more days of preparation and we were ready to go. The co-pilot, we called him The Don, asked me where we were headed.

"Somewhere in the jungles of Colombia, we're going to find a lake shaped like a heart. Simple. I know where it is. I was there four months ago for five minutes," I informed him. When I was in Colombia the first time the Colombians took me, in a small plane, to a lake one-hundred-fifty miles west of Rioacha near Mt. Cristobal and said, *"Jew jez come back to el lago ... comprendo? Lago similar Corazon ... heart, comprendo?"*

"Si."

No charts, no landmarks, nothing, just a compass heading out of Rioacha, traveling for over one hour at one hundred twenty miles per hour was all I had to go on. Perhaps I should have been more thorough during the advance expedition, but I hadn't gotten much sleep the night before. The Don seemed awfully quiet.

The next day, we fueled up and were on our way down to Colombia and the Guajira Peninsula. We crossed over the Colombian coast near Rioacha and climbed to 14000 feet to cross over the mountains. We had no emergency oxygen onboard. The Don began to moan, and when we crossed into the forested area, there were hundreds of lakes. The Don moaned even louder. I couldn't tell the lakes apart... I could if he'd shut the fuck up! The Don's mood began a slow descent.

Things were starting to look bad. Our mouths were bone dry, our eyeballs stuck in their sockets and our lips split from the dehydrated air. We were bleeding down the front of our Zig Zag T shirts and running low on fuel as we descended toward the jungle. Not to mention I couldn't find the freaking *Corazon-* shaped lake. We didn't have enough fuel to double back and start from the beginning. We were running on vapors and The Don was losing it. I told him to calm down, but he kept getting worse, muttering, "We're going to die; we're going to die!"

He may have been right but I didn't find the attitude helpful, so I told him to shut the fuck up or I was going to throw him out of the plane and ensure that he would die. He shut up, almost, for awhile, but finally Tony and I got tired of his droning. I grabbed The Don by the scruff of his neck, jerked him out of his seat backwards (it's better to surprise people in situations like this). I took him to the back of the plane. He started to struggle. I threatened to adjust his hair-do with the butt of a jungle gun I had on me and tie-wrapped him to the frame of the plane. I put one of Tony's socks in his mouth. One of Tony's used socks. Think waterboarding is bad? Try sock-boarding.

It didn't help the co-pilot's mood, but it helped ours. Nothing like a little peace and quiet if you're going to crash into the jungle and die.

Finally, I spotted the lake and pointed excitedly, too excitedly, driving my index finger into the cockpit windscreen and sustaining an injury. It was my nose finger.

"We're almost out of fuel." Tony said as we banked for our approach. Tony had decided to put her down no matter what. "It's better than crashing," he grinned through blood caked lips. I wasn't sure there would be much difference. I sat on my throbbing finger and listened to the starboard engine start to cough and sputter. It was going to be close. We dropped ass first toward the runway, but it wasn't a runway, it was a farmer's field and home to a herd of boney bush cows. We came in low enough to see flies swarming around a herd of boney cows. The engines scared them off the strip. It had looked like a runway from the air months before, hadn't it? The Guajira Indians hid in the jungle; they wouldn't come out until they knew what was happening. Gravity took over as we came around and turned on final approach. We came down hard. If we had had any cargo, the plane would have broken in half on impact. Eventually, Rita skidded to a stop in the bushes at the end of the field. We were alive!

It was getting dark as we taxied out of the bush and onto the flat. The Don was very quiet. We heard a truck start up and out of the jungle came the Indians in trucks filled with dozens of Army surplus, five-gallon "Jerry Jugs" to refuel the plane. Tony climbed up on the wing grabbed a steel can and started dumping the fuel into Rita. He emptied one can, slid it down the wing to an Indian then grabbed another being passed up. At one point Tony dropped a can; it hit the wing and bounced. When it came off the wing it hit an Indian in the forehead and peeled that native's scalp half way back. The Indian didn't miss a beat. He reached up, pulled the flap of bleeding skin back down over his forehead, held it like a toupee in the wind and waited for the next can. The simplest things can be very valuable in the bush, the cans were valuable, the Indians, not so much. By the time we fueled up it was dark but we decided to walk down the "runway," to check it out anyway. Don was loose but decided to stay in the plane. He was a little miffed. The idea of walking around in the jungle at night can be filed under "not too smart," and after a short walk and a brief discussion we agreed that the "runway" would be all right. Good to go. Besides, we were tired and hungry. "I think we'll be fine," said optimistic Tony sounding much like Vertical Vern in Vietnam. We trotted back toward the plane for a dinner of popcorn and water.

The next morning we walked the runway and loaded the plane with bales carried through the jungle by mules and horses. Within an hour we were full of cargo and a little Peruvian Marching Powder.

"Turn and Burn ... Flaps up ... Gear Up ... Baby to Mama ... Here we come!" we yelled at each other over the throbbing engines. Laughing like fools we taxied down to the end of the dungway, "FULL POWER ... FULL PITCH!" screamed Tony as The Don leaned hard on the throttle and pitch controls. We careened down the runway, our seat belts saving us from being smashed into the instruments. Bouncing up and down through the cow pasture and looking like a one legged high jumper we tried to get up enough speed to rotate. No joy, we were over gross weight and couldn't get off the ground.

However, we did manage to clear the runway of cow turds on that pass. Since we had what could be described as **NO CHOICE** we decided to turn around and try it again in the other direction. There was no wind; it was jungle hot. So far, so good. Unfortunately, we'd stirred up straw and bush leaves, not to mention a fine dusting of cow dung. As we headed back the other way we failed to notice the oil coolers sucking in wads of debris. We powered up and rolled back down the runway, Tony pulled back on the yoke, the stall alarms went off and the oil gauges were racing toward the redline. It was too late to stop so we went for it, "FULL POWER FULL PITCH! Rita shook and moaned; we pulled up and made it ... almost. We hit a scraggly palm tree that punched a frond through the nose cone but, unbelievably, did no damage. We'd snapped it off clean. Now we were headed over the mountains of Colombia with a six-foot palm tree stuck in the front of the plane and our oil coolers filled with straw and cow dung. It would be a long trip, or a very short one.

Tony figured there was no way we were going to make it back over the mountains. We had enough fuel but were too heavy and we were burning too much oil to go fourteen-thousand-feet. We had to weave through the mountains. The mountains were in the clouds; hence we had to weave through the clouds too, with no radar. Actually, we had radar but it didn't work. As we flew along, I spotted a dark shape out my side window.

"Tony," I said, "what the fuck is that?"

"It's a special type of cloud," he snorted, lips curled and bleeding again "We call it Cumulus Granite."

The hay and dung were burning off the coolers.

We flew through the mountains and across the desert on the other side. Tony and I had massive migraine headaches from stress, lack of food and lack of oxygen as we headed home on a wing and a Bayer. The co-pilot calmed down since being given the choice of staying in the jungle or flying back with us. He made the wrong choice but held the co-pilot's seat while I glanced at Tony's remaining sock.

We were Bahamas-bound and that was fine because we'd been assured that all the necessary Bahamians had been "well compensated."

All except for one Bahamian that is, a Biminian from Bimini, Mr. Mentor Pindling. He seemed confused when he signed us in to re-fuel after we landed. Pindling approached the small cargo plane. There was a palm tree stuck in the front, the oil coolers smelled of burnt barn straw and two pilots, bleeding from the mouth, who said they needed fuel, fast. Meanwhile someone moaned, "We're going to die..." behind mildewed curtains, covering the dung flecked windows. Looking back I suppose it was confusing.

Everything was fine; we were refuelling, almost home. Pindling, the curious Bahamian, said nothing, just stood watching us. Finally, he came around the plane, near the boarding ladder. He went up one step. I stood not too far away. He looked at me. I looked down at my right hand. He nodded. My hand moved slowly inside my Guyabera style shirt. I nodded. He looked at the plane. He looked at me. I looked at him. I looked at the plane. He looked at my right hand. I looked at the center of his chest. He went up another step. My hand was all the way in my shirt. Pindling went up to the third step. He looked at me and nodded; I looked at him and nodded. I slowly reached for the gun in my belt. Pindling got to the fourth step and reached for the doorknob. I grabbed the .45 and started to pull it out. He nodded at me and I nodded at him. He knew it would be my last nod and maybe his too. Time stopped. He turned, reflected, slapped at a black fly and slowly walked down the creaking steps. It was mostly for show. He passed me without saying a word; I passed him a thousand in cash without saying a word. We nodded one more time just for good measure. He was a clever double dipper.

Of course, we weren't simply refuelling, we were praying. Oh yes, we did pray. Lordy, Lordy! We dug the cow dung out of the oil coolers as best we could; it takes practice they say. We decided to leave the palm tree in place. We'd made it this far with it. We had to get back, no matter what. We were almost rich! We took off and headed for Fort Lauderdale. The oil coolers were badly damaged, cinders of burnt carbon sparked out during takeoff and the grim remnants of a sea bird, possibly an albatross, were mashed into a wing tip.

Rita groaned, like a tired lover who has no choice. We made it off the runway and headed for the Florida coast. Because of the damage to the oil coolers and our sincere desire not to get caught we flew low across the Gulfstream waters and headed west relying on the famous BONSAI altimeter. The altimeter gave us a bright red digital readout showing how many feet above the water we were. 40', 35', 30', 25'. We had to fly low enough to be below the US and Bahamian radar but just high enough to be above the water, always a good idea (*it's in the manual*) while trying to miss all the large freighters with their antennas, and sports fishing boats with their outriggers.

Our lips cracked open again. Tony wiped some blood off his chin, grinned at me, throttled up and stared intently at the BONZAI altimeter. "Here comes the fun part, you're gonna like this, man!" he shouted over Rita's groaning engines.

We crossed the Gulf Stream. I could see the lights of Fort Lauderdale on the horizon. They were getting bigger, quickly. Tony stared at the Bonzai altimeter and never looked up. I held the throttles and never looked down.

We came into Fort Lauderdale "balls to the wall," flying thirty feet off the water at 120 knots. Rita screamed in over the beach. We headed right for the large condos, it was the only way to get inland and avoid radar detection. We had to fly between the buildings, in their "shadow" (*not in the manual*). I opened the co-pilot's window; I thought I could smell French fries. We hadn't eaten in 24 hours. We gave what little food we had to the "scalped one" when we left. Who cares, we're almost rich!

With Tony at the controls we passed a large condominium, our wing tip was only twenty or thirty feet from a balcony. An elderly gentleman sat on his balcony, two stories up, having a peaceful evening meal with his wife. First he heard and then he saw a dark brown, twin engine, Lockheed Lodestar doing 120 knots coming at him with a palm tree sticking out of the front. We burned past his balcony. He panicked and bolted upright, but forgot to pull his chair out and dumped the table onto his wife. She struggled under the table; covered in food while he tried to figure out what the hell a plane was doing twenty feet from his balcony. It happened in much less time than it takes to tell it.

Rita was a class act but she was smoking like an old hooker in a biker bar as we scorched through downtown Fort Lauderdale, her oil coolers looked like sparklers while the remaining carbonic dung burnt off. We stayed close to the ground and passed over the Everglades. Now we watched for radio towers, then on to Opa Locka Airport where we made a low altitude pass across the airport, turned on final approach and executed a "touch and go." When we pulled up we appeared, on tracking radars, to be a local airplane taking off. We headed north for the Georgia border. There are no rear view mirrors on planes.

Rita was starting to shake as the fuel burnt off.

"That fucking palm's going to bring us down. " I burbled through the headset.

"Be cool," Tony sputtered through cracked and bleeding lips. He looked over and smiled, "We made it this far."

It was midnight.

The shuddering Lockheed Lodestar was over gross with too many pounds of herb in the cargo bay and a palm frond stuck through the nose cone.

Rita moaned as we dropped ass first through the clouds and turned for final approach at a remote airstrip in southern Georgia. Tony flashed our landing lights. Seconds later the black strip lit up.

"Flaps down!"

"Roger." I piped.

"Gear down!"

"Roger."

"FUCK IT!"

"Roger that."

We hit the ground hard, blew a tire and screeched to a stop, sideways in the dirt. Burnt tire smoke wrapped the plane. The stink gagged us. The engines backfired and died.

I kicked the cargo door open. A guy stuck his face in, "We'll take it from here. If anybody's got a gun, get rid of it" I kicked a few bales out and hurried to the terminal sixty yards away. Tony and The Don disappeared into the bush.

Something didn't feel right. I hesitated, looked back and dropped my .45 down a storm drain.

Inside, ground boss Full Buzz laid out a line of cocaine. I rolled a fresh hundred-dollar bill and fit it to my dehydrated nose. Buzz did the same. "We're fucking rich!" Buzz said. We got ready to dive for the line.

Without warning, glass shattered, doors slammed open and six black riot guns racked back. Locked and Loaded. We, on the other hand, were soon to be Loaded and Locked. They didn't need six shotguns; we were unarmed. But the lawmen wanted to let us know they had the firepower, plus the sounds of racking back are cool.

I looked at Buzz, Buzz looked at me. We dove for the line and hoovered the heady powder up our fear dilated nostrils as fast as we could. We started at opposite ends but went so fast that we head-butted when we met in the middle. Within seconds we were lying on the floor high as a kite, with hundred dollar bills stuck up our noses and bleeding profusely from minor cuts on our foreheads. Seconds seemed like minutes.

Half unconscious and surrounded by six well-armed Swamp Cowboys, I looked up the barrel of a 12-gauge riot gun and tried to focus. I had never looked up a gun barrel from the other end before. It looked big.

"You're all under arrest," said a DEA jacket, jingling his handcuffs.

No one seemed surprised.

Tony and The Don had run into the swamps but were captured later. It was a setup; the DEA controlled the airport. They followed us in their plane from the Bahamas in case we changed plans. We were busted before we ever left for Colombia. Damn, all that for nothing! Still, the vagaries of life persisted.

After a rather cursory body search (I had missed a few showers) and a refreshing frog-march with a well-fed deputy on each elbow I, along with my fellow co-conspirators were put, not very gently, into several police cars.

I had a wad of hundred dollar bills left over from the trip, minus the thou for Pindling. The money was stuffed in my underwear in a location that deterred even the most hardened cop. Even though my hands were cuffed behind my back, I managed to slip my arms under my legs and over my feet without the driver noticing. When I got my hands in front I pried the cash out of my Jockey Shorts, without hesitation I might add, and stuffed the wad between the back seat cushions. When the police searched us thoroughly at the Sylvania Police Station and Bait Store, I had nothing on me. It was, fortunately, a time when hiding things in your butt and searches thereof had not become fashionable. After booking us "Perps" we were put back in the cop cars. They took us to the Savannah County jail. Luckily, they put me in the same car, in the same seat. I reached back, dug my wad out, slipped my body through the cuffs again and tucked the money back down my tightey whiteys. I was quite flexible in those days. I slipped back through the cuffs and, sitting on my still throbbing finger, attempted to maintain some semblance of dignity as I was driven to the county jail. I was an Army Officer, for heaven's sake, a Captain no less, and a decorated fool. But it seemed to make no difference to the Sylvania Swamp Cowboys. To them I was just a red-haired loser, another notch in the gun.

When we arrived in Savannah I had the money on me. The jailer on duty was a woman who, at two in the morning, was not interested in patting down nine sweaty guys that included the loaders, truck driver, Tony, The Don and me. I took the wad into the jail cell.

"How the fuck did you do that?" my fellow Perps and co-conspirators asked me, pissed-off but friendly. "You've been searched twice man and now you've got money. How did you do that?"

"I can't tell you, but it's a short story."

The police couldn't take the money because once I was in jail the money was not illegal. That's good to know. It allowed me to offer gratuities to our jailers and get us some much-needed supplies, like a bottle of rum. In jail you need money. Anyway, after seven days in the Savannah County Jail I was out on bail with a hangover and a diary, etched with a toothpick, on a Styrofoam coffee cup. I marked the days. I drew a set of tits and a cross. Jail has a way of making you want to believe in God, if for no other reason than to feel there is a greater power than that of those who hold you captive.

Genius never sleeps, so while out on bail I went back to Key West and flew to Curacao, off the coast of South America. For three months I lived in a dingy motel room waiting for the "job" and learning all the possible dance step combinations to the tune "Ladies Night…Oh yeah its ladies' night… oh what a night…" There was nothing else to do as I waited for the plan to develop. I chased goats and sketched Divi Divi trees for fun. Nothing happened.

I went back to Savannah for the trial in January. In court I was referred to as a "Perp."

I should have stayed with boats.

Our gang was called "Operation Snack Bar" by the DEA, and according to them it was a multimillion-dollar drug smuggling ring. Not quite, it was me and some college guys from Shrimphead, South Carolina. Some of whom went on to greater heights in the smuggling world.

For reasons I didn't understand, Tony had a separate trial. The total value of the pot we'd smuggled wasn't a big deal we contended, and the attorneys argued that the substance we brought in was not the same exact chemical composition as the substance that was illegal. On the other hand the feisty prosecutor, who did say that, "The defendants have no lack of imagination when it comes to their defense," insisted that a ton and half of reefer exceeded the "personal use" clause. All the bales had been marked with X's according to quality. X bale, XX bale, and the XXXX bale, (that's the one we kept, or would have kept, for ourselves).

We each had our own lawyers and I had some problems with mine. Basically, mine were trying to cheat me out of as much money as they could, as fast as they could. I was stunned. A month earlier I was in a private airplane with my attorneys who, after I had paid them a retainer, said they needed *another* retainer or they were going to "drop my case." The pilot locked the doors from the outside before takeoff (That's illegal) or I would have "dropped their case."

Fortunately, my friend Smiley knew a lawyer from Alexandria, Virginia, a larger than life fellow named JZ. JZ was a big guy with long, curly black hair and a Moses beard. He was completely out of sync with what attorneys were supposed to look like back then. JZ met me in a Foggy Bottom titty bar. I told him I'd already spent all my money on lawyers and wasn't sure how I was going to pay him. We sipped our drinks in silence for a few minutes.

"Fuck it," he finally said, sounding like a judge who has just reached a difficult decision. "Don't worry about it Reef, let's have some fun!"

JZ was a big fellow, ex-Navy, a Vietnam vet and smart. When we finally got to trial there were the usual arguments, counter arguments, complicated pleadings and a symphony of whining.

During the trial, despite trying our best, we were still not fully reformed and had little Dristan bottles full of nose food mixed with water and, when the testimony took a turn for the worse, we snorted this liquid flight. At one point the judge, after listening to us suck snot up our noses for an hour, asked if everyone was feeling well enough to continue. "Oh, yes, Your Honor, ahh ... my clients have bad colds, probably caught them in the holding cell, that's all," an attorney quickly replied.

Ultimately there wasn't any doubting what we'd done. There was no way around it. So, in his closing argument, his only argument incidentally, JZ went up to the bench and stood before the judge.

"Your Honor," he said trying to look sorry for me, "my client is sorry for what he did. He knows it wasn't the right thing to do and he understands it was a mistake. But he hasn't been back from Vietnam but a couple years. He was a Captain in the Army; he got a Bronze Star over there. He's really sorry, your Honor. (I'm nodding). He didn't mean to do it and he regrets his actions." Then he turned, walked back to to our table and sat down.

I leaned over and whispered, "Ah excuse me. That's it? That's my defense? *I'm sorry?*"

"Shut up."

After a week, the trial finished up and we were out on bail. Several months later the sentencing took place, again in Savannah. A couple of guys got spanked heartily. I got six months, which was pretty good, considering. Some guys thought I had "ratted them out" to get such a short sentence, but they had their attorneys check and found that I hadn't. What they didn't know and what I didn't know was that a member of the judge's family had been in the Army during Vietnam and had died there. JZ said all that he needed to say, and in that moment the judge heard nothing else.

In my favor, during sentencing, was the fact that I had not accumulated any tangible assets (mental or physical) that the Feds could locate. As Jimmy Buffett put it "...I made enough money to buy Miami and pissed it away so fast, never meant to last."

Chapter 21

A Perp's Life or Once is Enough

I followed the terms of my bail bond and, after being re-booked in Savannah, I was put on a bus and taken to the Atlanta Federal Penitentiary where fights, murders, rapes and other unpleasant events were part of everyday life. I spent four weeks in the "Pen," where inmates naturally divided into ethnic gangs such as the Blacks, Latinos, Orientals, Jews, the Stoned, the Drunk, a few rump rangers and pickle smokers and of course the Aryan brotherhood. All locked up together, the felonious mixing pot made for spirited conversations and debate.

I made it through Atlanta where even gentlemen offenders, such as I, were shown how bad things could get if they decided to follow a life of crime. For some it didn't make any difference.

After ten days and a hot nine-hour drive shackled to a seat frame in a un-air conditioned prison bus, I along with fifteen other Perps arrived at Eglin Air Force Base, a minimum security prison in the western Florida panhandle.

The Eglin Air Force Base Prison Camp wasn't bad, although the Har-Tru surface on the tennis courts could have used an upgrade. It resembled a summer camp with open yard space, picnic tables, security cameras, a library, and large dorms that housed the prisoners in "cubes." We had a nice mess hall and the blue prison uniforms brought out the color of my eyes. It was much better than Savannah where I'd been held after our capture or the Atlanta Federal Penitentiary for that matter. Personally, I would not give either of the previously mentioned institutions even a 3-Star "Perp" rating.

I exited the bus and was ushered into a room for "processing," like lunchmeat. I stood, waiting. It was something I knew how to do. On the other side of a glass panel and across the hall was the discharge room. A convict was being released. He shook hands with the guard and walked out in his fresh civilian clothes. His new T-shirt read: "Once you lose your reputation it's much easier to live freely."

At Eglin, life was a little different, but even there groups fought for control. Without muscles or tattoos, accountants, lawyers, politicos, arsonists and the occasional tax evader fought a brutal battle of unsavoury words and unnecessary insults over the Ping-Pong tables, scrabble games and shuffleboard courts. Like many other inmates, I tried religion to help me find my inner spirit and, coincidently, to help out on my early release evaluation form. I attended the small prison chapel, once. Unfortunately, that day's theme was "As ye sow so shall ye reap." Huddled in a pew with other sorrowful sowers I knew there was no escape. I had sowed a felonious seed and must now reap the felonious fruit. I got busy reaping.

I was assigned a "cube" in a large dorm where I lived and slept. At Eglin, like in the daytime soap operas so many guys watched, somebody was always screwing with somebody else, just to see what would happen and to break the monotony and, like any prison, it was a good idea to pay attention. But the worst punishment was listening to bullshit stories about the next big caper. Still, everyone was well behaved because if you screwed up, you went back to the Federal Penitentiary. My cube had a desk and a bunk and was open to the rest of the dormitory on the aisle end.

Big Fanny, a guy four cubes down, had been a gynecologist before his arrest and had developed Tourette's syndrome while in captivity, or so he said. He had graduated from Harvard medical school and was in for tax evasion. Big Fanny was obsessed with various parts of the female anatomy and uttered colorful obscenities for an hour or two most nights. He had an extensive anatomical vocabulary and a pleasant voice. "Titty, tush, nookie, bush, nipple, vulva, pussy, clit, butt crack, jugs, knockers…" and so on, non-stop. It got old after a month or so.

During my stay at Eglin I developed a heavier demeanor, kept to myself and learned just how many crooks there are among us.

While at Casa Eglin I played tennis with Marvin Mandel, my doubles partner. I also met "Harry the Heeb," as he called himself. The Heeb and I became buddies. He was an older guy and had his shtick down pat. He'd made plenty in Medicare fraud, tucked it away and lived the good life until he got caught. He'd been to Eglin three times, so far. The

Heeb's plan was: 1. Defraud 2. Live good 3. Go to jail. 4. Get out. 5. Defraud. No amount of counseling could save the Heeb.

Friend of a Fraudualist

Eglin is one of the Ivy League schools for criminals. "Old School tie, don't you know."

I was friends with a fraudualist (as he called himself), an arsonist, a con man, the Reverend Bob Roy Kernal and other white-collar types.

The Heeb and I were on the Tree Squad. Five days a week, eight hours a day we rode around Eglin in a blue government dump truck. Our job was to cut and trim trees on the base. We were supervised by Sergeant White (no relation to my buddy) who, like many others, was greatly influenced by the Heeb. Together with three other Cons, we merrily rode around in the dump truck all day long, cutting down foliage at will.

One day, just before lunch, the Heeb said to Sergeant White, who was distracted as usual by the pet ferret he kept in his front pants pocket, "Sarge, we should go cut down that tree in front of the headquarters building because it is making a mess with all those leaves. The men think it might be diseased." The headquarters building was the showpiece of Eglin Air Force Base. At its front was the Commanding General's office. The Heeb was quite persuasive... TIMBER!

It was reported that when the General came back from lunch and looked out his window his curses could be heard in the nearby latrines. All he saw was a large stump. The General was furious, but wisely acting on the Heeb's advice, Sergeant White, who had not completed eighth grade, "disavowed any knowledge."

Every so often our squad of Perps, I prefer to think of myself as a *Perp* rather than a *Con,* which has a negative connotation, would go to lunch at the 20-acre tire depot where all the used aircraft tires were stored. A grand stinky rubber maze, thousands of big, black, burned-out tires breeding mosquitoes were stacked twenty feet high. It was designed by the convicts who ran it. We Perps were sometimes assigned to stack tires and perform other exciting tasks like squirting kerosene into the tires to kill the bugs.

We arrived at the tire depot two hours before lunch one day and the Heeb, leader of the Perp Aristocracy said, "Sergeant White, all we're going to do is work around here and then eat lunch. We've got our bologna and our orange, we're happy, you don't need to stick around and watch us, like what...we're going somewhere?"

"All right," said Sergeant White, aggressively stroking the pet ferret stuffed in the front pocket of his uniform pants. "I'll be back here in an hour or so to pick you up."

"Bye, Sarge," we chimed like good little peeping Perps.

The diesel exhaust smoke and tire dust billowed around us as Sergeant White pulled away, stroking his ferret. Immediately, the convicts who ran the depot and whose lives The Heeb had improved, came out of the tire barn and took most of the Perps into the main building. Another took the Heeb and me into the towering maze of burned-out tires. Round and round we went in the noonday sun, into the centre of the maze, where it opened into a tiny dirt courtyard. Under a camouflaged cargo net stretched overhead to provide some shade, stood a table set with an umbrella, white tablecloth, crystal glasses, real silverware, Gefilte fish, bagels, lox, Kosher wine and a bottle of Veuve Clicquot champagne, my favorite. Extension cords ran a few fans. Two black corner girls, friends of the Heeb's from the District of Colombia were also in attendance. The Heeb flew them in on a chartered plane. They say there are more whores in DC than anywhere else in the States, and that's not counting the hookers. The "girls" waited on the table and after the meal, we shared a chocolate dessert.

Lunch was finished. We walked out, quite relaxed, and there was trusty Sergeant White. He quickly stuffed his ferret back into his pants. Service members were forbidden to have pets on base. He knew that we could turn him in but...he loved his ferret.

"Get all your stuff done and have your lunch, boys?"

"Yes, sir," said the Heeb, sucking at the remnants of Bulgarian caviar lodged between his front teeth.

Eglin was a minimum-security prison; you could walk out if you wanted. Some did. But if you did and got caught you were sent to a Federal penitentiary and they doubled your sentence. Not many people walked.

Even though it was minimum security, I still did my 1000-yard stare and tried to look dangerous. It made me dizzy. I kept to myself because even a prison like Eglin can be bad and it was. I heard that the preferred method of "erasing" someone involved sneaking up on the sleeping person, sticking a pencil in his ear and hitting the eraser end with your hand. It didn't happen, but it could. I was there long enough to know.

Heeb had some contacts and I successfully smuggled some herb in on occasion, old habits die hard. I almost got caught one time, which would have doubled my sentence, but I smelled so bad after cutting brush all day no one wanted to search me.

We also drank a lot of booze when we were out on the job. The Heeb had his buddies hide or bury vodka (it's hard to smell on your breath) in various locations and some days we came back into camp pretty liquored up. The guards had a breathalyser at the gate. They randomly picked out cons and, on occasion, the more sophisticated Perps to check on the way back in. That's why we always had a few raw potatoes, provided by the inmate cooks, with us. We cut them up and chewed them just before we went through the checkpoint; they cooled off your breath and beat the breathalyser.

Bob Roy Kernal worked in the library and helped inmates with their well-intentioned but futile appeals. He liked to be called "The Kernal" and described himself as a "self-ordained minister of the people." He was, in fact, found guilty of ministering to several people's trust funds and now enjoyed the confines of Eglin with a select group of Perps that he called his "fucking flock." He was a rotund fellow about five-feet tall and looked like a Russia nesting doll in prison garb. With a slow waddling walk, a round, pink, hairless face and Tennessee twang Bob Roy approached a group of loitering inmates. When Bob Roy talked, the conversation always took an interesting turn. No matter what was said or who was talking Bob Roy walked up and began speaking. Each time his words were different but the last line was always the same.

"There's two rails on a train, boys, and you gotta ride em' both, you don't have to be good all the time, just when it counts. Look at me son! An early arrival meant nothing in those days and even the pumpkin needs more than I can give, may gravity pull your soul back to your bones...your bones! Good Lord! ...**Does that answer your question, son?**" Bob Roy never waited for an answer. He sucked his teeth, clucked his tongue and, with a quick nod, was gone to spread the Word.

Conrad, the arsonist, who lived a few cubes down confided in me one afternoon. "Simple, Reef," he said, " You dip a fucking rat in gasoline and fucking light it. The fucking rat freaks and bolts towards fucking cover, which is always going to fucking be somewhere deep in the fucking building, with all its fucking rat shit around, flammable fucking rat shit. So all they find when they go to investigate the fucking fire is a fucking burnt rat. Period, end of story, like it?"

"Fuck yes!"

Then there was Big Sam, a gregarious and likable fellow who ran Lucky Sam's Discount Grocery Stores. Big Sam would order merchandise, mostly non-perishable goods, pay for it, sell it cheap, going back and forth paying in full each time, pretending to do real business. Then, because he was apparently successful, or so it seemed to his creditors, he'd make a huge order, sell it off for cash without paying the invoice, torch the building, and let the insurance pay. The ideas sure sounded good, but wait a second, these guys were in jail.

I came to know another lad named T. Register, nicknamed Cash. He was a swindler who specialized in women.

Cash looked like a young Mickey Rooney with red hair and freckles; cute and harmless. He had a big space between his front teeth, like his head hadn't finished growing together. He knew how to pick women and take them for all they were worth, one after another. Later, after he got out, he came to visit me in Key West. I introduced him to my neighbor Caroline, who he immediately took a liking to and held hostage for a week, right next door. Every morning he waved at me from the double hung kitchen window, holding a gun up in the air behind Caroline's head. Caroline waved too. "Hey, how're you guys doing?" she chirped.

"Fine," I replied. "Why don't you come over for a coffee?"

"Oh," she sighed looking over her shoulder and smiling at Cash, "I guess I can't right now."

"Where'd you get the gun, Cash?" I asked

"Oh, hee-hee, "Caroline smiled sheepishly, "it's mine."

Cash waved the gun and smiled.

I felt bad about that. I had introduced them and next thing you know he had her at gunpoint, with her own gun, and was getting her to empty her bank account. He was a dangerous individual, but she really seemed to like him, at least it sounded like it late at night. "It was my mother's money anyway," she said later.

Chapter 22

Tropical Rehab

After four months and seventeen days I received an honorable discharge from "The Eglin Air Force Base Home for Wayward Boys." I had gone from being free and rich, to being broke and locked up in a cube. Once was enough.

It was 1982. I remembered I had a wife and a 2 year-old son and went back to Key West. The Feds had taken away my Captain's license so I couldn't do anything with boats. I could re-apply in ten years. Ten years... not acceptable! My dad suggested I park cars. "Something you can probably do without fucking it up."

My wife (#2) was parking cars with me ... she was a trooper; we had no choice. Six months removed from living a comfortable lifestyle, I was parking cars for tourists. The Yin and the Yang of life. I started "Yang's" valet service, my first legitimate business venture. I needed a random miracle.

Yang's valet parking service was located at the Casa Marina Hotel. I was parking cars and taking cash. There was no deal with the hotel, just The Bubba System. It was 1980.

We kept Quincy under the counter in a cardboard orange crate, and worked the business. But I wasn't just parking cars. I was trying to become an entrepreneur and was never short of bad ideas. Remember that fad, "The Pet Rock?" I came up with the even stupider idea of boxing up little hammers and selling them as a Pet Rock Killers.

"*Are you tired of that stagnant stone, that foolish fossil? Embarrassed by your ridiculous rock? Now here is your chance to save face!*" I went up to Alexandria, Virginia to produce "The Pet Rock Killer." I designed a six-sided box that looked like a coffin, to house the hammer. I also came up with the idea, like other pioneers, of bottling water. I invented a bottle that was shaped like a can. With the top pushed in, it would fit in a vending machine. When the can of water rolled out of the machine you pulled accordioned neck and it became a bottle. You popped the cap but it stayed attached. I called it the

Wrinkle Neck. I started on that notion and got some attorneys involved but, being incredibly smart people, they said, "Yeah, it's great, but nobody's going to put water in their vending machines." I didn't pursue it. Duh.

The US Patent Office in Crystal City, Virginia is a fascinating place. I was in the process of researching the aforementioned "wrinkle neck" bottle, and discovered there were thirty-two patents for baby bottle nipples. How I got into the nipple section remains a mystery.

While I was at the Patent Office I met a fellow who had patented the logos on professional football league helmets. That's where he made his money. He'd also invented a shock absorber that never wore out, but he couldn't sell it. Finally a big shock absorber company, said, "We'll buy it but you have to make it appear that we have to fix it." So he modified the design to require a special wrench to adjust the shock absorber.

"Don't ever invent anything that won't wear out," he told me, "because nobody will touch it."

With my rather lean and limited resume' job prospects were slim. So, in 1983, with no idea about how to operate a business wife #2 and I opened Perkins & Son Ship's Chandlery. With nothing but our personal belongings, a pair of Vise-grip pliers and some old books we embarked on the retail life. The Chandlery was located where Mel Fisher's Treasure Museum is now, at the foot of Whitehead Street in Key West. The store was across from the Audubon House where, all day long, I heard the toot-toot of the Conch Train as it carried tourists on a historic tour of old Key West. I also heard the amplified, singsong voice of the Conch Train drivers as they passed the chandlery "…and the White Crown Pigeon… was found DEAD… strangled in the Wires…" Hour after hour, day after day.

One afternoon, the owners of the building, held a meeting without advising us, and decided to cancel our lease, immediately. The situation appeared to be a total catastrophe. We had our whole life in that store, piles of used marine gear we'd collected or taken on consignment and nowhere else to go. We were nobodies. They gave us a month to move out. I knew we were screwed. I was wrong.

A couple days later my new friend, who I met at the Full Moon Saloon, and mentor-to-be, Southernmost Leonard, who I'd met at the Full

Moon Saloon, walked into the store. Leonard was, in addition to being a random miracle, a mild-mannered engineer and although he was an American, he called himself a "Scandahoovian." He had some money and good business sense. I spilled my guts and told him our tale of woe. "Well it looks like you need a place to move, " he said. "Let's go buy one."

"Right, Len, let's go buy one… ha ha."

"Yeah," he said. "Let's go buy one."

And we did. In 1984, we bought a store, an old building at 901 Fleming Street, built in 1897. Len put up the cash. We paid for our half of the building over the following years out of the store proceeds.

The Conch Train drivers were always making up anecdotes about the island's history.

One day, I was hanging a new fiberglass reproduction of a figurehead above the second floor balcony. It was still swinging on the lines when a Conch Train came by. The driver noticed the figurehead. He pointed up and announced to the passengers, "See that figurehead up there on the Chandlery, folks? It's been there for over *one hundred* years!"

Sometime later, a guy named Monkey Tom stopped by the chandlery, "Hey, Roof, you want to buy some rope?" He never did get my name right.

I'd known Monkey Tom for years. He was a world-class swimmer. He came to Key Weird and started to smoke a little too much of the hallowed herb. One night he bought a monkey from a desperate person. He and the monkey became inseparable and every sunset Tom jumped into the ocean off Mallory Square and swam across the main ship channel to Christmas Tree Island. Tom pulled hard against the tide with the monkey on his head. No matter the weather or the current, Tom and the monkey headed off across the channel. I was amazed at the pure adventure of it. They always made it, until one night on the island, when someone reportedly killed the monkey and ate it. Tom went over the edge. He never came back and was given the name Monkey Tom. His paintings are highly collectible to this day.

Monkey Tom led me down to the 'Toxic Triangle" at the end of Grinnell Street to see the rope. It was somebody else's rope, I guessed. Tom said he found it in the bushes. There was grass growing on it and bird-shit all over. It was nice rope, so I said, "Sure Tom, I'll buy that. How much you want?"

"Twenny bucks."

I bought it, peeled the grass off, shook the scorpions out, and toted it back to the store. The first thing #2 said was, "What are you going to do with that?"

"I'm going to use it on my tow boat," I said.

"You don't have a tow boat," she said.

"I know, but I will."

I launched a dramatic campaign at the USCG District Office. The campaign involved whining, moaning, good behavior, groveling and letters from friends. With the help of my parole officer (a good guy) I eventually got my Captain's license back and launched Key West Harbor Service. I wanted to operate a marine salvage business. It was the only thing I knew how to do, besides getting arrested.

Chapter 23

Friend or Faux

One afternoon, after picking up a six-pack, I met Mr. Clarence Hollett, also known as "Mr. Doodlebug" in the parking lot at the Winn Dixie super market. He was sitting on the rear bumper of his beat-up Dodge van trying to figure out how to reach his artificial leg that had fallen off and rolled under the van. The prosthesis was an old plastic model that he'd picked up at a pawnshop. The flesh tone paint was flaking off. I pulled the limb out from under the van and handed it to Hollett. "This dang stump jez don't fit quite right," he mumbled and eyed my beer. I offered to help, "No thanks son, it's between me an' my leg, dang thang," and kicked at the pre-owned prosthesis with his good leg. After he got his stump on Mr. Doodlebug introduced himself, "I'm knowed as Mister Doodlebug."

"Howdy Doodle, I'm knowed as Reef."

"Nice to meet you, Grief."

Doodlebug pushed his dog and two cats out of the way and rummaged through a pile of smelly cardboard boxes to produce these newspaper articles.

> *The Cumberland Newspaper, October 9, 1978*
> "Most dowsers seem to like nothing better than to regale skeptics with their accomplishments. Clarence Hollett of Willow Shade, Ky., styles himself as "Mr. Doodlebug." In the dowser lexicon, doodlebugs are a special breed — diviners for oil. Hollett, a rotund, barrel-chested man, says he has found wells that produce 1,000 bbl. a day and, if only he hadn't been swindled by so-called friends, he might be a millionaire. He also dabbles in healing and dowses for gold. "Don't believe me?" he asks, and promptly borrows a gold ring from a cynical listener. Hollett's divining rod is a single leaf of spring steel about 2 ft. long and weighted at the far end. Holding the rod in one hand

and the ring in the other he smugly watches as the steel bends toward the ring. "Guess you got gold there," he says, laughingly brushing off the suggestion that the rod's natural tension caused the bending."

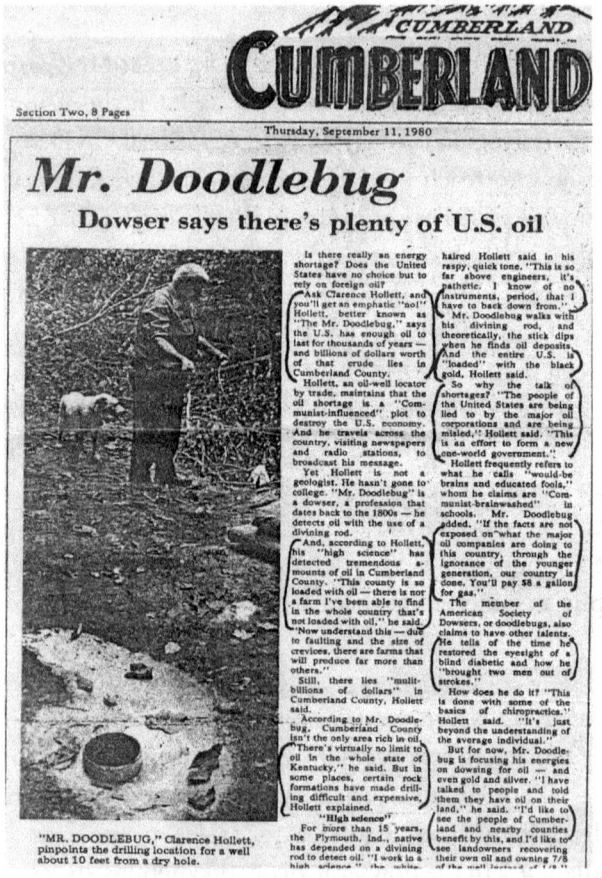

Doodlebug Story

I handed the papers back to Doodle, suitably impressed.

"I douse for gold, too, got me a resonator and I know where's there's a shit load of it, but I need some help getting to it." Mr. Doodlebug told me. "We'll need a boat, a couple guys, a magnetometer, a dredge pump and a bottle of whiskey."

"I got 'em all," I said.

"Let's be pardners, we'll split the gold!"

"OK Doodle, let's do it."

I went home and told #2 that I was going up the Keys with a professional dowser to find gold. As proof of my sanity and the potential value of the project I showed her the article. "Right," she remarked.

White-who had returned to Key West to work with me in the salvage business-and I gathered up all the necessary equipment, put my small boat on a trailer and headed up the Keys with Doodlebug following in his van. After the third time his van broke down, we loaded him and his menagerie into my truck and continued on. Doodle kept looking out the back window "In case," he said, "some sumbitch is following us, them needle-dicked bug fuckers been trackin' me for years, but I got their number."

We stopped for gas near Jewfish Creek and were about to pull back on US Highway 1. Out of nowhere a good-looking girl appeared; she stood by the roadside with her thumb out. She hadn't been there ten minutes ago when we pulled in.

From the backseat Doodlebug said, "You boy's best pick her up."

Things were getting weird. I thought maybe we were being set up, that she was working with Doodle and was going to pull a gun and take all our rusty, mildewed gear. But, she was good to look at, so we picked her up.

"Where ya'll goin'?" I twanged, testing the waters.

"Nowheres."

About ten miles up the road she said, "This here is close enough." I pulled over and she got out. There was nothing around us but swamp.

"Women!" Doodlebug said as the door slammed. We cracked a beer and headed up US Highway 1 towards the gold.

By now it was getting late. We unloaded all the gear and got ready to start "trolling for gold." Doodlebug pulled out his divining rods, two pieces of copper tube and two bent coat hangers. Then he pulled out the "resonator." He asked White to walk out into the water about fifty yards offshore and hold the resonator. Meanwhile, it was too shallow for me to get the boat in close to shore so Doodlebug had to walk along the mangroves and through the mud to get to it. About half way out his "stump" got sucked off into the mud. We heard it, *sluupsh* ... so White and I walked back in and with Mr. Doodlebug hanging off the guano-caked limb of a nearby gumbo-limbo tree. White and I dug in the mud for Doodle's stump.

We found it but he couldn't get it back on in the water because when he stood on his one good leg to put it on, the good leg sank into the mud. So we stuck an inner tube under his ass, inflated it, and towed him out to the boat. Doodlebug used his plastic leg as a paddle. Once onboard the boat we could hear Doodle's dog barking madly onshore as we went up and down the beach towing the magnetometer. We waited for the beeping sound to alert us that we had found gold. Mr. Doodlebug got to talking and told us about the gold. Doodle said he'd met an old swamp rat who had told him this story.

"Years ago this protected bay was knowed to pirates. The shortest route for a sailing vessel to cross from the Bahamas and get fresh water from the swamp. Someone buried a chest full of gold near shore, they didn't make it back and two brothers, who lived in the swamp, it was all swamp, somehow came across the gold buried in the sand right near the high tide line along the beach. For years the brothers came into a camp set up by the Florida East Coast Railway Co. They were building the Overseas Railroad. In the camp was a general store where workers bought their simple food and supplies. They paid with gold coins. None of the merchants told the other merchants about it. They each thought that only they knew about the gold coins. Some of the merchants set out to follow the brothers and, after numerous bug bites, found only each other, hiding in the bushes. The brothers were not fools. They knew they were being watched and screwed but didn't care. They had so much gold it didn't matter. When they needed money the brothers walked along the beach and, when the tide was right, dug up a few coins with their feet. They held them between their toes and kept on a walking." White looked at me and I looked at White. We smiled.

For three hours we hunted for the gold. I wanted to believe we would find it, but it was getting dark, the mosquitoes and no see'ums had joined the hunt. Finally Doodlebug said to me, "Grief, go get my gun, it's in my duffle." He never did get my name right. He thought we were going to kill him when we found the gold, we thought he was going to kill us. White and I looked at each other, not smiling. I went ashore, got the gun, a snub nose .38 revolver and gave it to Doodle. He never checked the gun to see if it was loaded. I had. The bullets are with the gold.

Finally darkness and the bugs overwhelmed us. In the end, Mr. Clarence Hollet, "the Doodlebug," went up the Keys and off into history, a remnant of Americana. It was a grand chase, one day in a life, all or nothing and then he was gone, but the gold was still there. I was sure of it.

I couldn't stop thinking about the gold and a few months later I brought two divers, twin brothers Bob and Bruce Lima into the hunt. They were treasure hunters from California living on their catamaran sailboat in Key West. The Lima's had experience in treasure hunting. I met them a few years before as they sailed through Key West on the way to Colombia, South America. Bob and Bruce looked like the Hardy Boys gone bad. They were both about five-foot-six inches tall, short guys, but built like rocks. Bald-headed squat pieces of rock. I wouldn't say they were world famous but, in certain circles, they were well respected. They were the treasure hunting world's version of a SEAL team. Nobody messed with them. They made their first treasure find at the ocean end of the Chagres River as it pours out of Colombia, South America. Diving at night in the river mouth where the sharks came to feed they searched for gold. If you got caught by the *Federales*, you were put in prison for the rest of your life, if not executed and your boat was confiscated. You disappeared off the wet, puckered lips of the planet earth.

When the Limas arrived in Key Largo to help me locate the treasure, the treasure that only I knew about....har! har! I asked Bob about the resonator.

"Oh, yeah," Bob said. "We've got one of those. We've been working on it for about six years." They performed a test for my benefit. I took my gold wedding ring and buried it a quarter mile away, underwater, along the east side of US 1. It took two hours to find it.

Bob and Bruce had heard about Doodlebug. They said he was the real McCoy.

Bruce most innocently asked where the treasure was. I made a big show of pulling out a chart. I unfolded it and said "It's right here, pointing at a five square mile area, I'll tell you when we gets there... I ain't no fool, you know!" There was some embarrassed laughter. We took my truck, went up to Key Largo and tested the area where Doodlebug and I had been. There were "very strong readings" in the area according to Bruce. Hoo boy, we're rich!

The resonator is based on the assumption that everything has its own resonance or frequency. The resonator sends out vibrations that are the same as the material you're trying to find. The vibes from the gold set up a resonant pathway that, according to Doodle and the Limas, can be located by walking back and forth between the resonator and the gold. You are on the line when the rods cross. Then you move the resonator and repeat the process. When these lines are laid out on a chart they will cross where the gold is. Theoretically.

The Lima brothers sailed up from Key West and crossed over into the Gulf of Mexico, at Jewfish Creek, then back up into the Everglades. They ghosted along through the mangroves and shallows eventually anchored in the Everglades National Park on the west side of Route 1 near the 18- Mile Stretch. Lots of people visited this area because it was legal to fish there. But it was illegal to do anything else, especially treasure hunting. The Marine Patrol came by several times and checked Bob and Bruce out. That was fine, because they weren't doing anything, during the day. You could search their boat and not find a piece of equipment. While in Colombia, they had all their gear built into hidden lockers so it wouldn't be confiscated; and even if you saw the equipment you probably wouldn't know what it was.

They sat around during the day, fishing poles over the side, pretending to fish, but as soon as it got dark, overboard they would go, into the night swamp. Bad beavers on the hunt.

Night after night they blew holes the size of a Toyota in the mud bottom looking for the Gold.

It was a mud bottom so they had to dig fast. With currents, and the viscosity of the mud, the holes filled in quickly, leaving little evidence of dredging. They went through the mud like earthworms in wet suits. The airlift worked well if you had an isolated target area, the dredge lifted the mud, but not the gold.

Although they worked for a month they never found the gold. Bob said he knew it was there. "We've never had such a strong signal and we've been doing this for seven or eight years. It works; it has to be here," they told me. It wasn't. Eventually, they gave up and went back to Key

West leaving the "treasure" for other fools to find. Or did they find it and not tell me? Treasure hunting is not a good hobby for the trusting soul.

I used to be, and probably still am, a dowser. My ex-grandfather-in-law said, "You can take somebody and show them the method, then they can either do it, or they can't." That makes sense to me. At grandpa's direction I cut a forked willow branch from a nearby tree. I held the "tines" and twisted the tip so that it was pointing slightly upward then walked around the yard. When I passed over what must been ground water the tip went down so strongly it wrenched the forked branch out of my hand, cutting me with the bark. I was a natural! I was a dowser! I was bleeding! Note: Be sure to empty your bladder before dowsing or you may suffer a nasty lick.

On one trip home to visit my dad, Bob, he said he wanted to put down another well somewhere on his four acres. I told him I could find the right spot.

"How are you going to do that?" he asked.

"I'll dowse it."

"Jesus Christ, Kid you've got to stop smoking so much weed, you smoke too much of that shit."

"Just let me find the water, Bob," I insisted.

He didn't have any willow tree and instead, I rigged up 3/8" diameter copper tubes with coat hangers bent at 90 degrees like Doodle's. With my divining rods I walked around our four acres of lawn. A little while later, "Right here, Bob, (kicking a hole in the new sod) is probably where the water is," I said.

"Fine, thanks," he stared at the hole in the new grass and shook his head, "see you later."

Bob didn't get around to drilling until a year later, but when he did, in the spot I showed him, the water was there, 25 feet down. He called me, which was rare. "You got lucky," he said.

"That's tough." I replied, smiling at the phone.

Chapter 24

Salvage Daze

I'd met Doc in the Cayman Islands several years before he came to Key West. He was a swarthy fellow with glasses and the gift of gab. He came to Key West in 1984. He'd been a teacher at a small college in New Jersey. He got bored. He wanted to stay in Key West, had come into a little money and asked if I wanted to go into some kind of business with him.

"Sure," I said, "let's start salvage and towing business! I've got the tow line!"

"Ah, Okay," he said, "Great! ... Ah... What's salvage?"

I quoted the definition of Marine Salvage by Captain "Black Bart" Bartholomew U.S.N.

"A science of vague assumptions based on debatable figures taken from inconclusive experiments and performed with instruments of problematic accuracy by persons of doubtful reliability and questionable mentality."

"That sounds good." Doc said.

But Doc was difficult as a partner, the kind of person who was overwhelmed by the concept of hard work, well, not so much the concept but the actual doing. I went down to our wrecking station in the Toxic Triangle at the end of Grinnell Street one morning where he hung out and lived. "Hey partner, I've got a job. Can you come out and give me a hand with this?" I asked.

"I'm pretty busy today."

"Oh, doing what?"

"I have to go to the post office." He was serious. For him going to the post office was a day's work. He could talk, though. He talked about building large ships; he talked about sailing around the world. He had been a teacher, so he could talk about anything. He was not a silent partner.

When Doc and I started the salvage business, it was up to me to find the boat. I looked around Florida but none of the builders were interested, or perhaps did not know how to build the boat we needed. I knew enough about the demands of the salvage business not to try and convert a lobster boat. If I didn't get it right the first time I would be out of business. We had to buy a new boat for the purpose, a custom-built towboat. I looked all over the country and finally found Tom Carney at Thomas Marine on Long Island in New York. Tom could build the boat we needed, the twenty-six foot aluminum salvage vessel *Ranger*. I named her after the *Lone Ranger*. *Tonto* just didn't sound right.

I flew up to Long Island and talked with Tom. I told him what I wanted, where to put the fuel tank, where to locate most of the weight, everything. I knew my shit. When I finally completed my summary Tom looked at me, "Them's some pretty good ideas, but I won't build it that way, Grief."

"Ah, it's Reef."

"Sorry."

"Why not? It's my boat."

"It's not your boat yet, son," he said. "And I'm going to build you the boat you need or you can kiss off." Crisp, down east, a point well taken.

"OK."

Of course, he was right and was enough of a gentleman to save me the extra $30,000 worth of junk that I had insisted he put on the boat, all of which would have proven to be totally useless. The one thing I asked for, and he agreed to do, was install an extra four inch diameter zinc on the keel to protect the aluminum hull. A zinc is a sacrificial anode that corrodes quicker than the aluminum and protects the aluminum from corrosion.

"Okay, Riff" (danged down-east accent) he said, "I'll put an extra zinc on the keel, but when you're done with the boat, send me the zinc back. I can reuse it."

Twenty-two years later I did. Tom Carney knew exactly what he was doing. If only I had been that smart.

During that winter on Long Island, before the boat was finished, I went to see how construction was coming along. The *Ranger* was in an unheated shed. I climbed into the boat and lay down on the frozen aluminum plate in the forward cabin. After awhile Tom came out to see if I was alive. He asked what I was doing. "I'm getting to know her, Tom. My life will depend on this boat and I want her to like me." Tom smiled and walked away.

When the salvage vessel *Ranger* was completed she was trucked down from New York to Miami on a trailer. I took my five-year-old son and a crew to deliver the *Ranger* from Miami to Key West. It was her first time in the southern ocean and she liked warm water. My towing business was officially started and now I had the boat to go with the towline! Although I had been trained in ship salvage I was worried my military experience might not apply in the civilian world of small pleasure boats.

Soon after the *Ranger* arrived in Key West, I was at the counter in the chandlery when I got a landline call from a taxicab company relaying a message from a cabbie up the Keys. The cab driver had overheard a call on his CB radio from three guys who were out fishing in the Atlantic Ocean. The driver notified the dispatcher and he in turn told me that some guys were adrift in their eighteen-foot bass boat about six miles offshore in what they described as the "Big Lake." I called White-working with me again-to meet me at the *Ranger.*" It's our first tow!" I told him.

"Oh boy, here we go!" said White

When we arrived on scene, we spied three cowboys complete with cowboy shirts, boots and Stetson hats. They were sitting in a small aluminum, fresh-water, inland lake bass boat. They had lost power and drifted into the Gulf Stream. It would be dark in three hours. They only had a CB radio, not a marine VHF radio and it was before cell phones.

"How much is this going to cost, Pardner?" were the first words out of their leathery lips.

"Are you going to charge us for coming out here?" one twanged.

"Absolutely," I said. "And I'm going to charge you for going back in, too." I started making ready to take them undertow. One cowboy looked at White, then at me, and started carrying on again about money, getting rude and downright insulting about how much it was going to cost. I looked at White. He grinned, nodded and kicked the boat away letting it drift farther into the Gulf Stream where, after a few months, the bass boat would end up in Nova Scotia. Good bass country. I wondered if this was how all my tows would begin.

After a brief but poignant conversation among themselves the whining cowboy's buddies jumped up off their western buttocks. They were shocked that we'd kicked them loose and began to sober up which stunned them even more. They took off their cowboy hats and started whupping on the rude guy. "Shut up, you dumb sumbitch," the remaining two twanged in unison. One of the guys reached into his pocket and came out waving a fistful of frog skins, the dollar bills were blowing all over the place, loose change falling in the bilge. "Don't leave us here, Mister! ... and you, you shut up, you dumb sumbitch..." They tossed their empty Bud cans at him and muttered profanities as we towed them back to port. They were a long way from a West Texas Grand Ballroom now.

In the beginning all the money I made in the towing business was going into paying rent, insurance, fuel and buying inventory for the Chandlery; I wasn't taking home a penny. It was twelve years before I got my first big salvage job. I worked the *Ranger* as much as I could. The rest of my time was spent helping with the Chandlery and doing marine surveys, all while being on call twenty-four-seven. I ran the towing and salvage company for twenty-two years until 2006 when my adrenalin began to run low.

One cold winter day, with a howling north wind, White and I were working a distressed charter dive boat, the *Lady Godiver* out of Cudjoe Key. The *Lady Godiver* had lost power and was driven aground north of Key West on the remote Content Keys. The passengers and crew had been taken off by the Coast Guard when we arrived. I anchored *Ranger*. White got into the dinghy and I let it drift back until he could jump onboard the rolling *Lady Godiver*. The winds and seas increased and, with White onboard, drove the vessel across the reef and into the mangroves a couple of miles to the south. I recovered the dinghy and headed back to port to load more equipment and supplies. The wind continued to increase. We would have to wait until the weather calmed down before we could tow the wreck out to safety. White "volunteered," using a loose interpretation of the word, to stay with the boat and guard it until we could proceed. Actually, he didn't have to guard the wreck, no one could get to it, but since I couldn't get him ashore, I tried to make the situation sound important. White doesn't remember it quite as fondly as I do. I called White on his hand held VHF radio. "White, old pal, I guess you'll have to ah ... guard the wreck! That's it, guard the wreck! ... ah, it could take a few days."

"A few days!" White remarked one night, years later, at a party. "It felt longer. I was stuck in those mangroves with a norther' pounding down on me for close to a week! To stay warm I crawled inside the small cabin while the *Godiver* pounded on the fucking mangrove roots. The anchor was hooked around the bushes somewhere to the east. The *Godiver* was heeled over on her side. I was going to be there for a while. The next day, after flipping over in the 17' Boston Whaler trying to get to me from shore, Reef swooped by overhead in a Cessna 172 high-wing airplane. The winds aloft were fifty knots or more. Fantasy Dan, the pilot, had removed the passenger door and Reef was hanging out on a harness holding a duffle bag. After several passes he dropped the duffle, holding supplies, near the boat. Near is the key word. I was there for three more frigging days, getting the odd aerial drop.

I was bored out of my skull. One re-supply mission, Reef dropped in a bag with an AM/FM radio, headphones and a little battery taped to it. I recovered the bag after it smashed into the mangroves, one earphone was broken and wires were hanging out everywhere. I stuck the remaining earphone in my ear and tried to get some music. It shorted-out and almost fried my eardrum, but it was something different and felt good in a way. The next time Reef came by, it was urgent because I was hungry, real hungry and had no fresh water and no CIGARETTES!" White looked up from his story for understanding and sympathy from the other smokers.

"Reef swooped in with the airplane, just like Snoopy and the Red Baron," White continued, "and after several passes he dropped a waterproof bag. But he missed, no surprise, he'd missed every time before. The bag landed deep in the mangroves. I could hear it crash through the bush. It was getting dark so I radioed him, "You missed, asshole! I'll never find it in the mangroves. It's lost, it's gone, I can't get to it...It's getting dark, goddamn it! I quit!"

Reef radioed back. 'You can't quit...You'll find it...Your Cigarettes ARE IN THERE! You've got a flashlight, go get it.'

I can't quit? I said.

"No."

Oh.

"Smokes?"

'Si, in the bag, nothing further, Out.' said Reef. After an hour in the mud I did manage to find the damn bag. I was on that boat for two more days… it was great fun if you like being alone in the bushes, eating cold smashed food and swatting bugs… I do." Four days after she wrecked we were able we put lift bags under the *Lady Godiver* and tow her out.

It was still winter and on the way back from another job, White spotted a small sailboat capsized and adrift and, some distance from the capsized boat, a girl was floating on her back. Her top had come off. It was winter. She could die from hypothermia. White, always alert and a man who could spot a set of tits a mile away cried, "Tits ahoy!!" We banked into a hard starboard turn, motored over and picked her out of the water. We got her onboard and made her as comfortable as we could. Meanwhile, her boyfriend swam over and scratched noisily alongside the *RANGER* pleading for help, his salt-soaked fingernails clawing at the new decals on the side of the boat. We'd just put them on. "Hep me, hep me!" he whined and sank lower in the water.

White, not to be distracted from his ministrations said, "Hey, cool it man, it's not all about you. Breast stroke, I mean swim, back to your boat and get it ready to tow."

Salvage work was never dull and that suited my mood. The promise of physical danger prevented boredom as it had most of my life. The minute you thought you knew everything, got too carefree, or thought you had it licked, that was the minute you were screwed. I always remember watching my little brother plough into the ski lift and the lesson I learned that day. The sea is always changing, always fickle, never predictable and without mercy or emotion. I knew that any day I could be gone. I gave up being afraid a long time before but I knew that in order to reap the benefits of any endeavor, you must be present to win. "Constant vigilance is a sailor's price for safety."

The Coast Guard called me one day in the early 90's. It was my first commercial dive job in Key West. A Coast Guard SES cutter (Surface

Effect Ship) backed down and wrapped one-hundred feet of two-inch nylon line in its starboard propeller and the line had melted onto the shaft. The ship's Captain was embarrassed because he backed over his own dock lines and instead of shutting the engines down, he'd spun the propeller faster trying to cut the line loose. Dumb. All he accomplished was to slam the ship into the pier, melt the line and lock up the prop shaft. The Captain had already requested the Navy Explosive Ordinance Disposal team to come over to have a look. They hadn't been able to fix it. The EOD's wanted to use explosives to blow the whole propeller off, but the Captain wouldn't agree. It was too dangerous. The regular Navy divers said they'd need a new $5,000 underwater hydraulic saw, and finally the Army divers came over and said, "Nope, that won't work; you're going to have to tow this boat up to the shipyard in Virginia."

Smokin' Joe McCollum, the Coast Guard engineering officer, called me as a last resort. That was comforting. He said, "Reef, do you have any other ideas that we don't know about, something above and beyond, because we've already had professional military divers here."

"Professionals huh…Ah…Yeah, I've got an idea. Give me an hour and I'll come over."

So I called Bob Lima, from the Doodlebug gold story. Bob now worked for me.

"Bob, we got a little job here."

I took a screwdriver and sharpened the end, then rounded the tip off. I brought along a short-handled mallet and a dull shark hook. Bob and I boarded the *RANGER* and motored over to the Coast Guard base.

"Ok, Bob, put these tools down the front of your pants." Bob was only wearing a sweatshirt and blue jeans for protection, even though it was winter.

We pulled up at 1600 hours; it was already getting dark and we saw fifteen Coast Guard guys standing on the dock. Everyone was ready to go home. They hoped the fouled line would give the Captain an excuse to delay their deployment. We motored in and tied up to the bulkhead behind the ship. Bob started putting his dive gear on and the Coast Guard guys looked at us like we were from Mars. Perhaps they had expected more sophisticated equipment than blue jeans, flip-flops and a sweatshirt.

I said, "Ok, Bob, go get her." He jumped and went straight down. Bob didn't bob.

We only had one tank of air. An hour passed. An hour and a half passed. We all stood around scratching ourselves. The Coast Guard guys were wondering what the heck was going on. Had Bob drowned? I wasn't worried. Bob Lima was a serious diver and he knew how to breathe. I call it "frog mode." Using the brain, you cut off oxygen to unneeded organs or muscles, except the brain. This can be accomplished with a little practice, and Bob had practiced.

The Coast Guard guys were bored and wanted to go into town. The Captain thought Bob had drowned and was worried about liability. The crew started out being gracious and polite, but an hour later they were sniping, "Who are these assholes, anyway?" They wanted me to hear them. I kept waiting for Bob. I could still see his bubbles so I knew he wasn't dead. The Coast Guard guys had given up, I think. All they knew was a guy had gone in the water with one tank an hour and a half earlier, he didn't have a single tool with him and there was no noise. I could hear them muttering on the concrete bulkhead nearby.

"Who are these freaking clowns, anyway?" was a not-so whispered, often repeated inquiry.

The Captain wouldn't let the crew leave because they were supposed to be departing on a mission as soon as the shaft was cleared. The Coast Guard guys were getting genuinely pissed off. They could smell the conch fritters and beer just a few blocks away.

The pungent harbor water was dark and cold, and the winter light faded fast. Finally, Bob bobbed to the surface behind *Ranger*. None of the Coast Guard boys could see any tools because Bob had stuffed them back in his pants. Bob came up holding a fifteen-pound collar of molten line. He'd cut and pried until he got through about three inches of melted plastic, cut it on a 45-degree angle, twisted it and BORK! There it was.

"Got 'er, Bob?" I said calmly, but loud enough for everyone to hear.

"Got 'er, Reef," he said back just as casually. He flipped the collar of melted line onto the dive platform. It made a *"thunk"* when it hit the aluminum plate.

The Captain stood nearby as Bob hauled himself up onto the dive platform.

"How the fuck did you do that?" he asked.

"I was just about to ask you the same thing," said Bob as he smiled and honked out a lugey.

After that, I got all the diving work with the military, the National Transportation Safety Board, FBI, DEA and NOAA. All kinds of ships, all kinds of initials and, all kinds of problems.

There were four Surface Effect Ships stationed in Key West at the time, operated and maintained by the Coast Guard. Smokin' Joe was the engineering officer for the USCG Surface Effect Ships and a very innovative thinker. I helped him in the research and development of these one-hundred-ten foot vessels that rode on a cushion of air trapped between two outer hulls. One problem was the big rubber seals, called fingers that trapped air between the hulls at the bow and the stern. The stern tube or seal weighed two-thousand pounds and needed to be custom cut to fit each hull.

One afternoon, Joe and I rode inside the aft bag while the ship was underway. We were trying to determine "the wrinkle factor" as he called it, so we could cut the seal to fit properly between the hulls. We sat inside the seal with our dive gear on in case things went south. This hadn't been tried before. Trapped in a pulsating, one-ton black rubber bag, under a one-hundred-ten foot ship careening down the Northwest Channel at forty knots, me and Smokin' Joe smoked cigars and laughed like kids, laughed like the fools we were. The kind of day I lived for. We kept those 100-ton whoopee cushions going for almost 5 years.

On the evening of August 8, 1994, the University of Miami, Rosenstiel Marine and Atmospheric Science School research vessel *Columbus Iselin* was conducting sonar research south of Looe Key Reef in a calm sea. It was 2330 hours. The ship was outfitted with the latest electronic navigation systems designed to research, monitor and protect the delicate coral reefs of the Florida Keys; one of the world's most highly protected ecological systems. The most modern and sophisticated navigation electronics known to man were installed onboard the *Columbus Iselin* as she motored along the front of the reef. It was nighttime, they could not see land, they could not see the reef and no one could see the tragedy waiting to befall them.

The incident started when someone farted on the bridge. As the unpleasantness wafted through the wheelhouse neither officer bothered to check the depth sounder as they exited the bridge. The *Columbus Iselin* hit the corals and abruptly came to grief on Looe Key Reef.

The salvage of the *Columbus Iselin* was both comical and sad. The USCG called for the tug *Captain Jim*, owned by Jimmy Felton to assist. I was the Captain. Duke Pontin, another salvor was on scene when we arrived. Duke came on board the *Captain Jim* and I radioed the *Iselin*. "What happened?" was the obvious first question.

"Somebody farted," the radioman replied. There was not much else to be said at that point. We anchored nearby, upwind, and I dove under the ship to survey the situation. It would be better, I thought, to take her off the reef and risk holing her rather than to leave her pounding on the reef to be taken off later when she would surely be holed…No?

Back onboard the tug I started pulling, full power ahead, on a four-inch nylon hawser.

Columbus Iselin

The roiling prop wash turned the sea white as *Captain Jim* tugged mightily. We were making progress, moving the ship backwards, inch by inch. We'd moved it about five feet when the USCG stopped us.

In certain complicated civilian situations the military is not schematically equipped to make quick decisions. Instead they stop everything, hoping for someone higher up to make a decision and therefore take responsibility for the eventual fuck-up.

The USCG decided to bring the Navy and a big salvage company into the job. A Coast Guard official boarded the tug. We were ordered to stand down and maintain a presence one-mile away. "But wait," I said, "it's moving, it's coming off, let's do it!"

"Wait, it could *possibly* have a hole in it!" he said.

"I know that, and it does have a small one," I said and pointed. "But look, it's moving, it's getting more floatation ...we...see... we're going to patch the hole. But we've got to get it off the reef before the *possible* hole can become an authentic hole."

"Huh?"

He made us stop. We were left on the job, but put under the "command" of a pipe-smoking young Lieutenant sent down from the Navy Supervisor of Salvage (SUPSALV) in Washington DC. We met on the bridge of the *Captain Jim*. The lieutenant had a computer with all the latest Navy salvage programs, the best in the world. He punched in his calculations and was working through the program. Finally, after I had been standing there for some time he looked over at me and puffed, "What are you doing?"

"I'm the salvager."

He looked at me as if I were a sea turd and turned his computer away to make sure I couldn't see his plan. I moved to the left, he turned the computer to the left. "Oh, you're the salvager, huh?"

"That's right, I am and I could have taken the *"Columbus Stink-bomb"* off the reef yesterday. Now it's been pounding on the coral for an extra twenty-four hours and it's pretty much assured that any damage to the reef or ship you could have prevented has now taken place."

"Oh, really," he said. "And just what was your plan?"

"Well, now that the ship is in this condition, I'd pump the forward ballast tanks, flood the aft tanks, transfer fuel from the port tank to the starboard side, manually shift any cargo aft and man the pumps."

He turned his computer further away from me. "That's the same as my plan," he sniffed suspiciously.

"I know that. I went to the same school you did, twenty-five years ago."

He puffed, but his pipe was out.

"The only thing to do is to pull it off the reef," I said softly, wondering which smelled worse: the legendary fart or his cheap pipe tobacco.

After she spent almost two days pounding on the once pristine coral reef, a tug out of Miami dragged the battered *Iselin* off. With a small hole in the hull and a large hole in the taxpayers' checkbook, the *Iselin* was towed to Miami for repair.

The story made national publications and after a three-and-a-half year investigation into the *Cause of the Accident* a panel of marine investigators described the incident as "an internal problem." The title of the article that ran in a Professional Mariner magazine summed it up: "Flatulence on the Bridge." A summary of the proceedings.

One of the two officers involuntarily "expelled a gaseous substance" in the confines of the ship's bridge. The unpleasant expulsion reportedly caused both crewmen to simultaneously, and rapidly, exit the area for safety. The helmsman exited to the port wing bridge, the navigation officer to the starboard wing bridge. Each officer then, reportedly, accused the other, yelling profane accusations and vile expletives through the wheelhouse from opposite sides of the bridge all the while facing upwind and, unfortunately, away from the reef. They described their actions as a safety precaution in an attempt to escape the "unpleasantness."

It was the official explanation and they were 'stinking' to it. The "fartee" was never identified nor did anyone confess. There was little evidence and no one seemed inclined to do any field-testing. Both men swore it was the other who committed the grievous act. Who was to be believed?

The insurer of the *Columbus Iselin* paid two million dollars to NOAA for the damage to the reef.

Executive World Headquarters, Key West, 1986

Wrecking Station in the "Toxic Triangle"

It was midnight at the approaches to the Northwest Channel jetty. The winter's cold, salt wind was blowing thirty knots out of the Gulf of Mexico. I listened to the VHF radio 24 hours a day for twenty-two years, waiting for the "big one," the salvage that would make me rich. Half asleep I heard the urgent call, "Mayday! Mayday!"

After a long sail from St. Petersburg, an elderly couple was making their approach, north of Key West. They were under full sail when they hit the Northwest Channel granite jetty.

The Coast Guard radioed back, "What is your position, how many people onboard?"

"We've run aground on the Northwest Channel jetty…" was the last, and only reply.

That was it. The man and wife were gone when we got there. They must have tired, trying to hold onto the rigging, and been swept out to sea. We're just food for the planet.

We searched all night for the crew with no luck. In the morning we went ashore to get more gear and eat, then returned to the sixty-foot wooden sailboat just after daylight. The USCG informed us that the wreck had to be removed; it was a hazard to navigation. The sailboat sank on its side after being holed as she washed across the jetty. Sea foam swirled like the top of a Piña Colada around the granite rip-rap rocks as White and I inspected the wreck to see if we could do anything to patch the hole. We attached two one-thousand-pound lift bags to the starboard chain plate and filled them with air. We weren't able to lift it off the bottom far enough to run a line under so I dove underneath the hull in my wetsuit and dive gear. I could see the hole in the keel but couldn't reach it.

I was trying to dredge a hole in the mud and marl to get a line through to the other side, so we could lift the vessel from the keel. I was digging away, using an air hose to blow out some of the mud and sand. In the middle of this attempt, the tank I used to blow the sand away ran out of air. The pressure fell off and the sand, faster than quicksand, suctioned back into the hole. This was bad. My arm was trapped under the keel. I couldn't pull it free without injury.

While I was under the hull, the lift bags were swinging back and forth, pushed by the breaking seas. One of them, on my side, caught a cotter pin on a lower shroud and it cut a hole in a bag. It deflated fast. This meant one side of the boat was supported by an air bag and the other one wasn't.

The boat rolled over on top of me and pinned me under the hull. Most of me was up inside the curve of the hull, where the hole was. It was unpleasant and it began to get on my nerves after a while. White rigged up another air bag and freed me. Now we were out of lift bags and there was no room for error. I went back down and got the line through. We towed the sailboat back to Key West. It sank six more times on the way in. It turned out not to be the "Big One." I was out of adrenalin and explored the remote possibility that I was beginning to age.

One sunny morning, in 1994, a Chalks Airlines airplane crashed into the sea immediately after taking off near Christmas Tree Island in Key West Harbor. The two pilots were killed.

A Nasty Affair

The National Transportation Safety Board called me because some other salvors, working on the plane, kept flipping it over and ripping pieces off. I jumped in and got it rigged quickly. There wasn't much damage left to be done, so I looked good. Timing is everything. After that I got every airplane job in the Keys that the National Transportation Safety Board was involved with. If a component failed on an aircraft, the NTSB wanted to do as little damage to the carcass as possible so they could find out what happened and whom to blame. They wanted the wreck brought up in one piece if possible. During most of these jobs I was the working salvage diver, the one in the water doing the work, because I was the one with the most training. Let that be a lesson to me.

During another job, we picked up a sunken plane, first using lift bags, then employed a fifty-ton crane to set it on a barge. Filling lift bags is an art. Lift bags are like industrial whoopee cushions. You sink them to the wreck, tie them around the hull, think about what might happen and start inflating. As the lift bag fills and rises, the air expands quickly and the lift force accelerates. It gets bigger and bigger and comes up faster and faster. We always tried to figure out how to do a controlled lift. We were rarely successfu

"I don't think she'll fly"

I survived on excitement, hope for a big salvage job, and a dismal cash flow. I did a variety of independent jobs until TowBoat US, a membership service that pays for non-emergency towing service and light salvage, was formed. A woman came down from Boat US Insurance Company and wanted to learn about towing. The Coast Guard was rapidly backing out of the recreational towing business. She spent a few days and I showed her what I did. I got the franchise. Not many small companies were undertaking open-ocean towing or salvage at that time. The Coast Guard had been doing most of it, but the calls for help had become overwhelming and diverted them from their primary mission of saving lives.

In the emergency towing business there was often a human element to deal with and it wasn't always pleasant. I once rescued a couple of guys in the dead of winter.

It was cold and windy when I arrived at a flat sea grass sandbar at the entrance to the Lakes Passage west of Key West. The boat was a go-fast type and was sitting high and dry 100-yards from deep water. I paddled in toward the grounded boat as far as I could in a little rubber raft until I started furrowing the marine landscape with my buttocks. I didn't want to get fined for "butt dredging" in the National Marine Sanctuary. I got out, walked to the boat and banged on the hull. No answer. The boat's name was *Bar Fly* and had been towed down from Detroit on a trailer. I unzipped a weather curtain and saw two guys in the forward cabin. One guy was all the way up in the bow and had a small pit bull dog in front of him. He was hanging on to the dog like a machine gun, one hand holding the dog by the back of the neck and the other holding the dog by the balls.

His buddy, probably the owner of the boat, was threatening Dog Man, yelling, "You stupid asshole!"

The other guy squeezed the dog's nuts and held it out in front of him. It was a fool's standoff.

"Excuse me," I said. "How's it going in here? You boys got a problem?"

"Yeah," said the owner, eyeing the pit bull.

"How'd you get so far up in the mud?"

"These stupid locals," laughed Dog Man. "We were racing one of them and they quit way back there," pointing with the dog toward deep water behind the boat.

"But this dick head wouldn't stop," said the owner, pointing at Dog Man.

"But we won!" chirped Dog Man. The guy was so intent on winning the race he failed to wonder why the other boat had stopped. He augured in.

I took a line back out to *RANGER* and pulled them off. As soon as their boat was in deep water they cranked it up and blowing mud and grass twenty feet in the air headed off at full speed for their next adventure. They made it about half a mile, "TowBoat US, ah...we're aground again," came the call over the VHF radio. These were my kind of people but stupid can get boring.

Chapter 25

A Cast of Characters

On the sea there is an unspoken belief in a greater power. A shapeless deity you can see, taste and touch, a force that gets "hands on" if you don't pay attention and sometimes even if you do. It's real and therefore, for me, easy to believe.

In the 1980's, Captain Edwin E. Crusoe IV was the bar pilot in Key West and responsible for guiding the newly arrived cruise ships through the main ship channel and to the dock at Mallory Square. When he introduced himself he said, "I'm Ed Crusoe, bar pilot, every bar in town." A rotund fellow who lived a hermit's life up the Keys, he loved good red wine and poetry. The Conchs (Conchs are people born in Key West-pronounced Konk) nicknamed him "Blinky." When you talked with him, he blinked continuously, as if he had never heard anyone say such a ridiculous thing before. Some said it was because he stuttered, which he did. It was funny, but not helpful when he gave orders to a tug driver. "C-c-c-c come t-t-t-to huh … h-h-half sp-sp-sp-speed!"

As a poet he wrote with the eyes of a seaman.

"The wind
blew thru
the coconut trees
shaking the leaves
a southeast breeze
through mangrove roots
of the Florida Keys
making waves
on Spanish Harbour."

In the early days Blinky had a navy surplus lifeboat with a one-cylinder Buda diesel engine. He used it for pilot duty. No matter what the weather, Blinky and his mate, JC, would head eight-miles offshore, just past the sea buoy, to rendezvous with a cruise ship. I was running Key West Harbor Services at the time and was occasionally hired by Blinky to take him out to the ship when his boat was busy or broken.

Blinky had a full set of buttocks and when I put him alongside the cruise ship, *Glutton of the Seas,* Blinky had to climb a Jacobs's ladder that hung down the leeward side. It was a forty-foot climb, on a rope ladder straight up a steel wall, a long row to hoe for a man of three-hundred pounds with a satchel on his hip. But no matter, it was his job. Blinky stepped off *RANGER* and grabbed the ladder, risking his life each time he did. As he went up, his pants came down, and by the time he reached the deck, half his butt was hanging out. My crew and I used to bet how much crack he'd show. We used a lobster-measuring stick for scale. From above, the ship's crew laughed heartily until Blinky was on deck. Once there he was in command of that ship.

I went to see him one day, down in the Pilot Shack, at the A&B Restaurant. The shack was smaller than a bathroom and anchored to the concrete by heavy steel cables. Blinky didn't want to lose the Pilot Shack in a hurricane, even though it would be under water. When I arrived he had just finished giving directions to a tourist family. No matter where someone wanted to go Blinky always gave them the address of the dirty bookstore on Duval. He was laughing to himself when I approached.

We walked back into the Pilot Shack. I'd been thinking about becoming a marine surveyor for some time. I and asked Blinky, who was a marine surveyor, how to be a successful surveyor. "Don't fuck up," he said. He pointed to a poster above his mildewed, paper-laden desk. It was a picture of the backside of a fat guy sitting on a park bench with his pants half way down his ass. The caption read, "Just say no to crack." Blinky was an honest man.

Another waterfront character was Choo-Choo Perez. He was a Cuban Godfather. He made a lot of money and he gave a lot away. Got a problem? ... Go see Choo-Choo. He also ran the only ship-docking tug in Key West.

One winter morning, a cruise ship was scheduled to enter Key West Harbor. I was working on a 1200-horsepower pusher tug with Choo-Choo at the helm. This morning an unusual fog rolled in, unusual but not unheard of. The cruise ship was at the sea buoy. Choo-Choo and I were on the tug pushing against the dock to maintain position near the local aquarium and Blinky was on the way out to pilot the ship in. The fog closed in around us. We couldn't see fifty-feet in front of the bow. Over the VHF radio Blinky called out in his best pirate voice, "They'll be no movin's til' I gives the word!"

We waited on the tug. Slowly the fog lifted. Everywhere, everywhere except where Blinky sat drifting westward with the fog. "I am seeing dee sheep, Blink." Choo-Choo accented over the radio.

"They'll be no movin's 'til I gives the word," Blinky's voice crackled back over the airwaves.

We could see the cruise ship six miles away and the cruise ship could see us. They radioed, "Halloo ... tugga boata we can see you!" meanwhile Blinky is reliving a scene from the classic pirate movie "Black Beard the Pirate" where Robert Newton calls out to his crew "They'll be no killin's til I gives the word!"

Slowly, in a thick patch of fog, Blinky drifted away to the west. He was the pilot and he was lost. Choo-Choo, who loved to rankle Blinky, couldn't stop laughing. Finally, I took the microphone from Choo-Choo, " Steer zero-niner-zero, Blink!"

"They'll be no movin's 'til I gives the word!" he hailed again, emerging from the fog a few minutes later. We all cheered.

As part of our work we provided launch service to tugboats and cruise ships.

The old cruise ship *HMS Britannia,* in route from Miami to Jamaica was "hove to" off the Key West sea buoy. The ship's agent called and asked for our help. According to the Captain, a female laundry technician had apparently gone "Kaboomski in her head," and the Captain thought she might be a distraction to the passengers and crew. We motored out to the ship and came alongside. Down the gangway two burly crewmembers carried and dragged a very large woman wrapped in a quickly constructed straightjacket made of garbage bags and duct tape. They were followed by extra duct tape, garbage bags and her personal belongings in a canvas laundry bag. DESPHINA was stencilled on the cloth.

Tombolo, one of my early salvage crew, was mostly deaf, blind in one eye and couldn't see out of the other. His real name was Tommy but I called him Tombolo which in Portuguese means "a dry hump between two wet spots." When Tombolo explained his nickname to girls they looked at him like "*What?*" I guess none of them spoke Portuguese.

Tombolo was waiting on deck when the Captain announced, "This woman, her name is Desphina, is prone to suicide and may attempt to take her life at any moment. Thank you for coming out. Cheerio and Bon Voyage."

"Roger, out," said I.

By the time Desphina was dragged onto our deck, the makeshift straightjacket made out of garbage bags and duct tape started to come loose. I squeezed Desphina into the cabin with Tombolo's help.

Now, instead of calming down, Desphina, the thirty-something, six foot tall, 250-pound crazy woman from Slovenia started to strip off her clothes. Apparently she'd just found out that her boyfriend had left her and she was inconsolable, not that anyone was trying. She pulled off her top, displaying areolas the size of saucers, then made wet, guttural, though not wholly unattractive noises and fondled herself, all the while flopping her monumental breasts around and moaning, "Am sad, am sad," over and over to Tombolo. Tombolo was sympathetic, or maybe just pathetic and wanted to help. He found the duct tape but Desphina took it away from him. She tried to tape Tommy!

"Bolo," I said, giving him a stern eye, "the Captain says she might jump, so block her if she goes for the door."

He gave me his most baleful look. "I don't know if I can take her if she comes at me, Reef." Tombolo weighed about 110 pounds and was five-foot-seven inches tall. "Just hang on, Tombolo, use your body if you have to."

"For what?"

But Desphina didn't go for the door. She went for her crotch. She yanked her uniform pants down right in front of two professional mariners and started masturbating, going at it something fierce, both hands, European style. Her huge eastern European bosoms were flopping back and forth with the sea, and it was getting ripe in the cabin. Tombolo was in the doorway but beginning to turn an unpleasant shade of green. The propeller lost its grip in the following sea and the RPM gauge red-lined as a wave crashed over the stern, flooding the cabin and deck. Things looked grim, and that was before the wave. In the midst of the madness Tombolo worked his magic and talked soothingly to Desphina as she groped for him in a moment of dark passion. Tombolo got Desphina calmed down. I steered for shore when, in a voice filled with unexplained emotion, he told me to go slow so we wouldn't "scare her." I throttled back and stared straight ahead. When we got to the dock an ambulance was waiting and it took four paramedics to get her off (so to speak).

"We gwine home now Tom," I said.

Tombolo looked lonely and watched the ambulance depart, it's drooping rear bumper slammed into the curb. "Am sad," he said with what sounded oddly like a Slovenian accent. Salvage of a different kind. After the Desphina incident I called him Private Parts. He called me Major Fuckup.

On another cruise ship launch service we were asked to take a Jamaican waiter ashore. As we pulled alongside the British Captain advised me that the waiter was "Simply not all there, don't you know. Bit of a bloody loon, what!"

The ship did not have a straightjacket, you would think it would be required, and they had run out of Thorazine, or whatever they use on crazy Jamaicans. The crew put him in a steel gymnasium locker and duct taped it shut. White was on deck. Reggae-Head was banging away in the locker as they lowered it down the gangplank with lines. We eased the banging box onto *Ranger's* rolling deck.

"We can't get the locker in the cabin White. Take him out," I said.

One glance told me this Jamaican was certifiably bug-shit crazy. I radioed the Captain and informed him I would not accept responsibility for a nut-case without supervision, so he put the ship's dive instructor, a stout lad, onboard *Ranger* to hold the Jamaican like a human straightjacket. Once onboard, the dive instructor pinned the Jamaican to the engine hatch and we made ready to head for shore. "Excuse me old chap," said the British Captain over the VHF radio, "but we have another bit of a wicket, a rather sticky wicket, I'm afraid." He paused for what seemed an unusually long time. "… um … ah … actually, old chap … an elderly female passenger appears to have had a bloody heart attack."

Before I could reply, a petite, frail older lady strapped in a Stokes litter was brought down the gangplank. The old lady's husband, the First Officer and a nurse with a cardiac monitoring system also came onboard.

"Thanks so much, *veddy* good show, well played," said the first officer with a jaunty salute as he hauled his British ass back up the gangplank, getting ready to leave us in their wake.

"Righto, no problem, cheers," I said in my best stiff-upper-lip accent.

The British habit of understatement can be dangerous to the inexperienced listener and more so to the speaker. We had seven people on board our twenty-six foot boat. We tried to follow the cruise ship while getting things organized, but we couldn't The ship was accelerating and if we stayed alongside too long the suction would pull us under. We turned away into the sea. It was blowing like hell's fury. We couldn't get the old lady into the cabin because she was strapped to a Stokes litter that wouldn't fit through the door and, even if we could, I didn't want to lay her down on top of the Jamaican. If we turned the litter sideways she'd tumble onto the hard aluminum deck with all her color-coded wires like an oversized marionette. Instead, we laid her down carefully on the deck behind the engine box. The deck was covered with three inches of cold seawater. Onboard were the old lady, the old lady's husband, the nurse with wires, the Jamaican, the dive master/human straightjacket, White and me. The *Ranger* started to take on water because of the all the extra weight. I wanted to power up but the faithful nurse was out on deck, hunched over Grandma, trying to keep her monitoring equipment dry while the old lady's husband gripped the cabin rail and puked into the wind.

White saw the problem, took off his foul weather jacket, sat down on the engine box and leaned over the lady with his jacket spread across his back, arms and knees to keep her and her monitors dry. I pushed the throttle forward. The only problem was White had on his Patagonia shorts and wasn't wearing any underwear. His nut sack slipped out of its assigned position and with his hands employed protecting the old lady and no other offer of assistance; it swung back and forth, above her head, in rhythm with the passing waves. White had to protect the cardiac equipment. He was Mission-Oriented. The old lady lay on the deck with water sloshing all around her. The Jamaican wrestled with the diver, who appeared ready to cry for help after taking a knee in the groin. The husband was puking, and the nurse was getting a cramp. After a few minutes of this, with the situation worsening geometrically, the old lady looked up and saw White hunched over her, his nut sack swinging to and fro in the beam sea. "Young Man! Are you trying to hypnotize me?" she quipped.

It was one of the greatest lines ever spoken at sea. She was alive and present to win. Everyone on the boat cracked up. Even the Jamaican stopped struggling for a minute. He felt it. What a tough old bird. I should write a book I thought.

It was March 1993 and the "Storm of the Century" was fast approaching the Keys. I was out at the sea buoy on another towboat, the *C.O. Jones*, trying to untangle a tug and barge. The tug was making its approach to the Key West sea buoy when the Captain learned of the storm. He turned to head out to sea but wrapped his two-inch steel towing bridle around the sea buoy.

I jumped in the water and rode the wire at the sea-buoy, signalling the tug which way to go to unwrap itself. We finally freed the tug and got underway for safe harbor. I got dressed as the storm closed in.

The cruise ship *Empress of the Seas* was anchored offshore and had a steel barge alongside, used to transfer passengers from the ship to the shuttle boats that took them ashore. The *Empress of the Seas* hailed us on the radio "PAN PAN...Can you help... Can you help? Cannot recover passenger barge." PAN PAN is called out prior to calling MAYDAY. We turned toward the cruise ship and found that they couldn't retrieve the barge because a large steel lifting hook had come loose. They couldn't lift the barge without it slamming into the side of the ship. We came alongside the barge and I tried to grab the lifting cable with a boat hook. It was lashing back and forth and I couldn't do it. There was no time to put on my wetsuit. I stripped down to my tighty whiteys and jumped into the chilly water. I swam over to the barge. It was rolling wildly and the thirty pound steel retrieval hook was beginning to show some interest in me. Other loose equipment was sliding around on deck as I finally managed to get a line around the cable and, after thrashing around like a mad man, re-installed the hook. I was a little shaken. I waited for the *C.O. Jones* to pick me up.

Suddenly, I felt strange, soft impacts all over my almost naked and rather trim body. They looked like flowers! They were coming from above! I looked up when someone shined a flashlight on my groin and I found the port rail full of young men looking down at me. It was a gay cruise out of Fort Lauderdale. They flapped their arms, threw flowers and yelled, "Yhoo hooo!" their thankfully distant crotches pressed against the cold steel life rail for balance. The flowers smelled good at sea but still, I was more shaken than stirred.

In the world of marine salvage almost all incidents are one of a kind and in some cases that is good. If you knew what was to come, you might not go.

Before the National Marine Sanctuary laws came into effect in the Keys, the Coast Guard found the shrimp boat *Lucky* floating, abandoned and adrift, forty miles out in the Gulf of Mexico. They towed her into port. The next day the duty officer called and told me they had recovered an abandoned shrimp boat. The Coast Guard couldn't keep it. There was no registered owner to be found and no bodies to kick start an investigation. Could Key West Harbor Service dispose of her?

We moved *Lucky* to my dock, stripped off anything we deemed of value and could be sold in the chandlery, then rigged her to be towed out into the Gulf of Mexico. It took two weeks to strip the *Lucky* down.

Just after we got under way a fast moving micro-storm came in from the north. We were barely away from the dock when the cell moved in. The *Lucky* went hard left pulling my towboat, *Ranger*, backwards along with it. We were still in the marina! A crewman named Deebs was on the shrimp boat, coiling lines and checking the towing bridle rig when the shrimper veered off course. He ran back to the wheelhouse only to find that my wife had taken the steering wheel off to sell in the Chandlery ...there was no way to steer the shrimp boat! While Deebs ran around looking for a tool, the eighty-ton shrimp boat plowed ahead without a helmsman.

"Deebs! I can't stop her now. We're headed for the jetty... I'm going to have to pull it hard the other way... try to get steering...get steering!" I yelled over the VHF radio.

Deebs stepped out the side door of the wheelhouse, the Sea Gods smiled and my faith in random miracles proved to be intact. He looked down and saw a pair of rusty Vice-Grip pliers on deck. Deebs clamped them onto the steering shaft and guided the seventy-two foot shrimp boat out to sea with a pair of pliers.

We made it out of the harbor and into the Northwest Channel just as the storm cell hit hard. In the fog and rain our visibility disappeared. I couldn't see the *Lucky* only sixty feet behind me, and forty-knot winds caused her to swing wildly on the towline. I turned on the radar and saw seven targets coming at me from the north. Seven steel shrimp boats out of Texas, it turned out. Ninety-foot monsters with their outriggers down because they're very unstable without them.

There were other stationary targets included on my radar screen. The shrimpers also had radar, so I figured they could see us. I was wrong, they couldn't, because we had stripped all the metal off the *Lucky*, the rest was made of wood and my boat was only twenty-six-feet long. Not a good radar target. We turned circles for an hour and let the big shrimpers pass. Somehow we survived and towed the *Lucky* into the Gulf of Mexico, about twenty miles offshore. Once the storm receded we could work. We cut all the hoses and opened the seacocks, assuming the old shrimper would flood and sink. Everything was great, neat and tidy.

We waited and waited some more, waited for the *Lucky* to make her final voyage.

The problem was we had not noticed that the deck was full of foam. The insulating foam underneath lifted the deck off as the shrimper took her last dive. Shit!

We drove our boat up onto the deck a couple times, trying to make it sink. The hull sank, but the deck popped loose, wheelhouse and all. The foam separated from the hull and the *Lucky* (at least the upper part of the *Lucky*) began its unintended journey along the coast of North America.

The Coast Guard tracked the deck for a month: it went out and around the Tortugas then turned north into the Gulfstream, bound for the cold and vast North Atlantic. Mariners kept sighting a big seventy-two foot "piece" of shrimp boat, reporting it to the Coast Guard. The guys at the Key West Coast Guard base called me often, too often. "Good day, Captain Reef, just to let you know, YOUR deck is now off Fernandina Beach."

It was in the freighter lanes; I figured some ship would run over it and chop it up. But it went on for a month, the phone calls, tracking MY deck. I later found out that the Coast Guard was not really upset; they used the unintended voyage of the *Lucky* to develop drift data for future rescues. It would have been funny, if it had been someone else.

Occasionally a job would come along that was so bizarre I can only laugh when I remember it. I wrote this story years ago.

Miss Dimple Sue Pankersly had no fear of the past or future. She had been living with her boyfriend on his sailboat, but tonight she stood with her tits afloat; chest deep in the summer sea backwaters, on the flats off Dredgers Key. The night sky was a dark backdrop to the blaze nearby that was her boyfriend's burning boat. He'd done gone and pissed her off. With a half empty bottle of Jack Daniels in her hand, the first half had been used to start the fire, she laughed with pleasure at the sparking wreck and with each snort another half gulp of Jack blew out her nose. The neck of a guitar, strings still attached, bobbed nearby. She knew no fear at that moment. Her fear was burning and sinking on the indistinct, sparking horizon. She wallowed in the mud and cheered the charred remains floating past. "FUCK YOU!" she bellowed again and again through whiskey-numbed lips. She loved to hear the echo in the nearby mangroves. Dimple Sue was finally arrested and hauled, half nude, drunk and laughing from the sea, turtle grass still clinging to her mud- caked feet and wedged in the crack of her ass. She never stopped laughing for as far as we could hear or see. She knew the next day would not be as much fun. We towed the smoldering remains away the next morning.

Not long afterwards, I came upon a mostly sunken Cuban lobster boat. I decided to check it out, see if it had any value. Only the work deck roof was visible as we pulled up. I stepped onto the plywood top. The weight of my body made the top go under. I looked around and saw it was a piece of junk. At the same time I felt something weird on my legs. "What the fuck?" I looked down and saw hundreds of terrified cockroaches trying to climb up on me, the dry one. The crawling bugs had been trapped under the roof for days and were hungry. My mind could not register the sight. It couldn't be, bugs at sea! I instinctively dove into the water and swam away at a brisk pace. For a moment I thought it might have been the mushrooms flashback from long ago. It wasn't. It was one adrenalin rush I could've done without.

It's weird, but the worst jobs always seem to occur on the worst days. It was just before dark in early May when a small tug boat called us on the VHF. They were north of the Northwest Channel in the Gulf of Mexico and couldn't control a barge carrying four metal containers. It was nasty out in the Gulf but, three hours after leaving port, we got the tug *Captain Jim* alongside the barge. Just as we came alongside the barge, the crew on the other tug threw the towline line off their boat. It floated back and wrapped up in our port propeller. We were tied to the barge and one of our propellers was fouled. The barge blew around until it was upwind of us. It trapped the tug and pushed us downwind toward the coral reef at Cottrell Key. The tug that called for help turned away and left us. They wouldn't return our call for help and headed for port. We watched them go, and cursed madly into the wind. I finally got the Coast Guard to hail them on the radio.

When the Captain of the other tug finally responded I said, "What's on the fucking barge, Captain, I need to know because we're probably going to go aground on Cottrell reef."

"Industrial dynamite...out," the Captain said.

There were four containers. It was going to be a long night.

I had a very competent, but very crazy young fellow, Jeff, working for me. I put him in the water between the tug and the barge. He was a certified nutcase but fearless, and in all fairness, only a person equally challenged (me) would ask someone to do this. The tug and barge slammed together in the six-foot seas, compressing the water between them and shooting Jeff out of the water like a squeezed grapefruit seed. Jeff was a tough little bugger and refused to accept defeat. He dove under the tug and unwrapped twenty-five feet of three-inch line from the prop shaft. We were only half-a-mile from going up on Cottrell reef when we pushed away from the barge and headed into the waves. We eventually towed the barge into port, tied it up, changed shorts and had a beer. The original crew had just buggered off, abandoned the job. Real pros!

By the 1990s, the small vessel salvage industry was changing rapidly, for the worse. Environmental concerns, more boats than people who knew how to run them and legal problems collecting for salvage work became the norm.

During that time, I salvaged a brand new one-hundred-ten foot mega-yacht that hit a reef off the Cuban coast. It was worth seven million dollars. She had been on her maiden voyage from Palm Beach. The yacht was powered by three large diesel engines. When the Captain hit the reef he tore the middle engine out the back of the boat. He was in Cuban waters and the vessel was not insured for Cuban waters. Punching the remaining engines full ahead he managed to get out past the 12-mile limit before the vessel rolled on her side. Air was trapped inside the partly upside down hull and she was floating on her side. I motored out and found the vessel almost upside down, 24 miles north of the Cuban coast. I was alone on the *Ranger* and had to swim away from my boat to get a line on the floating one. I didn't have enough horsepower to tow it but I could steer it and keep it away from the reefs. For 20 hours I pulled the wreck and slowly rode the Gulf Stream north toward Miami. I called my friends at the Fowl Salvage Company. A day later, the Fowls came with a big tug and hooked up to the Hatteras. We towed it north toward Miami, 120 miles of open ocean. The Fowls were well-connected in Miami and when we got the boat in and refloated, they billed the owner a large percentage salvage fee. A salvor is entitled to a percentage of the value saved. But my friends didn't include my name in the claim. They wanted to pay me on their own and then bill the owner themselves. I asked why and they said, "Don't worry about it. Trust us, it's better if you're not in on it."

"Why?"

"Well, we can't really go into it but trust us, we're your friends. We're the Fowls! It's just better if your name isn't on it." Hmmm, friend or faux?

That wasn't going to happen. "You're full of shit," I promptly replied showing little of the courtesy I'd been taught to employ. Almost immediately the Fowls, wanting to avoid a stinky affair, amended all the suits to include me. What are friends for? I did get paid.

The same day the Hatteras was towed to Jones Boatyard, it was immediately covered with shrink-wrap. The builders apparently did not want anyone to see how cheaply the vessel had been constructed once you got behind the big white finish panels. Later that night a security guard saw two men dressed in black exiting the vessel. They rushed across the yard and slipped over the bulkhead into the fetid Miami River. The guard rushed to the seawall but they were gone. He looked for bubbles but there were none. Re-breathers, military style? I wondered what was on the boat that prompted such action.

After years of head to head competition with other salvage companies in the Keys I tried to convince my rivals that it would be in all our interests to work together. Sometimes it worked, sometimes it didn't.

A year or so before I sold the business I was off Cuba trying to raise a boat that had been used for smuggling people. The thirty-five foot outboard powered "go fast" boat had a large tuna tower and wouldn't stay upright when we rolled it over with our towboat. The "free-surface-effect," the water shifting inside, continued to roll the boat over on her side each time we pulled. We were thirty miles off the Cuban coast and had a one-hundred-ten-foot Coast Guard cutter standing by with us. We needed their help. I radioed the cutter and got them tied up to the port side of the sports fisherman. I said to the Captain, "Look, we're going to roll it and the minute you see it coming over I want you to clutch in (engage the engines) and go ahead."

That was a fine plan and I got the sunken boat rigged up to the Sea Tow towboat (we worked together on this one) and to the cutter. The cutter left both engines running and I breathed in diesel, carbon-monoxide-rich exhaust gas. I wasn't paying attention as I worked on getting it rigged. On my command the Sea Tow towboat flipped the sports fisherman over and the cutter Captain did as I asked, he put the ship in gear at idle speed. I didn't know a cutter does twelve knots at idle. It does. When the cutter clutched in, both boats took off and all the water in the sunken boat rushed toward the stern and washed me overboard. No one was watching. No one saw me go.

The impact with a motor cracked a couple ribs and ripped the inflator hose off my air tank. The cutter kept on going as I had suggested. I had expected to stay with the boat. I didn't.

Left in the wake, I wondered why I had not provided better instructions to the cutter's Captain. The sun was going down while the cutter, in blind obedience to orders, also pulled the Sea Tow boat backwards.

The stern started to go underwater as the towboat Captain clawed his way toward the axe to cut the towline.

Off they went. Ciao! I was left behind. I tried to swim, but... I couldn't, my ribs hurt and my muscles were cramped. I couldn't take a deep breath and realized, a little too late, that I had been breathing the cutter's exhaust. I was wearing a wetsuit and it slowed down the release of carbon monoxide through my skin. I didn't have enough oxygen in my blood to feed my muscles. I didn't have any flotation because my inflator hose had been ripped off. I was hot and exhausted. I was tiring rapidly, sinking slowly, that blissful moment before death coming over me. But I was a professional, I reminded myself. That knowledge didn't help. I was still sinking downward, dreamily looking up at the beautiful blue... my Episcopalian upbringing suddenly kicked in, "If it feels good, it must be bad." I snapped out if it and kept trying to inflate my buoyancy compensator; I didn't know the hose was broken. It was behind my head. I tried to trip my harness buckle to get rid of the weight belt and my tanks. It wouldn't come loose; it bent when I belly-washed out of the boat. I was about fifteen feet down, sinking, and looking up at a fading sky.

I was exhausted but still found something to whine about. "Man, I don't want to die like this... it's lonesome out here, so quiet." Then I thought, "That's not a very original thought." I should have been able to come up with a better line, especially if it was my last line. Maybe I was too tired. Failing to find any humor in my situation, I snapped out of my deadly reverie, grabbed my knife, cut away the weight belt and harness and finally got loose of my gear. The wet suit farted me up to the surface. I still couldn't swim but I could float an inch or two above the surface and lay on my back, nose up, hovering in the air. The one thing I could do was move my hands and thank Neptune there was an orange Igloo cooler that had been washed out of the boat along with me, floating about a yard from me. I hand-flopped myself over, grabbed that Igloo and hung on. It saved my life. Once they realized I was gone they might not be able to see me, but they would see the cooler. Hopefully. It was getting dark as the cutter turned toward me. It wasn't that long since I'd gone overboard but it felt like I had been adrift for days. I was saved by an

Igloo in the Keys and I never did check to see if there was any beer in the cooler. I was definitely getting old.

The last time I nearly died, I started to think I should consider retirement.

Jeff, the one that dove under the tug, decided to sail down to Key West from Tampa. It was terrible winter weather. He got in trouble near the approaches to the Northwest channel and I went out to save him in a nasty storm. I don't know why, I guess it was the panic in his voice. Trying to save a fellow sailor is not something you can say no to unless you practice. I hadn't, so I went. I sort of owed him. During the time we worked together he was always the one that was ready to go when it looked like it was going to be a rough patch. At two in the morning when I described how bad it was going to be, how high the seas were, how dangerous the job, he always said, "Hot damn, what are we waiting for, Boss?" That kind of enthusiasm is very helpful when things get bad. Jeff had a limited education and therefore became a very innovative crewmember. He saved a half-million dollar sports fisherman from sinking by finding a coconut and stuffing it in the boat's broken exhaust pipe.

It was a "Holy Bat Shit" bad night. I'd seen some bad ones and this one got my attention. I had a newly installed GPS onboard and, to orient myself, I was zooming in to see where the Northwest Channel jetty was. However, when the manufacturers designed the new GPS they forgot to enter the jetty on the electronic chart. I zoomed in but there was no jetty on my GPS and I spent too much time trying to find it. It was pitch black; the waves so violent the boat was pretty much under water the whole time. I couldn't see out the windows and there was no visible horizon. All the lights were spinning. The ocean was everywhere, up, down, on every side. I had vertigo. I tried to see the jetty but couldn't so I popped open the side window. I was in the foaming breakers on top of the granite rocks with my crewman Arnaud, The Fearless Frog, screaming ... "Zee Jetty-Zee Jetty!" With the waves breaking over the stern, I hit reverse and backed down.

The *RANGER* started taking on big water, she was getting heavy. I was spinning, the GPS was spinning and the compass was spinning. I tried to go west; I knew west would get us out of there. I leaned forward and put my face down on the compass. I could see the compass card spinning madly.

That didn't help. I couldn't find the horizon or focus on anything for very long. The weather was getting worse. I finally found west on the compass and started to turn that way when I began a quick and uncontrollable ascent to "pukesville." I was going to be very sick. I knew what was coming. It was scary. When I slammed open the side window to puke, I saw a blue-black wall of water coming at me. The barf blew back on me, and as I looked up the face of a ten-foot wave the wet thunder crested and landed on top of the boat. The wave could have rolled us and that would have been unpleasant, but instead it came straight down and almost completely submerged the boat. The water hit so hard it knocked a couple of twenty-pound thole pins out of their transom holes. Somehow the *RANGER* dug her way out of that grave of water and surfaced on the other side. Six hours later we finished the rescue of J's boat and I swore to never do it again. I was getting soft and said to myself, "Perkins, I'm worried about you."

I got over being scared when I was young; it was a waste of time. I got scared after close calls; I got drunk after close calls, but never before or during. This was the first time I had been scared during a job and I was disturbed by that. I said to myself, "Hey, don't die and end up crab food" and thought again of my friend Mendoza at dive school. "Yes... I understand."

When I got home I slipped into bed with Roberta and weighed my options.

Option #1 - Die alone in cold/watery grave.
Option #2 - Come home and snuggle up with Honey.
Watery grave/snuggle ... dead/alive?
It didn't take long to decide and I slept well with my decision.

I put the business up for sale the next day. I reminded myself that ending up dead cuts down on the possibility of future pleasurable activities. You must be present to win.

After I sold the salvage business I became a "salvage consultant," semi-retired and working for insurance companies. One day, I found myself at sea again, climbing two and a half stories up the side of a listing ship on a pilot's ladder apparently salvaged from Noah's Ark. The eight-hundred-foot long RO/RO (containers roll on, roll off) ship, *Magoona Star* was listing heavily to starboard in eight-to-ten foot seas and not rolling back upright. The pilot ladder swung away from the ship, and then slammed back against the hull as I managed to climb thirty-feet up the side without plummeting into the sea. When I reached the main deck I slipped and fell into the passageway. My lucky day, the deck was covered in guano, both old and new, that helped cushion my fall. The boat had been laid up in Virginia for years and was full of bird shit, out-of-state bird shit. My hands were white with guano.

After meeting Joe, the salvage master, who chose not to shake hands, we slid down the guano-encrusted decks, deeper inside the hold, deeper, down two decks into the bowels of the ship. If our dim flashlights failed, we would be in cave darkness. Cave darkness means you can't see anything, even your hand. The naval architect onboard the tug said if the ship heeled over more than seven-and-a-half degrees it would capsize. It was at six degrees when the salvage master and I went down into the hold. We were trying to figure out where the water that was causing the list, was coming from. The ship groaned and creaked as she rolled heavily in the sea and there were avian snowflakes everywhere, each splatter different from the others. Death could be a bulkhead away. We found a rusted bulkhead seeping water but were afraid to touch it. It might give way. We went back up and I suggested the crew should keep pumping and get underway, there was nothing to be done at sea and she had to be moved away from the reefs. I returned home.

My son Quincy called and I told him my tale of woe: I told him that I was getting soft.

"That's tough," he said.

Then it hit me: I'm retired. I'm finished, it's over, finite, *nada mas*, I will never put my ass on the line again. That's it. Period. There are many more comfortable things to discover about the human condition, *no*?

Chapter 26

Winding Down

After I sold the business I had time to take care of other duties.

Ashes were the last thing I saw of my Uncle Jim. He came down to Florida to die in 1992. "You know Mark, I did all that shit, member of the New York Yacht Club (one of his life's goals), golf clubs, tennis clubs, blah, blah, blah, all that crap. But I really screwed up."

"Why?"

"Because what I really wanted to do was just work around boats."

"But you had all that stuff, all that great stuff, the house, the big life!"

"Yeah, that's what it was, but who cares. I'd have rather been doing this."

Uncle Jim died in Palm Beach, was cremated and boxed. For years we had his ashes on the bookshelf in our house. He was a great houseguest and held up one end of a row of seafaring books. This was okay with me and I think him too; ashes keep well and it takes time to let go. Six years later I awoke with a sense of closure, the time was right, and according to Uncle Jim's last wish, my wife Roberta and I took him offshore and spread his ashes at sea. I still had the use of the *Ranger* and motored twenty-five miles out into the Gulf Stream, where it was calm and the crystal blue water was bound for the Arctic. I was going to play a Scottish jig on my boom box, except it wouldn't work. I understand now. Uncle Jim wasn't Scottish. The last thing he wanted was to be "put to rest" with the sound of a bagpipe droning in his ears!

"What do you throw a drowning bagpiper? His bagpipes!"

"What's the difference between a bagpipe and an onion? No one cries when they cut up a bagpipe!"

As we tossed my uncle's ashes into the Ocean River, bits of the ash, of different densities, formed a vortex. It was as big around as a ping-pong table when it finished spreading. The lighter bits of ash stayed up and the heavier pieces fell more quickly, making a white cone shape under the surface. The western sun hit the proper angle and lit up the cone of Uncle ash.

Off Key West
The flying fish cavorted about
The day we took Captain Perkins out
To cast his remains to the deep blue sea
My uncle, my ship, my lover and me.
We slowed where the water was blue and deep
And spread his ashes for the sea to keep
The ashes sank from the surface slow and
 in the depths soon formed a luminous glow
he was happy and where he wanted to be
As the pipes played Skye Boat reverie
We watched the light and current's course,
He was under way... Northeast by North
The routes and figures are just mine but
He'll be off Old Lyme in three weeks time.
And should you glance at the waves just then
You may spy Captain Perkins ... at sea again.

A Millennium Trip

I had never been interested in genealogy but my wife, Roberta, changed my mind and my life. It is only since we met that I have been able to stop and look back.

During a vacation to Scotland, a few years ago, we rolled into the city of Edinburg one afternoon in a rented car. Roberta patiently worked her way through the ancient microfiche records at the Town Hall while I patronized a nearby pub and worked my way patiently through five pints of Guinness Stout. She found the address in Dunfermline where my mother was born. I found a taste for Guinness.

On the way to Dunfermline, to find my mother's house, we drove *mostly* on the left. I had to concentrate and hold the Guinness buzz at bay. The buzz combined with driving on the wrong side made for an exciting trip as I navigated the slippery roundabouts in the dark. It was raining and bitter cold. The roads were slicker than snot on a doorknob, the wipers were no match for the fog. It was just days before the millennium. We drove along a river, its icy water running to the sea. Near Hogmanay we saw the Millennium Clock on the bridge over the river. Fog clouded the giant digital numbers, tick, tick, as they counted down the last minutes of 1999.

When we arrived in Dunfermline, it was almost dark. Along the ridges of Gardener's Row the ancient houses were cemented together, row-by-row, stone-by-stone and life-by-life. Gardener's Row commanded the high ground for centuries and was named "Gardener's Row" because each house had its own small gardening space on the hillside behind the house, set for best light. It was wall to wall to wall, up and down the ridge like the Great Wall of China with cucumbers and tomatoes.

We found the house but it was locked, no one was home. We got ready to leave as darkness settled in, when out of the mist, on a part of the sidewalk brightened by a streetlight, an older lady trundled toward us. Bundled up and leaning into the cold, her dark practical shoes ticked along on the hard-walked cobbles.

"Good evening."

"Good evening."

"Are ye lost?"

"No, actually, I think my mother was born in this house." I pointed. "But no one is home."

"Well, my goodness!" I canna let you in next door, but ye can most certainly come in to my hooose. We sharre a wall, ye know." The Scottish "R's" rumbled off her tongue like rain off a roof.

As we walked into her home, she softly told us that her husband had "passed." I was a stone's thickness away from where my mother had been born. Out back I looked over the shared brick barrier and into the garden space where she had played and grown up. I absorbed the neat little terraced lots, full of fertilizer and memories. I put my hand against the shared wall and inhaled the highland air and imagined those days of my mother's life. Our hostess, Mrs. Tufts, had no idea who I was, yet gave me one of my most valuable memories.

Alpine Texas, Pop. 322. Birthplace of the post hole

I took a vacation after selling the salvage business. Roberta and I boarded **AMTRAK**'s *California Zephyr* in Chicago for a trans-continental trip to California. After we settled in our private sleeper car I induced our porter, in the universally accepted manner, to find me a place on the train where I could smoke a cigar. I knew which doors opened and I knew they opened inward.

Roberta was taking a shower when the tired train screeched to halt in Alpine, Texas. I moseyed off the train and walked across the street to a western store to look at saddle blankets and smoke a cigar.

While I was poking around in front of the saddle shop, I saw the reflection of the train in the window. It was pulling away from the station! No whistle. Damn. I chomped down on my cigar (never waste a good cigar) and hauled ass, running as fast as my old legs would take me. I hadn't run in years and it took awhile to get the old bones to rotate. Later someone said I looked like I'd been shot. I headed toward the front of the train, hoping to catch the caboose before it passed. I sprinted up alongside a door near the end of the train, grabbed the handle and pushed hard. It opened inward and I spilled into the car, rolling across the floor with cigar-body parts, smoke, dirt, sweat and spittle flying all around. The train stopped. I skidded across the floor in the other direction as the uncomprehending conductors and stewards stared at me. It was the conductors' private car, "What the fuck?" one steward asked courteously.

The conductor, "The Captain of the Train," had moved the train forward because some lout was abusing his kid in a rear coach car and the cops wanted to take him off in a discreet manner, away from the main walkway. I had been sure it was heading out. The next stop was three hundred miles away. Roberta missed the whole thing and almost pulled out of west Texas, hair damp and on her own.

I walked into our cabin after only being gone for fifteen minutes. I was cut up, sweating, dusty and covered in cigar ash, both knees were black. Her face took on a peculiar expression. I tried to explain, but it was still a blur to me. She shook her head gently and held out her arms for a hug. "Ahh ... that's tough," I swear I heard her say.

Later we went down to the observation car and a kid, who had witnessed my mad dash, approached me. "That was pr-pr-pretty ather..le..le..letic of you, M, Mm, Mister," he stuttered with a Texas twa..twa..twang.

"Thank you." I puffed out my chest, reached for the corkscrew and started to feel better.

"Are you in the ma, ma, movies?"

"No, son," I said, slicking my eye brows, (you can tell I have a big ego with a slow leak,)

"I'm not in the movies, yet."

"Well you d-d-danged well should otta b-b-be cuz that was just like in the 'venture movies… I kin do that kind of stuff!" he said, chin out, firm in his belief.

I remembered when I was his age, watching TV adventure shows under a blanket and thinking the same thing.

"Well thank ya young fella!" I responded as his mother rolled her eyes and dragged him away. I still had it!

The boy looked back over his shoulder, I nodded, "Go for it kid!" I said silently.

***

Reef Perkins

YOUR MOVE

Bonus

By going to The New Atlantian Library website (NewAtlantianLibrary.com) or Absolutely Amazing ebooks (AbsolutelyAmazingEbooks.com) and entering the password below into the Bonus Reward Section, you can read another story by Reef Perkins – for **free!**

AA1026

About the Author

Captain Mark T. "Reef" Perkins is a marine surveyor with a colorful past. From commanding a 150-foot 300 DWT US Army diving ship off Vietnam to smuggling in the Caribbean, Reef Perkins has become a living legend. A graduate of both the US Army Engineer Officer Candidate School and the US Navy Salvage Officers School, he's a man comfortable in or out of the water. Raised in rural Michigan, Reef now lives in Key West where he can get his feet wet.

There is no greater fear than being forgotten.
Live to be remembered

For sales, editorial information, subsidiary rights information
or a catalog, please write or phone or e-mail

AbsolutelyAmazingEbooks
Manhanset House
Shelter Island Hts., New York 11965-0342, US
Tel: 212-427-7139
www.BrickTowerPress.com
bricktower@aol.com
www.IngramContent.com

For sales in the UK and Europe please contact our distributor,
Gazelle Book Services
White Cross Mills
Lancaster, LA1 4XS, UK
Tel: (01524) 68765 Fax: (01524) 63232
email: jacky@gazellebooks.co.uk

www.ingramcontent.com/pod-product-compliance
Lightning Source LLC
Chambersburg PA
CBHW050640170426
43200CB00008B/1090